ONLY
HEROES
AND
HORSES

The heart-warming true story
of Park Lane Stables

ONLY HEROES

AND

HORSES

Natalie O'Rourke MBE

SPHERE

SPHERE

First published in Great Britain in 2022 by Sphere
This paperback edition published in 2022 by Sphere

1 3 5 7 9 10 8 6 4 2

Copyright © Natalie O'Rourke 2022
Text by Emily Fairbairn

Images page ix: Getty Images

The moral right of the author has been asserted.

This book is based on real events from the author's life.
To protect identities, some names and places have been changed.

A CIP catalogue record for this book
is available from the British Library.

ISBN 978-0-7515-8507-0

Typeset in Goudy by M Rules
Printed and bound in Great Britain by
Clays Ltd, Elcograf S.p.A.

Papers used by Sphere are from well-managed forests
and other responsible sources.

MIX
Paper from
responsible sources
FSC® C104740

Sphere
An imprint of
Little, Brown Book Group
Carmelite House
50 Victoria Embankment
London EC4Y 0DZ

An Hachette UK Company
www.hachette.co.uk

www.littlebrown.co.uk

For my dad, and my children, Alice and Woody

CONTENTS

PART THREE

PART FOUR

BONUS CHAPTER

This book is about an ordinary girl from Birmingham, who liked horses so much she wanted to grow up and run a riding stables. The girl wanted the stables to cater for children and adults with disabilities, additional needs and anyone who needed a friend. (This was because of various good reasons which we'll get to shortly – hold your horses.)

There would be lots of bumps and obstacles along the way, but the truth of the matter is, there's no good letting what you think you can't do slow you down. Because – no matter who we are – there's always something we *can* do.

That girl was me and it has been my privilege to run the Park Lane Stables since 2009. Together with my incredible students, colleagues, community and the British public, we have survived, survived and survived again. This is our story.

It is about hope,
about horses,
and about lots and lots of heroes.

PROLOGUE

From the very first moment I sat on a pony, I was hooked. I knew there and then that in the saddle was the place I was meant to be.

We were at a school fete, and amid the crowds and the cake stands and the coconut shy, I spotted the sign which would change my life: 'Pony rides – 50p'. I was just six years old, and I reckon it was probably the first time I'd seen a pony in real life. You don't get many horses in suburban Birmingham, which is where I grew up.

Dad gave me a shiny silver coin, and I eagerly approached the pretty chestnut pony, with its stocky legs and shaggy coat. I can still picture her now – how her soft brown eyes were full of kindness, and how she flicked her ears forward in friendly alertness, and gently swished her tail. It was like she was saying hello. I reached out my hand tentatively and touched the pony's velvet nose. She breathed out in a quick snort and I giggled as the rush of air tickled my hand.

Dad's 50p bought me a ride which must have lasted no more than ten minutes, to the edge of the school field and back – but I'd never in my life felt so serenely happy as I did perched in that pony's saddle, the sound of her hooves softly thudding on the grass.

As the ride came to an end, I saw Dad had been joined by Mum and my thirteen-year-old sister Julia, who had her face painted like a butterfly.

'Look at you!' Mum called as I approached, pressing her camera to her eye. 'Say cheese, Nat!'

The photo she took that day, which I still have, captures a life-changing moment. With my long blond hair resting on my shoulders, my face says it all: pure joy.

Dad says that for the rest of the afternoon they couldn't keep me away from the pony. I begged him for more coins, then patiently queued over and over again for more rides, until he eventually insisted it was time to go home. As our family car pulled out of the school car park, I pressed my nose to the window, trying to catch one last glimpse of my pony friend.

From that day forward, horses became my obsession. Now, I should say I'm not from a horsey family – far from it. Dad was a police officer, Mum was a caretaker and they'd never had riding lessons growing up. I think they both thought my horse fixation would be a passing phase, but if it was, it's one I still haven't grown out of.

When we went to the library, the only books I wanted were ones with ponies on the cover. At home, I drew endless pictures of horses, and made up little stories all featuring long adventures involving me astride a trusty steed. Mum stuck the picture of me and the little ginger pony on my bedroom wall and every night I'd stare at it until my eyes got heavy and I fell asleep, dreaming of horses.

Knowing how happy it would make me, Mum and Dad decided to find me some riding lessons. Our urban neighbourhood wasn't bursting with opportunities, but ever resourceful, Dad found a rescue centre where they took in animals from circuses. They had a few ponies, and the guy that ran the centre kindly agreed to teach me to ride. Every weekend, he would take me out on the roads and I just loved it. Sitting in the saddle of a little albino pony called Noddy, I felt like he and I had become one body, one brain, and together we could do anything or go anywhere.

As the years passed I became more and more horse mad. By the time I was ten I was spending my whole weekends at the rescue centre, mucking out stables and grooming ponies in return for an hour's ride. For me, it wasn't really about riding as much as it was about being with the animals. I just wanted to talk to them and stroke them and smell their reassuring horsey scent. As a child, the ponies were the realest friends I had. I was so obsessed with horses that the other kids at school thought I was weird. At break time, I'd linger on the edge of the play-ground, fiddling with the little pony figurines I always carried around with me. I'd watch the other girls playing pat-a-cake or skipping or whispering in each other's ears and feel a dull ache in my chest. Occasionally, the boys would hoof a football directly at me, scattering my plastic ponies. My face would burn as I hurried to pick them up, their laughter ringing in my ears. But I'd forget all about the hurt and the humiliation, as soon as I was back alongside the ponies again.

'You know, life isn't really about fitting in,' Mum told me, stroking my hair one evening when I told her how people at school were saying I smelled funny because I spent so much time at the stables. 'If you're kind, true to yourself and stay positive even when the world wants to bring you down, you'll always stand out – and that's much more important.'

'I don't know why I have to go to school,' I said, burying my face in her shoulder. 'I just want to have my own stables and spend all day every day with my own horses.'

Mum put her arms around me and drew me closer.

'If you work hard, Nat, I know you can do absolutely anything,' she whispered.

Thanks to Mum, I gradually learned not to care what people said. And I had everything else I could ask for: I had my weekends at the stables, a cool big sister, and the unwavering belief of my parents.

But not long afterwards, our little world, like so many others' before us, got turned upside down. I was still just ten when Mum was diagnosed with cancer. As she spent more and more time in hospital, Dad encouraged me to throw myself into riding in an effort to distract me. He even went so far as to buy me a pony, a gorgeous palomino (golden coat, white mane and tail) called Norman, who I was allowed to keep up at the stable yard.

That pony became my lifeline. I tried to put on a brave face so Dad wouldn't worry too much, but I was so scared about what was happening to Mum. When Julia turned eighteen, she went off to university and I really missed her. But Norman would always listen when I had nowhere else to turn. I spent whole days holed up in his stable, pouring out my heart and taking comfort in our pony hugs.

I was fourteen when we lost my lovely mum. She'd come home from hospital, because there was nothing more the doctors could do, and died peacefully in her own bed with Dad and her own mother, my nanna, by her side. I can still picture my dad's pale, stricken face at the top of the stairs, and hear the croak of his voice as he told me: 'I'm sorry, love, she's gone.'

I went in to see my mum's body laid out in the bed, her

beautiful dark hair lying on the white pillow like ravens' wings. As I held her cold hand for the last time, grief punched me hard in the gut and left me struggling for breath. Mum's absence felt like an overwhelming darkness, and I didn't know how to find my way through.

Dad seemed to know instinctively what would help his heart-broken, frightened daughter. The day after the funeral he packed a suitcase, rented a horse box and drove us down to Dorset. He booked us into an idyllic B&B on a farm where there were stables for Norman to stay too. Every day we'd gallop over rolling green downs, until my eyes watered and my lungs were clear, and I could finally shake off some of the oppressive weight of my feelings.

While I rode, Dad would go for a walk then get a pint at a pub, before we met in the evening for dinner. Neither of us had the words for how much we missed Mum, but even as we ate in semi-silence, I knew how lucky I was to still have him.

After two weeks on the farm, Dad said it was time we went home and 'faced reality'. He told me he was going to hand in his notice at the police because the hours as a chief superintendent were too long and he wanted to be there for me. I tried to persuade him not to – Mum had once told me confidently that Dad would be 'the big boss' before very much longer – but secretly I was glad that he was going to be around more.

As we drove back home along the motorway, I started to worry about going back to school. I'd always been a misfit, picked on by the other kids, and the prospect of coping without Mum's hugs to come home to felt too much. Almost as if he could read my thoughts, Dad said: 'I know there's going to be tough times ahead, Nat. But you're brave and strong, and you'll get through them. Your mum always thought you could do anything – and I do too.'

Dad kept his eyes fixed on the road, which gave me the chance to wipe my own.

'There's something in the glove compartment for you,' Dad went on. 'I wasn't sure when to give it to you but, well, maybe there's never the perfect time.'

Puzzled, I opened the glove compartment. Inside was an envelope with my name written in my grandmother's handwriting.

'It's from your mum,' said Dad. 'She was too weak to hold a pen at the end, but she dictated it to Nanna.'

I slit the envelope open and unfolded the paper inside. Mum's letter spoke of how I mustn't be sad for her, because she would soon be free from pain. She urged me to always be the 'happy little girl' I had always been, and to keep loving Julia and my dad. By the time I got to the part where she said how proud she was of me, I could hardly see the words through the tears that were pouring uncontrollably from my eyes.

At the end of the letter, it said: 'I know it is your dream to one day have your own stables, and I hope, my darling, that it all works out for you.' Then she had signed it, in her own frail hand: 'All my love, Mum.'

I clasped the letter close to my chest, imagining that Mum's arms were around me in one of her incredible hugs. I knew I'd read it again and again until I knew it by heart – and even that wouldn't be enough.

That letter has never been far from me since – and neither has the dream which I confided in my mum, and that she believed I could achieve even as she was dying.

That day I vowed that if one day that dream came true, my stables would be a living tribute to my mum – run with kindness, integrity and boundless positive energy.

Part One

Part One

CHAPTER ONE

A Shaky Start

To most people, Park Lane Stables didn't look like much – but to me, the first glimpse of this ramshackle collection of buildings was enough to make my heart beat furiously with excitement.

It was an odd place to find a stables – the squat, whitewashed cottage, adjoining stalls and tiny yard were squeezed in among blocks of flats and Edwardian villas on an ordinary road on the outskirts of London. But in my eyes, there was something about its strangeness which made Park Lane perfect.

'It's not going to be as posh as the Monopoly Park Lane, is it?' my husband Thomas had joked, on the long drive down from Birmingham. It certainly wasn't. This Park Lane wasn't the sweeping avenue of posh hotels and billionaires' mansions to be found in central London. No, it was just a normal street in quiet, residential Teddington, in the city's south-west. And now, in March 2008, it was about to become our new home.

'I can't believe we're finally here,' I murmured, squinting through the windscreen of our blue VW Beetle, and trying to imagine the street teeming with eager children, and a horse's head looking out over the stable door.

The advert for this place, which I'd ripped from a January issue of *Horse and Hound*, was still clutched in my hand like a talisman. In rather officious, old-fashioned language, it specified: 'Couple needed to run riding school, Teddington, Middlesex.' I'd written to the address supplied, and after a tough interview over the phone with the stables' landlords, Thomas and I had got the job. I had a brief flashback to the magical evening when they'd called to say we'd got it – how Thomas had picked me up and spun me round and round, both of us grinning so hard I thought our faces might break.

For Thomas and me, taking over the stables was a leap into the unknown. We'd given up our jobs at the dental surgery where we'd met, packed up our whole life and driven halfway across the country to have a go at making my dream come true.

I adored Thomas for signing up to my mad scheme – unlike me, he hadn't spent his entire life obsessed with horses. But since we'd married in 2005, I'd been impressed by what an interest he'd taken in my beloved ex-racehorse, a grey gelding called Prodney, who I kept at a livery yard near to the little house we shared in Birmingham. Thomas would come with me to the yard on Sundays and spend time with the horses – I even persuaded him to get on Prodney a few times. He said he liked the fresh air, the predictable routine of caring for a horse, and the social buzz you got around a stables.

I'd never have thought someone like Thomas would fall for someone like me. He was your classic tall, dark and handsome, whereas I was still a bit of a weirdo who always smelled vaguely of hay.

But somehow, the two of us just worked. Thomas made me

happier than I'd ever thought possible – and now, he was about to dive right into this crazy adventure with me.

'It's maybe a bit smaller than I remember, but I can totally imagine how good it's going to look when it's done up,' I said now, as Thomas continued to stare out of the car window, a strange expression on his face.

It had been Thomas who had encouraged me to take the plunge once I hit thirty, and study for exams with the British Horse Society. Once I was qualified as a riding instructor, he pored over magazines and newspapers with me, looking for potential stables we could rent.

We had this romantic vision of ourselves on a picturesque farm, surrounded by ponies, me teaching kids to ride while Thomas did all the practical tasks around the yard. 'It's definitely got to be better than dentistry,' Thomas would joke, as we sifted through endless details of acreage and outbuildings. Whenever we spotted a property that looked good, whether it was in Lincoln or Devon, we'd pile into the Beetle and tear off to look at it.

None of them were quite right – until Park Lane. Maybe it was because it reminded me of where I had learned to ride, along the urban roads of outer Birmingham, but there was something about the place that just spoke to me. I loved that it was right in the heart of its community, and had so much potential to reach people outside of the usual horsey circles. The stables came with its own living quarters, and the owners would pay us a wage to look after the horses and run the riding school. I knew it was the perfect place to build the stables of my dreams.

And now, we were finally here. Murphy, our new rescue dog, was thumping his tail on the back seat, keen to get out. We'd only had Murphy, a leggy Labrador-lurcher cross with searching brown eyes, glossy black coat and floppy ears, for two days.

Thomas had insisted that moving to the stables was the opportunity to get a pet – and the moment I'd set eyes on gorgeous Murphy, I'd had to agree.

'Come on then, what are we waiting for?' I said, giving Thomas a friendly nudge and unclipping my seatbelt. 'We've got a new life to start.'

'Nat . . . ' he began, and I stopped, because his voice sounded like a stranger's. 'I'm sorry. I can't get out of the car.'

'What do you mean?' I said, the goofy smile I'd had the whole journey still lingering on my face.

'I can't do it, Nat. I'm not getting out of the car. I'm in love with someone else.'

My smile flickered and faded, but I couldn't quite understand what he was saying. It was like he was speaking another language.

'Nat. Look at me. Say something, please.'

A thousand thoughts were rushing and colliding in my head, as I tried to grasp what was happening. I thought of the moving van, stuffed with all our shared belongings, whizzing its way down the M40 at this very moment. And the horse box, containing my beloved Prodney, which was following close behind it. Just this morning I'd whispered into Prodney's alert ears about how happy we'd all be in our new home.

Thomas put his hand on my arm, and at last I turned to face him.

'You can't just back out,' I said quietly, trying to keep my voice steady. 'Our whole world is packed up. You said you wanted this. We wanted this.'

Thomas sighed, and ran his hand through his ruffled dark hair in that infuriatingly charming way he had.

'I thought I did. And I'm sorry. I never planned it like this. It's just that me and Freya . . . '

Freya?

'Wait – you're telling me you're having an affair with *Freya?*'

'Well, yes, but it's not an affair, it's—'

Suddenly, disbelief became white-hot anger. Freya helped out up at the stables where I kept Prodney, a bubbly blond woman who was never out of a crop top. I wrenched open the car door, needing to breathe different air to my faithless husband. I pounded down the street, feeling the blood hammering in my ears.

I could hear his footsteps behind me, hurrying to catch up. I spun round to face him, my blond ponytail whipping over my shoulder. It struck me that we'd been in London for less than five minutes and we'd already found ourselves in the middle of some kind of dreadful scene from *EastEnders*.

'For god's sake,' I began.

'Please, let me explain.'

'Go on then,' I thundered, feeling red spots rising in my cheeks, but the cogs in my brain were already whirring. All the times Thomas had been 'painting his mum's bathroom' or 'playing golf with the lads' over the last few months ... I'd been so busy, getting things ready for the big move, that I hadn't noticed what was going on right under my nose. How could I have been so stupid?

'Actually, don't bother,' I said, feeling like all the wind had been knocked out of me. Thomas was staring at his feet, and I could see exactly how he must have looked as a little boy caught doing something naughty. 'I don't want to hear it.'

'I really am sorry, Nat,' he said, eyes still on the floor. 'I never meant to hurt you.'

We stood in silence for several long minutes on that quiet street in Teddington, both of us lost for words. I had been too shocked at first to cry, but now I could feel the tears building up and threatening to blind me. I had pictured today over and over in my mind as I eagerly counted down the days until we moved to Park Lane. Never in a million years would I have thought that this was how it would play out.

'How could you?' I said at last, barely recognising my own choked and quavering voice.

Finally, Thomas lifted his chin to look me in the eye.

'I just . . . couldn't help it,' he shrugged.

I nodded slowly, then walked back to the car, opened the rear door, and helped Murphy jump out, clipping his lead on to his collar.

Thomas followed behind me, jabbering about how we'd sort out our stuff later but I should have whatever I wanted, and it wasn't too late to pull out of the stables job, but it was up to me to decide what I did next. I didn't say a word, just handed him the car keys.

'Oh, right,' he said awkwardly, seeming to understand what I was trying to say. He got into the driver's seat and rolled down the window.

'Goodbye then,' he said, in a way that I found almost ludicrously calm, given that he'd just detonated a bomb on our entire life. 'Will you be all right?'

All right? Here I was in a brand new city, where I didn't know a soul, more than a hundred miles from home. My husband was about to drive back to the arms of a woman I had thought was my friend, wrenching my heart to pieces in the process. Oh, and I had a stables to run – alone.

I didn't know if I'd ever be all right again. But I'd have to find a way to survive.

CHAPTER TWO

Home is Where the Heart Is

Looking back now, I can hardly believe I found the strength to get through those first few weeks in Teddington.

Obviously, with hindsight you know everything happens for a reason, but at the time, I felt like I'd pretty much hit rock bottom. The heartbreak was the kind that gets right into your bones. It lay like a heavy weight on me in bed, leaving me exhausted but unable to sleep. It squeezed pointless tears from my eyes for hours on end, leaving my lashes gummy and my cheeks red raw. It played horrible tricks on me, causing me to temporarily forget what had happened and leading me into unsuspecting daydreams about Thomas, only for the crushing reality to return with extra bite.

I've always been a keen runner, and in this new, unfamiliar place I took to pounding the streets in the chilly twilight, trying desperately to make myself feel better. But I couldn't outrun the fact that I didn't know anyone, and I didn't have any friends.

'Come back to Birmingham.'

That was my best friend Jenny's immediate verdict when

I rang her and told her the whole sorry tale in between big, gulping sobs.

'Just come back. There's no shame in it. You can't stay there when you don't know anyone, and you certainly can't run a riding stables all on your own.'

What I hadn't told Jenny was that the owners of the stables had in fact moved the goalposts, telling me on arrival that they had decided they weren't going to be reopening the riding school after all.

There had been horses on Park Lane since the 1830s, when the local fire service kept them to pull the fire wagon, before it became a riding school. But riding lessons had fallen out of favour in recent years, and now the current owners were more focused on horse trading and livery. As well as the small yard on Park Lane, which included a tack room and nine stables, they had a big farm out at Esher in Surrey, where the horses grazed. They wanted me to forget Park Lane and focus on the day-to-day running of the farm, training horses they bought before they sold them on and looking after the ones whose owners paid for them to board there. I found that I didn't have the energy to argue.

'So no husband now then?' the landlord had said as he gave me the keys to the cottage, his eyes running nervously over my tear-streaked face. 'Are you sure you can do this on your own?'

'Yes,' I'd said, with more certainty than I felt inside. 'I'll do the work of two people, just you wait.'

I was trying to look on the bright side – I'd still be spending all day, every day with horses. There were around sixty horses currently up on the farm, and it was no time before I started to get to know and love their varied personalities. Already I had a soft spot for a skewbald pony called Oaky, who was always snuffling round my pockets in the hope of a Polo mint, and a bay cob called Frank, who would whinny at the top of his lungs when he saw me approaching. In my down moments, of which there were quite a few in those early days, I told myself the farm work could be a good learning experience, which I'd eventually be able to channel into my own stables.

Something else I was trying to put a positive spin on was the accommodation. The cottage was, to put it nicely, pretty rustic. In fact, it was really a stable, which had been given the bare minimum of renovations to make it fit for human habitation. Long and thin like a canal boat, it had windows on only one side, looking out over the street, meaning it was pretty gloomy even on a sunny day. There was a kitchen/living room area with cheap, mismatched furniture and three bedrooms, all as damp and musty-smelling as each other. The bathroom had a horrible raggedy carpet and an old-fashioned bath with a hand-held shower. The exposed bricks of the cottage walls were painted a grubby off-white, and there wasn't a proper ceiling, just bare rafters.

It was a particularly cold March that year, and it became immediately apparent that my new home had no heating whatsoever. I'd spent my first night there shivering in bed, wrapped in every coat I owned and under a manky old rug of Prodney's. I couldn't help but think how if Thomas was there we would have found the whole thing hilarious, and would have relished hunkering down together as if we were camping. At least I had Murphy snuggled up beside me, to keep me warm.

'You can't even have unpacked yet,' Jenny continued. 'Just call that van back and come straight home. You can live with me for a bit until you're sorted.' Jenny and I had been mates since we were teenagers. Her horse lived in the adjoining stable to Prodney's and would kick the wall between them. She'd been one of my first real human friends – someone who shared my passion for horses and understood what it was like to not always fit in. Now we were in our thirties, but Jenny still had my back – just like I would always have hers.

I hesitated. It was a really tempting offer. In fact, any offer would have been quite tempting considering my current prospects were some backbreaking work and a lonely, chilly house! But even then my hesitation was only for a second. I just wasn't ready to give up the dream yet.

'Thanks, Jenny,' I said, and really meant it. 'But I've worked so hard for this. I can't just give up now.'

When I hung up the phone, I pushed my feet into the green wellies I kept on the doormat, and wandered the ten yards from my front door to the stable yard, Murphy trotting behind me. However rudimentary the living conditions were, this was a novelty I imagined I'd always enjoy. I found Prodney in his stable, calmly chewing a mouthful of hay. Nothing would ruffle the feathers of this old boy, who'd already seen a fair few ups and downs himself and had been the calming influence I needed during my turbulent teenage years.

'Hello, boy,' I said, snuggling into his white neck and breathing in his warm, grassy smell. 'I've got us into a mess, I'm afraid.'

As I sat with Prodney, absent-mindedly stroking his tousled mane, I could feel my heart rate instantly slow. For me, it's always been this way – horses have such a powerful effect, they can literally take my worries away.

I've had Prodney since I was seventeen – and it's fair to say it was love at first sight. When I first saw him there was something about him that took my breath away. He's tall – sixteen hands – powerfully built, with an elegant Roman nose. You can tell he has spirit from the curve of his neck and the way his ears flick around. He was born and raised in Russia, where he was used for harness racing, and got his rather unusual name when he arrived in Birmingham and no one could read what it said on his Russian papers. The strange characters looked a bit like they said Prodney, so that's what he'd been called ever since.

After my first pony Norman sadly died, I bought Prodney with the wages I'd saved from working part time at an orthodontist. Dad persuaded me to take the job when I was kicked out of school at seventeen for bunking off too much, so in a way Prodney is just another of the very many things I have my father to thank for. I used every last penny to pay for him, so I couldn't afford a saddle at first. It didn't matter though – because I knew I just belonged on Prodney's back. It was almost like we could read each other's minds, and right from that very first moment Prodney and I were perfectly in sync. I used to ride him bareback through the woods at twilight in that first winter we had together, feeling wild and free.

Fifteen years later, Prodney and I were both a bit older and wiser but we were as tightly bonded as ever. I'm yet to meet a living creature who is as good a listener as he is. Over the years, he's heard me pour out my heart about all sorts of things, from family to work and romance, and he's never judged me. He is just this constant, solid companion who I know will never let me down.

As I leant into Prodney's shoulder I knew I wouldn't change my mind about moving back home. Yes, my carefully laid plans had been turned upside down, and sure, my heart felt like it had been totally shattered. But the one thing I've always known to be true is that horses have the power to heal, in ways us humans could never hope to understand.

Tomorrow I'd start the day at the farm, feeding and mucking

out and grooming, and I'd end it here with Prodney, just sitting and listening to his gentle breathing. All I could do was take each day at a time and try my very best to keep the dream still flickering in my chest alive.

'I think you're right,' I said to Prodney, because I've always felt I can tell what he's thinking. 'I've come this far – I can keep going for a bit longer, can't I?'

CHAPTER THREE

Smile Though Your Heart is Aching

I was very lucky that the horses at the farm in Esher gave me a very important reason to get out of bed every morning. However bad my dreams or sleepless the night, I knew that when I arrived at the 140-acre farm I'd start to feel better. Murphy would ride shotgun beside me on the drive over as I slurped black coffee from a flask. Working on the farm was gruelling, but seeing the contented faces of the horses as they tucked into their breakfast made it feel worthwhile.

While the horses ate, I'd scribble up a plan for the day on the blackboard in the tack room. Then it was time to turn the horses out, me walking two of them at a time up from the yard to the paddocks, before starting the endless mucking out. The laboriousness of forking out wet straw and horse poo, my arms aching and sweat trickling down my back, was a comfort I came to rely on. It was hard to think of how much my heart was aching when I was deep in the physicality of the task.

After that I would tack up the horses that I was exercising or schooling and ride or lunge them on a long line for several hours. Then it was time to fetch the rest of the horses in and rub them all down and groom them, which was my favourite part of the day. You really get to know a horse's personality when you're up close to them, and you can feel them start to trust you as you hold their hooves in your hands and pick out their feet.

Next there were more feeding buckets to make up, the floor to sweep, the skips to empty and the tack room to tidy.

The horses up at the farm were a mixture of liveries – those owned by other people, who paid to keep them there and have them looked after – and those that belonged to the landlords, who planned to sell them on. It meant that there was a fair bit of coming and going, but every new arrival found a way to steal my heart.

As well as Oaky and Frank, I fell hard for a little-and-large pair who were inseparable. The landlord had picked them up cheaply at an auction and didn't know their names. So I christened them Simon and Louis, because *The X Factor* was big at the time and they'd sometimes playfight like the two judges did.

There was so much to do at the farm that I rarely got a spare moment, but when I did I'd lean against a stable door or a paddock fence and just watch the horses, dreaming of what it would be like if I ran the place instead of just working there. I loved being with the animals, but I still longed to run a riding school. I could picture Park Lane busy with children and volunteers, and imagined how good it would feel to help forge those remarkable human–horse relationships that can change the course of a life, like it had done for me.

As it was, Park Lane was mostly empty, but I'd sometimes ride one of the horses back from the farm in the afternoon, with Murphy trotting obediently next to us. Having a horse sleeping on the other side of the cottage wall helped me to imagine my dream one day coming true.

I'd usually arrive back at Park Lane around seven in the evening, just in time for my daily phone call with Dad.

As I had predicted, Dad was horrified by what had happened with Thomas. He took it as a personal affront that anyone could have humiliated his precious daughter so badly. 'But he was so lucky to have you,' he said, bewildered. 'What on earth is he playing at?'

Every night, Dad would ask the same question: 'Have you been to the pub yet, love?' The nearest one was a scruffy-looking pebbledashed Edwardian building on the adjoining road to Park Lane. It was very literally a stone's throw from the stables, so in my dad's opinion there was really no excuse for me not getting myself down there and making friends.

'No, it's too tragic,' I'd always groan. But I knew he was right. If I was serious about staying, I'd need some human companions to go with the four-legged ones.

So it was that about a month after I arrived in Teddington, I finally decided to take the plunge. After a typically taxing day at the farm, I told myself I deserved a drink. I peeled off the grubby jeans I'd been wearing for about a fortnight, and after a chilly shower, changed into skinny black trousers and my best stripy jumper.

'Just one drink,' I told Murphy, firmly. 'Then we're allowed to come home.' He licked his nose, which I took for agreement.

As I walked the 300 feet from my front door to the pub, with butterflies in my stomach, I felt immensely grateful to have Murphy at my side. Now I could see that Thomas was probably so enthusiastic about us getting a dog because he knew I'd end up needing some company. But he did me a favour, because without

Murphy I may not have had the confidence to walk into the Queen Dowager that April evening.

Once I reached its red front door, I took a deep breath, and stepped into the pub. It was pleasingly retro inside, with lots of wood panelling and walls lined with black-and-white photographs of old Hollywood stars. I could tell it was a proper locals' pub, with loud chatter and mates calling across to each other from the bar. I ordered a glass of house white then pushed my way to a small table in the corner where I perched on a stool, taking in the noisy scene with Murphy at my feet.

When you're alone in a pub it can be easy to imagine that all eyes are on you, wondering why you're such a loner. But I quickly realised that nothing could be further from the truth, with the other drinkers all absorbed in their own banter. A couple of lads at the next table made a brief fuss of Murphy, before turning back to their mates to continue a discussion about how badly Chelsea had performed at the weekend.

I sipped my drink slowly, feeling a small glow of pride spread through me. Here I was, in a pub, on my own! I was a strong, independent woman. Today I had single-handedly run a farm, and here I was enjoying the fruits of my labour.

That night I stayed for just one drink, but over the coming weeks, I started to go to the Queen Dowager more and more often. It was partly due to the relief in my dad's voice when I told him I'd gone, and partly because the pub was so much warmer than my draughty cottage. As the surroundings got more familiar, I began to relax. The landlord, Mark, started to recognise me, and would always hurry over with a bowl of water, and sometimes a biscuit, for Murphy.

Then one evening, as I was shrugging my denim jacket on and preparing to leave, I heard a voice at my shoulder.

'Want to stay for another?'

I looked up. It was a skinny lad in his late twenties who I'd seen in the pub on several evenings, always with another bloke with dark curls and a wicked grin, and a tall girl with long chestnut hair, who I took to be his housemates. They were about my age, and always seemed to be having such a laugh. I was so taken aback I glanced behind me to check he was talking to me.

The guy laughed. 'Sorry, I didn't mean to startle you. I'm Barney, and that's Pasty and Sam.' He gestured over to his mates who were watching us from a table across the bar. 'I mean, come over and join us! You don't have to always rush off after one. Sorry, I probably should have asked you over sooner. But we weren't always sure if you were waiting for someone.'

I cleared my throat awkwardly and could almost hear my dad's voice in my ears: '*Go for it!*'

'No, not waiting for anyone,' I said. 'It's just me ... and Murphy. But that would be lovely, thanks.'

Barney beamed. 'Great, what are you drinking?'

I helped Barney carry frothing pints over from the bar, Murphy's lead looped over my arm. He introduced me to Sam and Pasty – so called because he was from Cornwall – who both had the same warm and easy manner he did. I felt instantly at home with them, as they talked over each other and laughed loudly at their shared in-jokes. While they were fascinated to hear that I'd moved into the stables, they didn't grill me with questions about horses or why it was that it was just me and my dog, instead treating me like they'd known me for years.

I stayed that night until closing time, and as I wandered back to the cottage I felt a strange sensation. I put my hand to my cheek and realised what it was – I'd been smiling, for the first time in months.

CHAPTER FOUR

The Only Way is Up

I started to smile more and more in the months after that. My dad was right – with a group of friends to hang out with, everything seemed easier, and Teddington finally started to feel like home.

Up at the farm, I found my rhythm. Every day that went by I felt more tightly bonded with the horses, and I loved how Prodney had fitted straight into the herd. As the weather warmed up the work seemed more enjoyable too. Yes, it was physically gruelling, but you can't complain when you're out in the sun all day doing something you love.

It felt like a thousand years ago that I'd been working nine to five as a dental hygienist, and I could honestly say that I didn't miss it one bit. Dentistry was something I'd fallen into, mainly thanks to that part-time job at the orthodontist I told you about – my boss there had told me I could make a career beyond the reception desk, and had encouraged me to retake my exams and go to uni. Obviously, I'd never stopped spending all my spare time surrounded by horses – but now I got paid for that, too.

As well as all the physical work involved with running the farm, I found there was lots more to think about too – making sure visits from the vets and farriers were booked in, deciding how much feed and bedding we needed to order, planning how long each horse should spend in its stable or the field. But I was getting the hang of it – and every day that went past I felt more confident that I really could run my own stables.

I had plenty of time to imagine exactly what those stables would be like, too. The people who kept horses up at the farm were a privileged few – but my stables would be open and inclusive, with the horses there for anyone that needed them. It's one of the reasons I liked to have some of the farm ponies stabled at Park Lane from time to time, so people passing by could see them – in my experience, even a quick pat of a horse's neck can drastically improve your mood.

The days passed in a busy blur of hard work and horses, and by the time seven o'clock rolled around and I'd chatted to Dad, I was often ready for a drink.

From the first night I'd met them, it became an established routine that if Barney, Pasty and Sam were in the pub, I'd join them at their table. We never planned when we were going, but it always seemed to work out that whenever I was there at least two of them were too. I had guessed correctly that they were house-mates, and it turned out they lived in one of the flats opposite the stables. Their living conditions sounded about as basic as mine, which might explain why they preferred to spend the evening at the Queen Dowager instead of in front of their own TV.

They lived what I thought of as a sort of *Friends* lifestyle, working long hours at jobs they hated but living for the evenings and weekends when they'd talk and laugh until they were hoarse. One or other of them was always going on a bad date which they'd then regale the rest of us with afterwards, and they were always short of cash but happy all the same.

When I wasn't at the farm or the pub, I'd entertain myself riding Prodney in Bushy Park. I couldn't believe what a beautiful green space I had on my doorstep. A vast expanse of over 1,000 acres, Bushy is the second-largest of London's eight Royal Parks. I'd trot Prodney alongside its maze of waterways, through magical gardens and carpets of daffodils, marvelling at the herds of red and fallow deer that wandered across its rolling grasslands. King Henry VIII used to ride at Bushy Park, and as I sat astride my beautiful grey steed, the spring breeze on my bare shoulders, I felt a connection to that distant past. Prodney was such a lovely horse to ride, as eager and energetic as me. I always told people Prodney was the horse equivalent of a real gentleman, his outline effortlessly graceful, and his responses quick and precise.

Before I knew it, fresh spring days lengthened into long, hot summer ones, where the scent of freshly cut grass hung on the air and up at the farm horses crowded into the shade, lazily flicking their tails. Then autumn arrived with hedgerows heaving with blackberries, children trick-or-treating at my door and gloomy twilight setting in before I'd even finished grooming.

Winter at the cottage was, as I had predicted, pretty brutal. I'd made it as cosy as possible but when the cold weather hit, it was like an ice box.

Even so, the cottage had begun to feel like a proper home. With time I started to find its idiosyncrasies funny – and no matter how rough and ready it was, at least it was mine. I'd filled the place with shelves and shelves of books – I'm an avid reader – covered every windowsill with photographs of Dad, Mum and Julia, and plastered the fridge with snaps of silly nights out with Pasty, Barney and Sam. A trawl of the charity shops of Teddington had supplied pretty, mismatched crockery for the kitchen and a couple of nice vases I filled with fresh flowers when I remembered. The squashy sofa was piled high with blankets. They weren't always enough to fight off the icy winter chill, so I spent more and more time in the cosy embrace of the Queen Dowager until I felt brave enough to face another unheated night, grateful for Murphy's hot doggy breath beside me.

I don't think I saw it like this at the time, but in a way it was a blessing that my house was so inhospitable. If it had had heating, I'd probably have spent more time on my own watching telly. As it was, I was always down the pub, in the heart of the community. Pasty, Barney, Sam and I were a proper little gang by then, but during those dark winter nights we started to make friends with lots of the other locals, of all ages, and there were a fair few raucous lock-ins at the pub. Mark, the landlord, was always happy to see us – probably because we spent so much money there – and we'd often invite him to come and sit with us and share a drink. But we couldn't resist being a little cheeky too. Sam devised a game where we'd challenge each other to nick one of the Hollywood photos off the wall, and then see how long it was before Mark noticed. Luckily, he saw the funny side – and got his revenge by ringing first thing in the morning when he knew we'd be hungover, asking for the speedy return of Ava Gardner or Sean Bean.

As December approached, I felt like I'd put myself back together like Humpty Dumpty, picking up each shattered piece that Thomas had left behind. I had the beginnings of a great life here – a happy home, a farm full of horses, and a great circle of friends. But there was still one piece missing.

I still wanted to open a riding school. But how would I do it?

CHAPTER FIVE

Have You Herd?

The idea of taking over the stables was like an itch that I couldn't quite scratch. I spent many weekends that winter absent-mindedly wandering around the tiny stable yard, picturing it full of children ready to ride. During my hacks round Bushy Park, I thought about the different routes I'd take novice or advanced riders.

I knew the landlords didn't want to pay me to run the riding school – but what if I paid them? In theory, I could take over the lease for Park Lane, set up my own business and pay them rent.

But that would be easier said than done. I had no idea if they'd agree, and it would be a huge risk for me financially. I'd never run a business before – at the moment I worked for the landlords as an employee – and was I really ready to take on that level of uncertainty so soon after my whole life had been blown apart by my marriage breakdown?

Even so, every month, I squirrelled away more and more of my hard-earned wage. If I was going to do this, I'd need money. And that wasn't the only thing – I needed horses too.

'If I can, I want to give homes to horses who really need love,' I told Jenny on the phone. 'I'd want the stables to be welcoming to all – and that includes the ponies too!'

'You should definitely try the meat man then,' Jenny said. It was exactly what I'd been thinking. 'Meat man' is the name the horse world gives to a dealer who buys up cheap and unwanted horses, takes them for a (supposedly) humane death at the abattoir, before the meat is exported and sold for consumption in Europe. Sadly, lots of horses bred for racing that don't make the grade are disposed of in this way – as are unwanted pets that are sick or lame. Calling out a vet to euthanise your horse is expensive, whereas getting the meat man actually makes you some money – so, some owners do go down that route.

I hoped Jenny would be able to use her equestrian contacts to find out if there was anyone local to me who was buying horses for meat – in the hope that I'd be able to save them from their fate. I knew that you could pick up horses for a good price from a meat man – you just needed to pay more than the abattoir.

Sure enough, a few days later Jenny rang back with the name and address of a bloke who had a yard not far from the farm in Surrey. I drove over there right away, Murphy by my side.

The yard – really just one tumbledown barn and a scrubby patch of concrete – looked as unloved as you'd expect. It also appeared to be deserted – apart from one solitary horse, tethered to a rusty post.

'Well, would you look at that,' I said to Murphy, feeling my blood pump faster. Now, one thing you should know about me is that I fall in love with horses very easily. But this skewbald – that means with a coat of white and brown patches – had my heart before I'd even got out of the car.

I parked up, leaving Murphy in the back, and let myself

through the metal gate into the yard. I approached the horse slowly, so as not to scare him, but he turned to look at me with such a confident and curious gaze that I knew he wasn't the kind to get easily spooked. He was slim and tall, and seemed young and in good health – he certainly wasn't the kind of pitiful nag you'd expect to find in a place like this.

'Hi, boy,' I said softly, reaching out to pat his neck. The horse happily accepted my attention, and delightedly chomped up a chunk of carrot I found in my pocket.

'Can I help you?' came a voice. I'd been so transfixed by the horse I hadn't heard the approach of this thickset man, dressed in a ripped Barbour jacket and muddy boots.

'Oh hi, my name's Natalie,' I said, putting out my hand for him to shake. He didn't take it, still eyeing me suspiciously. 'I heard you might have some horses to sell. And, well, I'm looking for some horses.'

'You're out of luck,' said the man, who had longish, greasy hair which he tucked behind his ears. 'I took the whole lot to the slaughter yesterday. This is the only one I've got left – arrived this morning.'

I turned back to the skewbald horse, who was gently nuzzling the crook of my elbow, perhaps in the hope of another bit of carrot.

'Well, how much for this one?'

The meat man raised an eyebrow. 'You sure you want him? He's got stringhalt, you know – the woman who dropped him off reckons he's no good.'

Stringhalt is a neuromuscular condition that causes horses to have an abnormal gait – their hind legs will move upwards in an exaggerated motion. But I knew that especially if the horse is young – which this one clearly was – it doesn't necessarily mean they are a write-off. If the condition is mild, it's perfectly possible for the horse to have a good life and be wonderful to ride.

'Do you mind if I walk him up and down, to see how he moves?' I asked.

The meat man shrugged. 'Suit yourself, love.'

I untied the horse and led him around the yard. There seemed to be no problem. And I could tell how patient and gentle he was by the way he kept his pace exactly with mine.

'He's broken in, I take it?' I asked the man, referring to the process by which horses are trained to accept tack and a rider. It's not actually a phrase I like – if I am training a horse I like to say I'm 'starting' them, as in starting their education, because I'd never want to break anything about a horse's unique spirit.

'Yep – was going to be a showjumper before the vet diagnosed his problem, apparently,' said the man. I felt a stab of sadness for this kind-hearted horse. The moment he'd been unable to serve his purpose, his last owner had cast him off like he was a piece of rubbish.

'How much do you want for him?' I asked the meat man, who still hadn't introduced himself but had softened his body language slightly, now that he could see I was someone who knew horses properly.

'You can have him for £300,' he said. I knew I probably should have haggled, but I was so desperate to make the horse mine I agreed on the spot. We arranged for me to come back the next day with a horse box and the money in cash.

'Did his last owner say what his name was?' I asked, as I gave the horse one last pat.

'Yep, it's Noah,' said the meat man. 'I was calling him Noah-chance-in-hell – until you came along, that is.'

Noah turned out to be a wonderful horse – every bit as

generous and sweet as I thought he would be from the moment I saw him. It was devastating to think that if his ex-owner had dropped him off just one day earlier, he'd already have been mincemeat. The idea of it broke my heart – as did thinking about all the horses I didn't get to in time. I left my number with the meat man, urging him to call me if any other horses well enough for a second chance crossed his path.

The landlord was fine with me keeping as many horses as I wanted up at Park Lane and turning them out in the fields in Surrey, as long as I paid for their upkeep. I bought Simon and Louis from him, and not long after that I came across Samson, a stocky little bay pony, and piebald Dermot, who had to be named after the X Factor host because of how he immediately clicked with Simon and Louis. They weren't expensive horses, but to me they were priceless.

With the weather so cold, my little herd spent a fair bit of time inside, and when I went into the stable block first thing in the morning and saw all the horsey heads looking over the doors, I'd feel a glow of excitement – followed by a rush of nervousness about whether I'd ever be able to convince the landlord to let me take over the lease.

With all the new horses to look after, as well as my responsibilities at the farm, I wasn't going to be able to go back to Birmingham for Christmas. Eight months ago I'd have found that a depressing thought, but while I'd miss having Christmas dinner with my dad, I was actually excited to be spending the festive season surrounded by my new friends and my beloved horses.

Birmingham wasn't my home any more, Teddington was – and I loved how this little corner of the capital came alive when December arrived. The streets were festooned with fairy lights, the counters at the local deli groaning with panettone and sugared almonds, the pub blasting out festive tunes on the jukebox every evening.

It had been one of the most eventful years of my life, and in many ways I could hardly believe I'd survived it. I'd faced challenges I never expected but I'd overcome them, and now I felt like I deserved to see out the year in style. Christmas 2008 should be one of my most memorable ever, I told myself. And boy, how it was.

CHAPTER SIX

Fire!

A week before Christmas, Jenny and her husband Doug arrived for a long weekend with me in Teddington. We spent the Saturday afternoon wandering around central London, marvelling at the lights on Oxford Street and pressing our noses up to the windows of Fortnum & Mason's to take in every detail of their amazing display. I had booked for us to go skating at the ice rink at Hampton Court that evening, and we headed back to the cottage to get changed first.

I was sitting on the floor in the living room writing Christmas cards when the power went off. Jenny was in the shower, and she yelped in surprise as the whole cottage was plunged into darkness.

'It's not funny, you guys!' she called. 'Switch it back on!'

'Sorry, Jen, that wasn't us!' I said. I could see a shadowy shape I assumed was Doug, fumbling down the passage from the bedroom.

'Where's your fuse box, Nat?' he asked.

'It's just over here . . .' I used the light of my mobile phone screen to find my way to where the box was, in a cupboard by the front door. One of the trip switches was facing the wrong way, but when I tried to flick it back up, it just wouldn't budge.

'That's ... not a good sign,' said Doug, crouching beside me. He was trying to wrench the switch back into position when there was a hammering at the door.

I got to my feet and tried to pull the door open, but as often happened at that time of year, I found it was stuck. The wood swelled up when it was cold or damp and I'd spent many frustrating mornings doing battle with it as I tried to leave.

'Sorry, the door won't open!' I called. 'Give me a minute!'

'Stand aside then, I'll kick it in,' came a voice from the other side.

I opened my mouth to protest that this was a bit extreme, and I just needed to give the door another try, when there were four thunderous kicks and it came crashing in. As the cloud of sawdust cleared, I saw that the kicker was a man I didn't recognise, wearing a commuter's uniform of suit, tie and thick overcoat – and his face was a livid white.

'What on earth did you do that for?' I said angrily. 'Who are you anyway?'

'Your house is on fire.'

'What?'

I stumbled outside, and stared up at the roof of the cottage in horror. The stranger was right – it was alive with dancing red and orange flames, every bit as bright and dazzling as the Christmas lights we'd seen earlier. The fire cracked with sinister rage, and my nostrils were filled with the putrid smell of burning.

'Oh my god,' I breathed, as Murphy, Jenny and Doug rushed out behind me, Jenny wrapped in nothing but a towel.

'Didn't you smell it?' the stranger asked incredulously.

'No, we didn't smell a thing!' I said. It was so weird really, to think we had been in the cottage oblivious to the fact my home had become a giant bonfire, with the flames inching towards the stables. 'Oh my god, the horses . . .'

Without even thinking I threw myself back towards the cottage, vaguely aware of Jenny screaming 'Nat, no!' behind me.

The man tried to grab my arm but I wriggled free.

'The fire brigade is on its way!' he yelled. 'Don't go back in there, it's too dangerous!' But I was already diving through the broken doorway, and covering my mouth with my sleeve as the black clouds of smoke engulfed me. I grabbed the stable keys from the hook, and sprinted back towards the stable yard.

It had been so cold that week that all the horses from the farm were inside, and I currently had six of them up at the stables, including Prodney and Noah. All I could think of was them, how their hearts would start racing as they smelt danger in the air. I had to get to them, I had to keep them safe.

I had reached the big black gate which led into the stables and I was fumbling with the padlock, trying to get my key in, but my hands were shaking so much I couldn't do it. 'Come on, come on, come on!' I yelled angrily at myself, trying to stop fear from taking over.

The panic was really flooding through me now but my eyes could hardly focus and the key kept slipping from my grip. It was such a simple thing to do – why was my body letting me down now? I took a big gasp of air and briefly shut my eyes, imagining I was on Prodney's back, galloping over a rolling green meadow. Flicking my eyes back open into the smoky, dark reality, I found a new determination, and finally got the key into the lock.

I stumbled across the yard, covering my mouth with my sleeve, as clouds of rancid black smoke poured in from the direction of the cottage. Inside the stable block it was so dark I could only tell the horses were there by their panicky, shuffling hooves and the glint of their big, frightened eyes. As my eyes adjusted, I remembered with a jolt that Prodney was the furthest away – meaning he was probably safest for now. I had to take the horses which were closest to the cottage and therefore in most danger.

'I'll be back for you all, don't worry,' I told the rest of the horses, as I grabbed the halters of the two closest ponies, Simon and Louis. 'Come on, little ones,' I told them, trying to keep my voice soothing as they whinnied and stomped their feet, their ears pushed back in fear. But despite their panic, they chose to trust me, and I pulled them out on to the road.

'Nat, thank God!' Someone had found Jenny a tracksuit to wear, and she and Doug were rushing towards me. I handed them a pony each.

'Take them to the Dowager. There's a garden there.'

The fire engine had arrived and a team of yellow-hatted firefighters were unfurling an enormous hose. A small crowd of neighbours had gathered to watch, fear dancing on their illuminated faces. 'They're going to make a wall of water between the cottage and the stables,' I heard someone say. 'It should stop the fire from spreading.'

The noise of the hose when it was switched on was deafening. Water rose in an enormous plume, crashing on to the walls and roof of the cottage. I could only hope it would be enough to stop the flames reaching the straw and hay in the stables. If that were to catch light, the whole thing would go up like a tinderbox. But I didn't have time to stand and watch. Everyone was so fixated on the firemen, I don't think anyone noticed as I turned back into the stables, praying that they'd be able to stop the blaze in its tracks. I grabbed two more ponies – a little grey called Cloudy and Dermot – my heart aching to leave Noah and Prodney behind.

When we emerged back on to the street, I saw that half the pub had come to help.

'We just yelled in and they all came,' said Jenny, taking the halters from me. 'Are the horses secure in that garden, do you think?'

'Safer than here, that's for sure!' I said, wiping the sweat from my brow. Pleased to see Doug had Murphy on a lead, I turned to go back for Prodney and Noah, but a fireman stopped me.

'It's too unsafe, madam,' he said firmly, blocking my way.

'There's still two horses in there!' I screamed, terror threatening to suffocate me.

I glanced up at the wreckage of my home. The cottage was completely black, and although water was pouring down on it, a few stubborn flames still crept along the spine of the roof.

'The water may have weakened the structure of the stables,' the fireman warned. 'It could collapse. We will go in for the horses – but you must stay here.'

I wanted to protest that I could do it, but instead I felt all the fight drop out of me as if I was a rag doll. The thought of Prodney and Noah, scared and abandoned in the stables, just horrified me. I pictured rubble collapsing in on them, and I could almost hear their high-pitched neighing as they realised what was happening. Guilt tightened around my throat like a noose – if Prodney died, it would all be my fault. After everything he had done for me, all the joy he had given me, had I really left him in there to suffer such a terrible fate?

Jenny was suddenly at my side, and wrapped her arms around me – without her support, I'm sure I would have fallen to the floor. We watched breathlessly as three firemen, their yellow helmets glinting, disappeared through the black gate.

Every second they were gone felt like an hour. The clouds of black smoke were so dense now you couldn't even make out the outline of the stables, and it was hard to imagine that either men or horses would ever emerge from that hellish scene. In reality the street was filled with deafening noise, but to me it seemed that the air went silent as I waited. My breath was caught in the back of my throat like an iron ball, and my limbs felt like they no longer belonged to me. I don't believe in God, but all I could do was pray. I couldn't lose Prodney – I just couldn't.

'Please, Prodney, come back,' I whispered. Jenny gave me a reassuring squeeze.

Then all of a sudden there was a clatter of hooves and the two horses were right in front of me, each led by a fireman.

'Thank you, thank you!' I exclaimed, throwing my arms around Prodney's neck and showering his nose with kisses.

'Get them to safety,' barked the fireman nearest to me, and I didn't need telling twice. I ran down the road, Prodney trotting beside me, Jenny and Noah following close behind. At the Queen Dowager we turned them out into the beer garden, long abandoned for winter. It was only once I knew they were safe, along with the other four who were grazing among the picnic tables, that my mind turned to what had happened to my home.

My legs felt like lead as we walked back towards the fire engine. The firefighters were still battling the final flames, and I could see that they had won the war. But what of the wreckage that was left behind?

A young bloke I'd never seen before but would later discover was Anwar, a resident of the flats opposite, offered me a mug of tea – an act of kindness I'll never forget, because tea was exactly what I needed right then. Clutching the mug in my trembling hands, I felt numb as I surveyed the shell that had been my cottage. Yes it was cold and old-fashioned, but I'd come to love it. I'd worked so hard to make it a home, but now everything I owned was reduced to ash. So many of my photos, the postcards Dad sent me from his holidays, the old copy of *Black Beauty* I read every time I felt blue, even the wonky Christmas tree standing proudly in the corner, laden with gifts – it was all destroyed.

'It's just things,' I told myself, trying to hold back childish tears as I realised that the only belongings I had left were the jeans and silly Christmas jumper I was wearing.

The firemen had saved what really mattered. Jenny and Doug, Murphy and I and all the horses were safe. In contrast to the cottage, the stables themselves, miraculously, had survived relatively unscathed. There was a clear line where the water had been – the roof on one side, where I lived, black and burned, the other, where the horses did, dripping wet. The stables stood firm and intact, as they had done for several centuries. Once the walls dried, you'd barely be able to tell what had happened.

I had a funny feeling as I looked at the building, this small, solid survivor, so out of place on its suburban street. The stables were too important to be simply a boarding house where the odd horse spent a winter's night. They had too much dignity, too much history, to be an afterthought.

I knew then as clearly as I'd ever known anything: I was going to start a riding school here, and I was going to run it on my own. The stables would rise from the ashes.

CHAPTER SEVEN

Out of the Ashes

The blaze had been a freak accident, and we were lucky, really, that because of where it happened we had enough time to get out of the cottage.

Even so, I'd lost almost everything I owned, and now didn't have anywhere to live either. While the landlords did the necessary renovations to the cottage, Murphy and I moved on to the sofa of the flat over the road with Pasty, Sam and Barney. I would get dressed in the darkness in the early hours, trying not to wake my friends as I left for another long day on the farm. It wasn't exactly ideal timing for making major life decisions, but if the fire had taught me anything, it was that life is fleeting – and you have to grab each moment when you can. And I'd lost everything in the blaze – so I really had nothing to lose.

Before it happened, I'd been holding off approaching the landlords because I didn't have enough money, or I wasn't sure the timing was right, or I didn't have the confidence they'd sell me the lease. But I wasn't prepared to wait any more. Throughout January I stayed in the flat in the evening while the others headed to the pub, working on my business plan and sweating over budget spreadsheets. One welcome side effect to the fire was that it seemed to wake up the community to the fact that there was someone in the stables again. The *Richmond and Twickenham Times* reported the blaze on the front page, and it served to alert people that there were horses in the area once more.

The day the paper came out, I was mucking out at Park Lane when there was a knock at the black gate. Wiping my hands on the back of my trousers, I went to open it – and found a little girl of no more than nine standing there with her mother.

'We're sorry to disturb you,' said the woman, her hands on her daughter's shoulders. 'We just wanted to say how sorry we were to hear about your fire. And, well, Lexi wanted to know if you really keep horses here?'

I beamed at the little girl, who regarded me with big blue eyes. 'I certainly do,' I said. 'Would you like to come in and meet them?'

I might as well have offered her a trip on Santa's sleigh, such was the delight that this gave Lexi. She stood close to me as I introduced her to Samson, Prodney and Noah, reverently stroking their noses with my encouragement.

'She's absolutely horse mad,' Lexi's mum said, and I could tell this was true. Lexi was like me at that age – with an absolutely one-track mind for ponies.

'Do you do riding lessons?' Lexi asked shyly, when it was time for them to go.

'Not yet,' I admitted. 'But I will do before too long, I hope.'

It wasn't just Lexi – after that, I started to get a steady trickle of visitors who would come with apples or carrots for the ponies. If they expressed an interest in lessons, I'd scribble down their numbers, tucking them into a folder marked 'potential clients'.

By the first week in February, the work on the cottage was finished and I could move back in. And when I did, I didn't return alone – I had my very first housemate.

Her name was Jenny, like my friend from home. But I always called her Jenny Bear, because she worked at the kids' toyshop Build-A-Bear, and was as cuddly and comforting as a teddy too. Jenny Bear was a friend of Sam's, who had just split from her partner so was in desperate need of somewhere to live. In fact, she was so desperate that she agreed to move into the cottage without even seeing it – despite being warned that it was small and lacking in central heating.

If she was disappointed when she saw it for the first time, Jenny didn't let on. She wore little glasses and had her hair tightly drawn back into a bun at the back of her head. Her face was round and warm, and I could tell she was one of those people that invites confidences. She looked like she wouldn't judge you, whatever you said.

I watched her awkwardly as she looked into the three bedrooms, each with the most basic furniture. I said she could have whichever one she wanted – I didn't mind. I was half expecting her to say she didn't want any of them, because there's no doubt she could have found somewhere better!

'I'll have this one then,' she said, once we got to the middle-size one, and put her bag down decisively. I beamed. And that was that – Jenny Bear had moved in.

At first we were shy around each other, having polite conversations in the kitchen and diligently sharing the housework. But the rather survivalist nature of living in the cottage soon forced us into closer quarters. It was so cold that when we were watching TV, we'd have to snuggle up under the same blanket for warmth. And there was always some new household disaster – whether it was the discovery of a nest of mice or the collapse of the shower curtain rail – that we had to tackle together. Before long we were laughing uproariously and swapping break-up stories late into the night.

Jenny Bear turned out to be one of the kindest, most big-hearted people I had ever met. She wasn't really bothered about horses but showed a polite interest in Prodney, and she adored Murphy. She gave the best advice, and was always thinking of others. Even when she went to the corner shop, she would never come back without something for me – whether it was a bunch of cheerful daffodils or my favourite Cadbury's Caramel.

By March 2009, I considered her one of my best friends. So when she suggested that one of her closest pals, Lou, move in too, I didn't hesitate to say yes.

Lou worked with Jenny at Build-A-Bear, and she had long dark hair and a laid-back attitude to life. I quickly learned that it was best to avoid talking to Lou before 10 a.m., such was her extreme grumpiness in the mornings. But when you caught her in the evenings, watching one of her beloved musicals, she was so much fun. Lou had always dreamed of being an actress and had an encyclopaedic knowledge of Old Hollywood.

Like Jenny Bear and me, Lou was single, and she introduced us to one of the first online dating sites, Plenty of Fish. She and I would sit playing it like a game in the evenings, trying to get as many matches as we could. I always failed miserably, while she would rake in loads every night. 'Look, this is your problem, Nat,' she would say, gesturing at my rather lacklustre dating pro-file. 'This' – she waved at my profile picture, which showed me in a baseball cap with my arm round Murphy – 'and this' – she gestured at my interests, which were 'horses and reading' – 'is not what men want to see, I'm afraid.'

I didn't care really, it was all just a bit of fun, and I loved to laugh at Lou's indignation over how hopeless I was. The three of us had such a laugh in those days. Lou and Jenny were both younger than me – eight and ten years respectively – so I felt like I was in my carefree twenties all over again. With the girls in the cottage, it started to feel like a home again – Jenny filling it up with pretty knick-knacks, and Lou always cooking something delicious at the stove.

Murphy, meanwhile, loved having three 'mums', and would always try and squeeze himself between us on the sofa so he could get the maximum fuss. It was still freezing, of course, but we'd all snuggle up in the same bed on the really cold nights, woolly hats and scarves wrapped around our faces, watching water trickle down the icy walls. I couldn't believe that the girls actually wanted to pay rent to live in a place like that, but I guessed they loved living there as much as I did – cold and damp notwithstanding.

The fire could have proved a major setback, but instead it had been the start of an exciting new chapter. I spent my weekends researching things like riding hats for children, or looking for fields which I could rent for the horses once I no longer had access to the Esher farm. And, of course, I continued to work on my pitch to the landlord. I knew I couldn't stay and run the farm for ever, but I also couldn't bear the idea of leaving Teddington. I loved it here – how little old ladies would knock on my door and ask for leftover manure for their roses. Or how young dads would hoist their kids on to their shoulders when they were passing by, so they could see over the stable yard gate and watch the horses chewing their hay. The greengrocer would always insist I take an extra bag of wonky carrots, free of charge, 'for that big white horse of yours'. In Bushy Park the rangers had got to know me, and always gave me a friendly wave when I was out for my daily ride. I didn't want to say goodbye to all that.

I finally decided I had enough money and confidence to make an appointment to see the landlord in May 2009. It was make-or-break time.

All my friends knew what I was up to and how much was at stake. Pasty sweetly planned a celebration party in the Dowager afterwards, and invited everyone I knew.

'What if it's not a celebration, though?' I said anxiously, when I found out what he'd done.

'Well, you'll need plenty of mates to help you drown your sorrows, won't you?' he replied. Knowing my friends were all behind me gave me a boost, but even so, I was incredibly nervous.

The night before I barely slept, instead lying awake in my bed reciting my business plan under my breath. I didn't know how the landlord would feel about me going from employee to leaseholder, but I had to persuade him I could make it financially worth his while. I had already proved I was a hard worker – now I had to make him believe I was a businesswoman too.

CHAPTER EIGHT

A Twist of Fete

When I opened the door to the pub that evening, all my London friends were gathered there – just as Pasty had promised. There he was with Barney and Sam, and Lou and Jenny Bear, a few other locals I'd become friendly with, and even Mark had put on a shirt and tie for the occasion. The chatter fell silent as I stepped inside, and a sea of expectant faces turned towards me, all trying to read from my expression the result of the meeting.

I decided to ham it up, looking down at my feet and sighing.

'They didn't accept my offer,' I said.

'Oh Nat—' said Jenny Bear, getting to her feet, her eyes full of concern.

'—But they did say I can have the lease for an extra two thousand pounds!'

The pub erupted into cheers and the girls bounded over to hug me. In the grand scheme of things, two grand wasn't too much, and I had expected the landlord to negotiate. They were sorting out a contract with their lawyers now, and within weeks the riding school would be mine. I was over the moon.

Pasty's party turned out to be the best idea ever, and I was so happy to be surrounded by all my friends as I celebrated what felt like the biggest achievement of my life. I rang Dad just as the rest of them burst into song – I think it was 'Mr Brightside' by The Killers – and he could barely hear him over the din.

'I did it, Dad – they said yes! I got the riding school!'

I could hear just enough to catch him saying how proud he was. 'And your mum will be smiling up in heaven too – it's all she ever wanted for you,' he said. 'Now you better get back to your friends – sounds like there's some partying to do!'

After a raucous evening of celebration, when Mark finally chucked us all out, the girls and I staggered back to the cottage. Jenny and Lou fell asleep on the sofa but I still felt wired even though it was 1 a.m. I pulled on a denim jacket and took myself next door to the stables. Prodney was in there, and I could see he was awake, his eyes watchful in the moonlight.

Stroking his handsome face and pressing my face into his mane took me back to that first week in Teddington over a year ago, when I had barely been able to stop crying and I'd been tempted to pack up and leave. Now I was about to start a whole new chapter with my own business.

It was terrifying and exhilarating all at the same time. If it all went wrong, I really would lose everything, and I'd be forced to leave this lovely life I'd built myself in London. All my savings were going into the stables, and I'd never done anything like this before. There was no back-up plan, no safety net. But for now, I just wanted to enjoy the moment with my faithful horse, knowing I'd never regret taking this chance.

Over the next few weeks, I'd be glad I took that moment of stillness – because as the stables got started, I found I barely ever had a single minute to myself. Although I'd planned for it and dreamed about it for years, nothing could have prepared me for the work involved in starting the stables from scratch. The first hurdle was all the paperwork I had to file. I had to establish the business with Companies House, apply for a licence from the council, and write countless risk assessments.

Then there was the stable block itself, which was very unloved and scruffy. If I wanted to persuade people to pay for lessons here, it needed a facelift, so I roped in my mates to help paint it. Barney, Sam and I spent the entire May bank holiday weekend in there, fuelled by Lucozade and Walkers crisps, painting every square inch until it looked – almost – brand new.

I was still on the lookout for more horses, because I wanted to make sure that none would be overworked once we were up and running. To my burgeoning herd, I added Dodi, a powerfully built grey horse of about seventeen hands, and Diana, a little caramel dun pony, small enough that she'd be perfect for younger children.

I'd never worked with kids before, but I somehow just knew that I wanted to focus the lessons on young people. Horses had been so important to me as a child; my first passion, my best friends, and then my saving grace when things got tough. I wanted to pass that gift on to other children, knowing that spending time with horses when you're young can create memories that last a lifetime.

Of course, there was no way I'd let a child, or anyone for that matter, get on a horse of mine unless I was sure they were completely safe. Safety has always been one of my guiding principles in my approach to horses – ever since I lost a close friend in my early twenties. I knew Mandy because she kept her horse at Prodney's yard, and she was an experienced and highly skilled horsewoman, as well as a kind and fun person to be around.

Then one day she'd gone on one of her usual rides, and for some reason we'll never know, her horse got spooked. He'd bolted before coming to a dead stop in a cul-de-sac, throwing Mandy off as he did. She hit her head on the pavement when she fell, and tragically died. She was only thirty-two, and left behind two children. It was a horrific shock and a terrible loss, one I've never forgotten.

Because of Mandy, I have always been very conscious of what horses are capable of, and the awful consequences when something goes wrong. When you spend a lot of time with horses it can be easy to get complacent, but ultimately you have to remember they are big animals with minds of their own and it's never worth taking a chance.

To me, that meant testing each one of my horses in every possible situation before I'd let anyone else ride them. Until I knew them inside out, I'd never know if, for example, Noah didn't like it when the wind was high, or if Simon wasn't keen on yellow cars. I had to know what would spook them, so I could make sure that it wouldn't happen when they were being ridden by someone else.

It meant, as I prepared to open the stable doors, I spent an enormous amount of time with the horses, getting to know their personalities and making assessments over what kind of rider they'd be most suited to. I got to know their little quirks – for example, how Dermot never got any sleep if he was next to Noah, which meant he'd be in a huge grump the next day. After I figured that one out, I made a note to always keep them at opposite ends of the stable block.

But completed paperwork, perfectly trained ponies and a freshly painted yard would all be pointless without any pupils. And that was my next big challenge. How to put us on the map?

Yes, I had the numbers of a few people who were interested, but nowhere near enough to make the money I needed for my rent.

'You should speak to Richard Sharp,' Sam said to me one day, as she helped me load Dodi and Diana into the horse box to take back to the field I'd rented in Oxshott, Surrey. She was always happy to help out with the odd favour and we'd been discussing how to get the word out about the stables. 'He knows everyone in Teddington, and he knows about marketing too.'

I'd never heard of this Richard, but it turned out I was pretty much the only person in Teddington who hadn't. He was retired now but had worked in marketing for Transport for London for years, and he had since become a community powerhouse.

Sam arranged for us to meet for a drink, and I clicked with Richard straight away. He immediately got what I was trying to do, which was to create a stables which were friendly and inclusive – welcoming anybody and everybody, no matter what your experience around horses, your background or how much money your parents had in the bank.

'As far as I'm concerned, horses make magic happen – and I want to spread the opportunity to experience it as widely as possible,' I said.

'Well, with that I can help you,' Richard replied, smiling, and we clinked glasses.

In a way, Richard was Park Lane's first volunteer – even though it was very much behind the scenes. He helped in a really important way, which was networking on our behalf, and spreading the word. One of the first things he did was design and pay for leaflets for us to hand out – but he was insistent that a leaflet would never be as powerful as a real-life experience.

'And you know what that means?' he told me, one early summer afternoon. 'We've got to get you into the school fetes.'

I grinned, delighted – of course! Hadn't it been a school fete where I first fell in love with riding? Doing pony rides was the perfect way to reach out to kids who might not have thought about horses before.

'I know governors at just about every school in the area, and let me tell you, school fete season in Teddington is absolutely crazy,' said Richard, his mouth twitching at the absurdity of his own sentence. 'If you're prepared to give up every weekend in June I've got a hunch we can reach a lot of kids this way.'

I loved his plan – and I was delighted when he secured us a spot at our first fete the very next weekend. I got up early that morning to make sure I had hours to get Diana looking just perfect – her mane plaited, her coat brushed until it gleamed, and her tack gleaming.

Jenny Bear had agreed to come with me to help, and I felt strangely nervous as we drove over to the school on the other side of Teddington. We were early, and the wait for the guests to arrive didn't do anything for my nerves. It was a typical school fete – a cake stand, a tombola, skittles, balloons, the works – and typical British summertime weather: grey, with a chance of drizzle. Families soon started to trickle in, and it wasn't long before I spotted a determined-looking little girl making a beeline for us through the crowd. Her hair was in neat bunches, and her face was glowing at the sight of Diana.

'Hi there!' I said, feeling strangely emotional to find myself on the opposite side of the scene that was so burned into my brain from childhood. 'This is Diana. What's your name?'

Her name was Amelia, and although I didn't know it then, I'd be seeing much more of her over the years to come. For now, I just got to enjoy the magic of a ten-year-old girl having her first ever pony ride – and loving every minute.

After Amelia, we found we had quite the queue of children, and we were busy all afternoon. Diana was as sweet and gentle as I knew she would be, accepting the pats and strokes of the children with evident gratitude and clopping along beside me with boundless energy as we walked up and down the length of the field. Jenny Bear was busy giving out Richard's leaflets and taking down numbers – our potential client list had more than tripled by the end of the day.

As we led Diana back to the horse box, waving goodbye to the PTA volunteers dismantling trestle tables and bagging up rubbish, I felt a glow of pride.

'You know, Jen, if you'd told me when I was a kid having my first pony ride, that one day I'd be the lady with the pony – well, it's more than I could ever have hoped for. I wish I could go back and tell my younger self that it would all turn out okay.'

Jenny grinned and put her arm round my shoulders for a quick hug. 'I reckon it's going to turn out more than okay,' she said. 'You're just getting started.'

CHAPTER NINE

The Pavement Ponies

The fete had proved so successful at getting kids to sign up for lessons that I started attending every similar event that I could. Richard was always ringing with new dates for my diary – Remembrance Sunday, Christmas bazaars, the summer carnival – if it was possible to take a pony, he got us an invite. One of my favourite events was a Tintin-themed day at a pub in nearby Hampton Hill, where everyone wore Tintin T-shirts and I somehow managed to put grey pony Cloudy's mane into a rough Tintin quiff.

Pasty, who had a new job almost every other week, did his best to drum up some custom, haranguing any new colleagues with age-appropriate children to look me up. And Lou and Jenny Bear admitted they were always dropping it into conversation at Build-A-Bear – they had a captive market of children, after all! All our efforts meant that before I knew it, I had a waiting list of children aged eight to seventeen who all wanted riding lessons.

I was so nervous before the first lesson I took, but the moment we got going, everything just fell into place. The four children were taking it in turns to ride Noah, and I was showing them how to hold the reins and how to sit with their heels down, toes pointing up and backs straight. I remember the massive grin of the first little girl as Noah broke into a trot, me jogging alongside. Noah too was carrying himself with such pride – I could tell how much he was enjoying being with the children and getting to work.

As word started to get out about what we were doing, things snowballed. My motto was that we would be 'the friendliest stables in London – if not the world', and it turned out that there was a real appetite for riding lessons that weren't snooty or elitist. If I saw someone lingering on the street outside the stables, I'd rush outside and invite them in to have a look around, urging them to tell anyone they knew about the ponies and that lessons were available. I wanted Park Lane to be a stables that was open to all – and especially people that needed us. When I was a grieving, lonely kid, my local yard had been my safe haven. And that was what I wanted Park Lane to be too.

I remember one lad of fourteen who was always hanging around on his bike, keeping his distance, when I was taking the Saturday morning lesson in Bushy Park. He had that surly way about him that teenage boys do, but I could tell he was curious. After he'd watched from a distance for three weeks, I just marched over to him and told him to come and join in. He acted like he wasn't interested, but he took me up on my offer and as I helped him into Dermot's saddle, he smiled despite himself. From then on, he was a regular pupil.

As demand grew, I found myself spending seven hours teaching back to back in Bushy Park every Saturday and Sunday, my voice hoarse from shouting across to the kids. But I loved every minute.

Most of my pupils were complete beginners when they came to me, but their enthusiasm meant that they progressed fast. Once they could ride independently off the lead rein we could really have some fun. I have a clear memory of a gorgeous autumn day in 2009, when I took a group of teenagers for a long ride all the way down the river until the stunning facade of Hampton Court Palace came into view. I was on Prodney, and it was such an incredible feeling to ride alongside these newly confident kids who were starting to master their riding, their faces flushed from the autumn chill and the joy of being out with the horses and their friends.

As the months progressed, I started booking lessons after school as well as the weekends, which meant I was more and more frantic on weekdays doing all the jobs and chores I had to do to keep the horses happy and healthy. For me, the welfare of the horses had to always come first. No matter what the demand or how busy we got, I vowed they would always get their rest. My horses loved to work, but they also needed time to be, well, horses. That meant making sure they had plenty of time away from the stables to play and graze. I devised a complicated rota whereby the horses would do four days' work, during which they'd stay at Park Lane, and five days in the field in Oxshott. It meant I was constantly playing horse Jenga – driving between Park Lane and the field in an old, second-hand horse lorry every few days, swapping horses round so none were at the stables for too long. I also made time every morning to give each working horse a good groom and a once-over to check they were fit and healthy, and every evening I'd spend ages in the stables making a fuss of them so they knew how much they were loved.

I believe horses have a voice – and if you spend time getting in tune with their behaviour, you know what they're trying to say to you. Sometimes, when I'd go to pick up a horse from the field, I'd realise he or she wasn't ready to come in – so I'd let them have a bit longer. Other times, a horse would act in ways which were out of character – and you could tell they were tired or under the weather. Even if it meant cancelling lessons and losing out on business, I would always prioritise their needs, and I knew my riders felt the same way. (Sadly, while I had been studying for my British Horse Society exams and training at a range of stables, I had realised not everyone took the same approach.)

With more and more people signing up for lessons, I needed more horses, to make sure none were overworked. Not that I had much money to pay for them – but in this, the timing worked in my favour.

In 2009, when I was getting the stables going, the country was still feeling the effects of the recession. That sadly meant a lot of people were getting rid of horses because they could no longer afford to keep them. As a result, I was able to either take ponies off people's hands or rescue them, or even borrow them from people while they got back on their feet. Once, I was riding Noah past a café near the edge of Bushy Park, when a man came rushing out.

'Do you want another one?' he yelled.

'Another what?'

'Another horse! I can't afford to keep my daughter's horse!'

'Okay,' I shrugged. 'Bring him to Park Lane Stables in Teddington and we'll see what we can do.'

The next morning, I woke to a clattering of hooves outside. I poked my head out of the door to see a bay cob tied to a lamp post. It seemed the man from the café had followed through. We called him Benny, and he became a much loved member of my equine family.

My horses were a motley crew – rescued or begged or borrowed, some short, some shaggy, some lanky and some a little tubby. Some were a little unruly, like a cheeky grey gelding called Eddy who needed a lot of training before he was ready to be ridden by the kids. But what they all had in common was that they were safe and reliable and kind. Sure, they were hardly going to be showjumping at Hickstead, but that's not what they were there for. And I wouldn't have had them any other way.

Locals started referring to my little herd as the 'pavement ponies', because we'd always be clopping up and down the street, an incongruous sight in London. Even though I ran the place, I had to agree there was something surreal about our set-up. You'd be walking down this perfectly normal suburban street then suddenly you'd see a horse with its head hanging over a stable door. Sometimes I even put a horse to graze in the communal gardens of the flats opposite, and there's definitely something strange and magical about seeing a pony rolling around in the shadow of a tower block.

When I dreamed of running my own stables as a child, I'd pictured neat white fences and a spotless yard and acres of rolling green paddocks. Then as I'd got older I'd realised that kind of stables wasn't for the likes of me, and I'd set my sights on a more realistic dream – running something modest with the husband I loved.

I'd never have pictured this – a handful of misfit ponies, a tiny, tumbledown block, rides that took you past traffic and into a busy park – and doing it all on my own. But now that I had it, I realised this was what I'd been searching for my whole life. Park Lane might not have been conventional – but to me it was perfect.

CHAPTER TEN

The Kids are Alright

As we got up and running, I offered lessons to riders of all ages, and by teaching adults I made some good friends. One woman I got particularly close to was Ali, who was about my age and, like me, was single. She worked in celebrity management, so her world was completely different to mine, but we hit it off straight away anyway. We'd go riding together and then usually head to the pub afterwards and put the world to rights, as only two single women in their thirties know how.

Riding with adults was fun and sociable, but I found my real passion was teaching children. While adults mostly came with some background in riding, with children, I was usually offering them their first ever experience with horses. It is a true privilege to be there as they discover the joy of bonding with a pony. And also an incredible opportunity to teach them how to treat animals with respect, and how to use what they learned from riding to grow as people.

Take Amelia, for example – the little girl from the fete. She started coming for lessons and I saw her confidence blossom. At first she was shy and nervous, and would want her mum to stay and watch her. But as the weeks went by she'd rush through the gates and straight to Flo's stable with barely a backward glance. Flo was a little chestnut mare I had recently bought from a family that no longer wanted her, and she'd needed to be put on a diet because they'd fed her lots of ice creams! With her patient nature and pretty face, she'd been a huge hit with the kids, and especially Amelia who had fallen head over heels in love with her. She started staying on after her lessons to help around the yard, and she was so diligent and caring around the ponies.

'I love Flo so much I don't even mind her poo,' she told me one day, her face shining, as she wheeled another overflowing wheelbarrow out through the gates. I had to laugh – it's how I've always felt about my horses too.

Park Lane's unusual setting meant that we were able to reach the sort of kids who probably wouldn't usually have had the opportunity to ride. I knew some people looked down their noses at our ramshackle facilities and oddball ponies, but that suited me down to the ground. Instead I ended up with ordinary kids who were shy, or lonely or cheeky or silly or total bloody teara-ways – but I loved them all.

I never wanted to turn anyone away, so if a kid turned up whose parents didn't have the means to pay for their lessons, we usually found a way to make it work. I knew from my own teenage years how important horses can be to children in diffi-cult circumstances. I had kids turn up who were being bullied, or constantly fighting with their parents, or struggling at school. But the stables were somewhere they could escape all those prob-lems. For many of them, it wasn't even about the riding – it was about being around the horses, who give you that special kind of love that is hard to define. A horse can make you feel like the most important person in the world; even when the rest of the time, you feel like anything but.

There's one girl that particularly sticks in my mind. She was pretty much dragged to the stables by her mum, who told me quite plainly, in front of her daughter: 'I don't know what to do with Amy.'

I looked at the thirteen-year-old girl, sullen-faced and caked in make-up. Her mother ran me through her alleged problems: she was constantly getting into physical fights with other girls, she'd been caught by the police shoplifting, she was on her last warning before a permanent suspension from school. 'And I just can't get through to her,' said the exasperated mother, who I could tell was so hurt and exhausted by trying to fix her little girl.

I looked at Amy, chewing gum and trying to look like she didn't care one tiny bit that her mum was saying these things about her to a stranger. I didn't see a girl who loved being bad – I saw a child who was lost and deeply unhappy. She'd been referred to the stables by a kind-hearted PE teacher, who also happened to have a daughter who rode with us.

'This is kind of a last resort,' said Amy's mum, exasperated.

Amy finally lifted her chin and caught my eye. 'Well, I don't know about last resort, because it's kind of a privilege to spend time with my horses,' I said, keeping my eyes on Amy. 'But we do have a few rules around here. Work hard, respect the horses, and be kind to each other. Break any of those and you're out. Now, would you like to come and meet Mini? I think she's just the right size for you and you could be a brilliant team . . .'

Amy followed me into the stables without looking back at her mum, who called after her that she'd pick her up in two hours. I knew Amy's mum was just a parent trying her best who was at the end of her tether, which probably meant she couldn't see what I could. I don't think many people had taken an interest in Amy before – not in a way that wasn't constantly questioning her about all the ways she'd messed up. I decided not to address that at all, and simply explained how Mini particularly loved being tickled under the chin, and how she was super speedy when she cantered. I asked Amy what she thought about horses, and she shrugged a surly 'don't know'. But I could see how her face had lit up now we were in the stable block, surrounded by gentle, sweet-smelling beasts.

Amy took to riding like a natural. For a girl I'd been told was out of control, she had an astonishing amount of self-discipline, which you need when you're on a horse. She was fearless but also sensitive, seeming to tune into Mini's mind when she was in the saddle. I was amazed by how quickly she progressed, and told her so often. Her bright, girlish smile was the best reward I could ask for.

Two hours a week quickly wasn't enough – and Amy would spend the whole weekend at Park Lane, helping muck out, make up feed buckets, and even leading some of the younger kids on the little ponies. I watched her transform into an articulate, responsible and hardworking young woman before my very eyes. I didn't even need her mum to give me gushing progress reports on how Amy was changing every other aspect of her life – which she did – because Amy proudly told me herself. She knew I'd be impressed that she was on top of her school work and out of trouble – and I was.

There were plenty of other kids like Amy – such as Jordan, who'd fallen into a bad crowd of kids who were smoking too much pot but found purpose and direction at the yard, and a real friendship with Noah. I remember the day he jumped Noah for the first time, and how he punched the air with excitement as they successfully landed as one. When I'd first met him, Jordan had no hopes for himself – but here he was, brimming with pride and confidence.

Philippa was a sunny-natured fifteen-year-old with additional needs who was brought to the stables by her worried-looking mum, who seemed unconvinced that we'd be able to accommodate her. But when I started off by asking Philippa what she could do – rather than what she couldn't – her mum almost burst into tears. 'No one ever asks that,' she told me afterwards. 'They always just see her learning disabilities, and that's it.' Philippa fell in love with the stables and we fell in love with her – she was so friendly and positive and friends with everyone, that you really couldn't have a bad day when she was around.

Then there was Ruby, whose parents simply weren't interested in her but found that horses really were. Unlike some of the kids who had a favourite pony, Ruby loved them all – and would always arrive with her jacket bulging with carrots and apples, bought with her pocket money, because she wanted to make sure they all got a treat.

Astonishingly, Ruby's mum once dropped her off at the stables for an afternoon then rang to tell me she had gone on holiday to Lanzarote and wouldn't be back for a week. Ruby was only twelve. We had to hurriedly ring social services and get their permission for her to stay in the cottage. What really broke my heart was her reaction to the news. Shrugging, she said: 'Mum will have just forgotten. She never thinks about me.' That week, I made sure Ruby and I always went out for a special ride together after school, just the two of us trotting through Bushy Park, and I could tell by the contented look on her face that it was the one hour of the day she didn't think about the fact her mum had abandoned her.

I was proud that the stables became a kind of safe haven,

although there was soon a running joke with Lou and Jenny Bear about how many calls I got from the local police station. It was always one of my older kids who'd got in trouble – usually over drink or soft drugs – and afraid to call their parents, they would give my number instead.

Teenagers will always find ways to get into trouble – you just have to be there to catch them when they fall. I remember one girl of about seventeen, Leila, who was usually the life and soul of the party when she turned up at the stables. Then one day, she was suddenly quiet and withdrawn. I could tell she had a secret she was carrying like a burden – and I also knew the way to help her open up. She usually stayed after her group lesson to help with jobs around the yard, and I found her in the tack room, polishing a saddle.

'Hey, Dermot's rider didn't turn up today and I think he could do with a stretch of his legs – would you help me?' I asked her. 'You can lead him round the block, and I'll come with you with Murphy.'

Leila's face instantly brightened. 'I'll get my jacket,' she said.

We walked in silence for a bit, but Dermot was tossing his head gently and snorting, which made us both giggle. There was something about keeping step with a big horse that I found very soothing – and I hoped Leila did too. We did one turn around the block and then without discussion we kept walking – and Leila started to talk.

It turned out she was pregnant, and didn't know how to tell her mum and dad. 'They're going to be so cross,' she said, in a half whisper. We came to a stop and she buried her face in Dermot's neck, wiping away her tears. I put my hand on her shoulder, and told her I'd be there with her when she told them, if that's what she'd like. 'Can Dermot be there too?' she said, with a weak smile.

'Maybe not, but he'll always be here for a cuddle when you need it,' I replied.

Leila wasn't the only girl who came to me over the years with a surprise pregnancy, and usually, some time with a gentle horse could make even the most overwhelming news bearable.

If the older ones were a challenge, the little ones were a joy – I loved watching five- or six-year-olds get on a pony for the first time, and that rush of excitement and pure happiness flood their faces. Many of these city kids would never have dreamed they could learn to ride, but thanks to Park Lane, they could. I remember one little girl, Amala, who was about seven and lived in a tower block in Hounslow, riding into Bushy Park for the first time. 'Is this where God lives?' she'd said, her eyes wide with wonder as she took in the vast green space.

In the rapt faces of the little children, I saw myself at their age. I'd often wonder, as I watched a class full of children master a rising trot or take their first little jump, which of them would make horses a lifelong passion. Most children do grow out of it – that's just life – but then there are others, like me, for whom those first few riding lessons can be the spark that alters the course of their life. It was my job to light the fire.

CHAPTER ELEVEN

Support System

By the summer of 2010, I had a pretty thriving business on my hands. It wasn't making huge amounts of money, but was enough to give my horses the comfortable life they richly deserved, plus enough left over for fun nights in the pub and even a holiday to Greece with Jenny Bear. There was no long-term plan for the future, but I was busy from dawn to dusk, and I was happier than I had ever been.

While I was officially running the riding school on my own, my amazing friends and family all pitched in. Sometimes I'd have to go into the cottage and beg Lou and Jenny Bear to come and help because I had a birthday party full of kids or something, and they would always just sigh, put their Crocs on and throw themselves in. Luckily for me, they were brilliant with children because of the job they did, and were CRB checked so they could help at a moment's notice.

In the school holidays, when I was running a pony camp, the girls both took annual leave to help me, arranging games and running T-shirt-making workshops with the children in between rides. Pasty and Barney would pitch in when there was heavy lifting to be done, and Sam would help me with driving the horses to and from the fields. Dad came down as often as he could, and would make platters of sandwiches for the kids. They all loved him, naturally, and he was like a kindly grandfather to them all. Murphy adored having so many children around too, and would be bouncing around like a mad thing lapping up all the attention.

I also increasingly relied on the enthusiastic band of young helpers who first came to the stables for lessons but never wanted to go home. These were kids who, like me at their age, would happily spend their whole weekends at the stables, doing whatever jobs I asked them to do as long as it meant spending more precious hours around their beloved horses. One of my most dedicated volunteers was Rowena, who was only ten when she started helping out but was always begging her dad to let her stay 'just five more minutes' when he came to pick her up after a seven-hour stint.

It was Rowena who helped me deck out Park Lane in England flags and bunting that June, in celebration of the World Cup which was happening in South Africa. The weather was brilliant and there was a lot of excitement about the England team that year – you could almost taste the anticipation. Ultimately, as is so often the case with England, those hopes would end up being dashed – but we didn't know it at the time.

Jenny Bear, Lou, Sam, Pasty, Barney and I of course watched every game at the Queen Dowager, dressed in vintage England shirts and with flags painted on our faces. I mention this because it was during the World Cup that I encountered someone who would end up being very important in my life – Dickie – although I didn't know that at the time either!

Actually, according to Dickie, it wasn't the first time we'd been around each other; he says he'd noticed me in the pub lots of times before. But it's fair to say that the World Cup was the first time I noticed him. It was hard not to – because he turned up to each game with a trumpet, and would play 'Three Lions' for us all to sing along before kick-off.

Dickie was quite a bit older than my friends and me – in his mid-fifties – with broad shoulders and twinkly, mischievous eyes. He knew I ran the stables and when I went to the bar he'd always find an excuse to stand next to me and make some dreadful joke about horses.

As the tournament wore on, he started to come and sit at our table uninvited, causing Sam to roll her eyes when he went to the loo. 'What's wrong with Dickie?' I asked her once, genuinely puzzled – he was funny and chatty, with an encyclopaedic knowledge of football and music, so I liked having him around.

'He's just a weird old guy,' she said. 'Like, he could be our dad.' I pushed her and said age was just a number. It's funny to look back on all that with hindsight, when you see how things turned out!

Dickie was a handyman, and throughout that summer he kept pitching up at the stables where he'd take it upon himself to fix something. I came back from driving the horses to the field one day to find he was once again at the stables, just mending a fence. 'Oh please leave that,' I said to him – a little crossly actually, which probably sounds a bit ungrateful! But at the time I was totally skint, and I didn't know how I'd pay him. 'I can't afford to have that fixed right now.'

'I'm not expecting payment,' Dickie said, straightening up. 'I'm just a mate helping out a mate. But maybe you could keep my company at dinner tonight, to say thanks?'

What a charmer, you're probably thinking – but it worked. I didn't see those early dinners with Dickie as 'dates', but looking back, that's kind of what they were. He'd tell me stories and make me laugh, I'd chat to him about the ponies and my dreams for the stables and we'd stay there drinking until closing time. It had been a long time since someone had looked at me the way Dickie did and, well, one thing led to another.

I saw it as just a bit of fun – nothing serious. Dickie was more than twenty years older than me, and my friends certainly didn't approve. As far as I was concerned, it was just a summer fling.

The stables only got busier over the next few months, and at the beginning of 2011, I took on my very first member of staff. Her name was Izabell and to be honest, it was she who insisted I give her a job – not the other way round.

I first noticed her watching a class I was taking with some of the older teenagers one Saturday, and I assumed she was after lessons. She was young-looking, with tanned olive skin, bleached blond hair cut in an edgy undercut and tons of earrings.

'If you want to sign up for lessons it's best to come by the stables on Park Lane one day in the week,' I told her as she approached me afterwards, trying to wrangle two horses whose reins had been handed to me by departing teens.

'No, I don't want lessons,' she said, in an accent I'd later find out was Cypriot. 'I want a job.'

There was a directness in her manner which I found dis-concerting – and a little bit rude. 'Well, that's very nice but unfortunately there are no jobs going,' I said.

'You do all this by yourself?' said the girl, raising a perfectly manicured eyebrow. 'No. Better if you have help.'

'That's for me to decide, wouldn't you say?' I said.

The girl shrugged, looking supremely unbothered. 'Fine. But I help you with these horses now.'

I found that I couldn't find the words to argue with her, and it was actually quite helpful to have her lead a couple of the ponies back to Park Lane behind me. But it was still pretty cheeky, to just demand a job like that. I'd coped for this long on my own, and I didn't need any help – did I?

A month or so later, Izabell was back. I almost ran into her on the street as I hurried out of the front door of the cottage, heading round to the stables where I could hear one of my newer ponies, a little strawberry roan called Rusty, whinnying at the top of his voice.

'Hello, I came to ask for job again,' she said.

I sighed with exasperation. 'The answer is still no,' I said. 'Now, excuse me, I've got to urgently see to a horse.'

But Izabell didn't get the hint, and trailed after me into the stable yard.

'I think this horse would be better down at the other end,' she said bluntly. 'You see, this brown one? They're fighting, I think.'

What was extra annoying was that she was exactly right. Rusty and Samson did always wind each other up if they were too close to each other, and I'd forgotten that when I'd put them in the stables this morning. But I didn't feel like letting on to this strange girl, so I gave Rusty a new haynet which would keep him quiet instead.

'Why do you want to work here anyway?' I asked her.

'My boyfriend lives in Teddington,' she said, rubbing Noah's neck with a naturalness that spoke of years of experience around horses. 'I want a job near him. And I know about horses. My family always had lots back home in Cyprus.'

'Well, I'm afraid I don't have anything to offer you,' I told her again. 'There's just no job at the moment.'

'Okay,' she said, sounding unconvinced. 'If you change your mind – my name is Izabell.'

On her way out, Izabell stopped by the whiteboard where I wrote up the names of kids in each class and which pony I had assigned them for the lesson. She took a marker pen and wrote her name and number in looping cursive in the corner. Then she was gone.

I waited ten seconds, then moved Samson to the other end of the stable block, muttering under my breath about the fact I certainly didn't need any help.

When she turned up again, it was when I was unloading Prodney from the horse box.

'Not you again!' I said, when I spotted her, leaning against the outer stable door.

'I thought maybe you lost my number,' said Izabell, matter-of-factly. 'Because you didn't call.'

'I just think,' I searched around for more reasons, 'you're probably a bit young, aren't you?' I guessed she was only about seventeen.

'No, I'm twenty-two,' she said. 'Riding since I was two. Twenty years' experience.'

I had to admit, I was impressed. Izabell hadn't given up – so she must have really wanted to work at my stables. And after years of working in the industry, I had a sixth sense for people who were good around horses – and Izabell was one of them. Plus, the truth was, at some point I was going to have to accept that I couldn't do everything myself.

'All right,' I said. 'You win. When can you start?'

Izabell started the very next day – and I have to say, employing her was one of the best decisions I ever made for the stables. She knew exactly what she was doing, and was as good with the kids as she was with the ponies. She even knew how to handle the most difficult of the parents, never taking any nonsense from anyone. Admitting I needed help was something I didn't used to be very good at – although I've got better at that over the years. So I'm so grateful that Izabell wouldn't take no for an answer.

The real reason she was so insistent that I take her on was because she could tell that a time was coming when I would really, *really* need her, whether I liked it or not. She'd spotted that under my striped sweatshirt I was quite clearly pregnant.

CHAPTER TWELVE

It Takes a Village

If you didn't see that one coming – well, neither did I. I found out I was pregnant with Dickie's baby in November 2010, which was just five months after I'd met him, so you can imagine what a surprise that was.

Discovering I was pregnant knocked me sideways. I barely knew Dickie, we weren't in a relationship – and I certainly didn't expect him to be involved as a dad. But I knew as soon as I saw the thin blue line on the pregnancy test that I wanted to keep the baby – however hard that would be.

The girls were as shocked as I was when I told them. Lou thought it was funny, but Jenny Bear was cross – although only for about five minutes. We didn't really question the fact that we'd be bringing up the baby together. I pictured it like that movie, *Three Men and a Baby*, except it was three women and a whole lot of horses too.

Plucking up the courage to tell my dad was harder. I was so scared about how he'd react – but I shouldn't have been, because he was as supportive and non-judgemental as he always was.

'I know you'll make a wonderful mum, Nat,' he said. 'No matter what the circumstances.'

But as it turned out, I didn't end up being a single mum after all. I'd made assumptions about Dickie that simply weren't true – although to be fair, so did everybody else! No one thought he'd stand by me. When I told him the news over drinks at the Dowager – pint of bitter for him, Diet Coke for me – I was expecting him to ask me to get rid of the baby, or maybe do a runner. But instead he just raised an eyebrow and said: 'Well, we'll have to do something about the cottage then.'

'What do you mean?' I said, confused.

'Well, Nat, it may have been good enough for baby Jesus, but I can tell you now – no child of mine will be born in a stable!'

Over the next few weeks, I realised Dickie hadn't been joking. In the winter before the baby was due, he found a flat for us three girls to rent temporarily while he did up the cottage to what he considered an acceptable standard. He ripped out the manky old bathroom and replaced it with a fresh suite and clean white tiles, put in a proper ceiling, plastered and painted the walls, filled in the draughty gaps around the windows and, best of all, installed underfloor heating throughout.

When Jenny, Lou and I moved back into the new-look cottage just before spring arrived, Dickie moved in too. I don't think we ever really discussed it, but it just seemed the obvious thing to do. And that was that; we were a couple.

It was unconventional, but it worked. Yes, Dickie was older than me, but he made me laugh, could still make my heart race, and always made me feel safe. He loved horses and was passionate about music. Dependable, big-hearted, cool-headed and kind – I knew he would be a wonderful father.

I worked, of course, right up until the moment labour arrived.

Throughout the winter and into spring my belly expanded and swelled like a balloon, drawing fascinated stares from the children at the riding school and slightly furtive ones from the parents. As far as I was concerned, I had a riding school to run – and the small matter of a pregnancy didn't change that. I continued to shout myself hoarse in Bushy Park at the weekends as I taught the kids, then I'd tear between the stables and the Oxshott fields during the week, making sure the ponies were as well taken care of as ever.

With Izabell at my side, we were able to offer more lessons than ever. Together, we made an amazing team. Izabell was always coming up with new ideas to engage the children and was brilliant at organising the teens who volunteered into an extremely efficient rota. When I'd been running the stables on my own everything had been a bit haphazard and frantic, but with Izabell on board I felt like we'd finally hit a rhythm.

Typically, my waters broke while I was holding the lead rope of a horse – and our daughter Alice was born in May 2011. I loved her the moment I saw her – this tiny, unexpected, spectacular gift the universe had given me.

With Dickie, Lou, Jenny Bear and I all living under the same roof, Alice became somewhat of a communal baby. It helped that Alice was a very laid-back child, but having so many adults who adored her on hand was invaluable. Jenny and Lou worked different shifts at Build-A-Bear, and Dickie was his own boss so he worked flexibly, meaning there was always one of them around to help me. If I was desperate for a nap after a sleepless night feeding, Jenny would take Alice for a walk around the park in her pram. When the washing stacked up, Lou wouldn't mind putting another load on for me. And Dickie, far from being the hands-off dad everyone assumed he would be, threw himself into fatherhood head-first, dirty nappies and all. I felt so blessed to have these amazing people in my life – and now in my daughter's, too.

I worried that Murphy might have his nose put out of joint as he was so used to being the house baby, but he accepted Alice without question. On the day I brought her home and put her in her Moses basket, Murphy settled himself next to it like her protector. From that day forward, it became his favourite place to snooze.

Those first few weeks with Alice were magical – although I was missing spending whole days with the ponies terribly. I still went in to see the ones in the stable block every day, and Izabell and I had daily discussions about their care. With her in charge, I knew they were in good hands. She also kept the lessons going in my absence, meaning I didn't need to close the riding school. By the time I went back to work just a few months after Alice was born, I knew I'd never be able to let her go. She was my right-hand woman – and the person who made me realise just how hard it had been doing it on my own.

They say it takes a village to raise a child – but in my experience, a stables will do too.

CHAPTER THIRTEEN

Foxy

While my own family was growing, the Park Lane family was too. Not long before Alice was born, a very significant horse entered my life – and in turn, he was the reason I met a very important human.

It all began in unlikely circumstances. It was the summer I got pregnant, and England had just crashed out from the World Cup 4–1 to Germany, when I got a phone call that was far more distressing than that dismal result. A member of the public had spotted a horse on the side of the road in a terrible state, and wondered if I'd be able to help. I didn't hesitate for a minute, grabbing the keys to the horse box and driving as fast as the speed limit would allow to the main road near Kingston where the horse had been seen.

When I arrived, I realised things were even worse than I'd been told. The young horse – not much more than a foal – was at death's door. He was so skinny you could see every rib, and his coat was filthy and rubbed raw in places. The poor thing was so weak that he could barely stand and he was leaning heavily against the splintered fence he'd been tied to. Amy, who'd come to us as a troubled teen but was now one of my most trusted helpers, had accompanied me, and as we parked up, she looked like she might cry.

Catching sight of us, the poor horse's ears flicked back in fear. I could tell this was an animal who had known nothing but cruelty from humans.

'Shh, shh, we won't hurt you,' I said soothingly, as I approached him slowly, and untied the threadbare rope from the fence. 'You're safe now. We're taking you home.'

With gentle coaxing, the colt managed to take unsteady steps towards the horse box. I wasn't sure if he'd let us lead him in, but the smell of fresh hay seemed to be enough to tempt him.

On the drive back to Park Lane, I told Amy with a lump in my throat that she could give him a name.

'Let's call him Foxy,' she said decisively. 'Do you think he's going to make it, Nat?'

I didn't know what to say. I'd seen enough sick horses in my time to know that this one probably didn't have long left. The best we could do for him was give him a comfortable place to see out his last hours.

I had Foxy seen by the vet, who agreed with my verdict, put him in the stable furthest from the gate and told the kids to leave him in peace. And that's where he would have stayed – if it hadn't been for a parent, who noticed Foxy there while he was waiting for his daughters to finish their riding lesson. Brian, a music producer, was a real stalwart of the stables, a proper animal lover, who was as enthusiastic about the horses as his girls Maria and Susannah were – and he also wasn't afraid to speak his mind.

'I don't think you can leave that horse there to die,' he told me in a worried tone, following me as I led Simon back into the stables. 'It's upsetting for the children.'

'Well, what would you suggest? I'm not going to put him back on the side of the road,' I said, a little crossly.

'Oh no – sorry, I'm not criticising,' said Brian quickly. 'It's just – I have a recording studio out in Surrey with a barn and a paddock. The girls have probably told you about the little Shetland pony, Dobby, that lives there – he's a pet of my business partner's. I'd be happy to take Foxy there and look after him – following your advice, of course. He might be more comfortable, and he'd have Dobby for company.'

I was blown away by his generosity. It's true that Brian was one of our kindest clients, but to offer to take on the cost and responsibility of such a sick animal with no hope of reward was something else.

'I mean – that sounds wonderful, but are you sure?' I asked him. We'd walked to Foxy's stable and I felt my heart break now as we looked at him lying in the straw, breathing heavily, his eyes unfocused.

'You've made my kids feel part of something really special here,' Brian said earnestly. 'So of course I want to help, if I can.'

We made arrangements for Foxy to be taken out to Surrey, expecting that he'd probably last a few more nights but hoping against hope that he might take a turn for the better. It seemed so unlikely listening to his ragged breathing and patting his skeletal body as we loaded him into the horse box. But Foxy was a horse that confounded us all. Once he was settled at Brian's place I would check on him most days, as it wasn't far from the fields in Oxshott. And to my astonishment, every day Foxy seemed a little bit stronger.

'I just can't believe it,' Brian said to me, about seven months after we'd picked up Foxy from the side of the road. We were leaning on the fence of a paddock where Foxy was happily chewing grass, his coat now growing back fluffy and new, and his eyes sparkling with alertness. He was still skinny, but his bones didn't jut out so painfully, and he was no longer unsteady on his feet.

'Well, it's thanks to all the amazing love and care you've given him,' I said. 'And some kind of crazy spirit of his own. You know, I reckon we should start thinking about making him a riding school horse before too long.'

Foxy was young, and almost wild – now that he was a bit stronger, he wasn't even that keen on a head collar, and had clearly not been trained to be ridden. But he was sweet-natured and willing, and I knew he had the potential to be a brilliant horse.

Usually I'd want to start him myself – but as I rubbed my ever-expanding belly, I knew that wouldn't be possible.

A friend of mine from the horse world had a few months ago mentioned to me that he had a mate, David, who lived not far from me, and had urged me to look him up as he was good with training horses. I hadn't got round to it until now, but I remembered I had David's number in my phone – and decided there could be no harm giving him a call. Could he be the one to tame Foxy?

There's no time like the present, so I rang David from Oxshott, perched on the gate to the field watching Prodney and Samson playing together.

I liked David's manner immediately. He had a wonderfully calm voice and was incredibly easy to talk to. He told me he was a retired mental health nurse, but had always been passionate about horses – especially those that other people considered difficult.

'There's always a way through to them, if only you take the time to listen to what they're trying to say,' he explained. It's exactly what I've always thought too. He talked me through how he would approach starting a horse, saying he preferred to build trust and the bond of touch before gently building up to training, rather than trying to assert human dominance over the animal. I was delighted to hear him describe a method which was nearly identical to my own.

David and I met a few weeks later at Brian's place, and I introduced him to Foxy. I could have talked to David for hours – it was clear we shared the same philosophy on horses. There was no one I'd have been happier entrusting Foxy to than him.

I'd met David just in time, because it wasn't long after that when I went into labour, and Alice was born. With the whirlwind of welcoming a new baby, and knowing he was in good hands, I stopped worrying about Foxy so much and concentrated on the matter at hand.

Until, that is, one beautifully sunny Saturday morning in June. I was on the sofa, burping Alice after a feed, and Lou was chatting away to me from the kitchen, where she was making us a pot of tea.

'Oh – Nat!' she said suddenly, cutting her own sentence short. 'Come quickly and look at this!'

'What?' I said, alarmed by the urgency of her tone. I lay Alice across my shoulder and kept patting her back as I joined Lou at the window. 'Oh!'

There, coming down Park Lane, was an extraordinary sight. It was Foxy – and riding him, as if it was the most natural thing in the world, was David. Spotting me at the window, David grinned, and raised a thumbs up.

I couldn't believe it. Foxy looked sleek and muscular, his neck elegantly curved, and his ears flicking around as he responded to David's aids. He was barely recognisable as the feral, half-dead colt that we had brought here just under a year ago, who we'd never expected to survive. I felt like my heart might burst with delight.

Lou opened the cottage door and we went out on the street, whooping as David and Foxy got closer.

'Look at you!' I said. 'What an amazing job you've done, David!'

'It really was a pleasure,' he said. 'This cheeky chappy is going to bring a lot of joy to a lot of kids, I just know it.'

I reached out with my spare hand and stroked Foxy's handsome neck. He seemed to recognise me, blinking slowly and leaning gently into my hand as I gave him a good pet. Alice wriggled against me, so I turned her around so she could see Foxy properly. The two of them looked at each other, and then Alice started to smile.

It was a magical moment. Life certainly throws some unexpected situations at you – but with a bit of hope, a lot of love and the support of some good people, there's really nothing you can't overcome.

CHAPTER FOURTEEN

Baby Bombshell

David became a bigger part of the Park Lane family after that. He was right about Foxy – who really did become a huge hit with the kids – and having seen the impact he'd had David wanted to do more. Together, we would find and train so-called 'problem' horses, and turn them into much-beloved members of the Park Lane herd.

While he was brilliant with horses, David was also great with humans too. It's why I asked him if he'd consider taking his exams to become a riding coach. He knew how to help people who were having a particularly tough time to open up, which with the sort of kids I had around, was really important.

With David on board as well as Izabell, Park Lane had gone from being a one-woman operation to a real organisation. We were busier than ever, with a waiting list for lessons, but by early 2012 we had increased our horses to about twenty, meaning we were able to cater for more kids. Juggling running the business, looking after the ponies and raising a baby, I was in a state of near exhaustion most of the time – but we were making it work.

I felt like I'd dealt with my fair share of curve balls – but then, in January 2012, I got another one. At thirty-six, I was pregnant – again. And if Alice had been a surprise, this was an out-and-out shocker.

'Jesus, Nat, Alice is only eight months old! How can this have happened?' Dickie said, when I told him.

'Well . . . I didn't do it on my own,' I said wryly.

A second baby was very much not in the plan. We'd already got rid of most of Alice's newborn stuff to make room in the increasingly crowded cottage. Although Lou had recently left to go travelling, it was still chaos in there with Dickie, Jenny Bear, Murphy, Alice and me. Oh, and Liam – one of my teenage riders, who I'd suspected was sleeping rough. It turned out I was right – he'd been chucked out by his dad. So I'd invited him to stay for a week, which had turned into six months.

'We really do have enough on our plate already, you know,' Dickie sighed, pacing up and down our small bedroom, almost tripping over a set of Alice's plastic bricks. 'The baby, the riding school . . . how far along are you anyway?'

I didn't actually know the answer to that question, so with Dickie's encouragement, I booked in to see the GP, who referred me for a dating scan the following week.

The drive over to the clinic was bad-tempered, with Dickie trying to get me to agree that if it was still the very early days of the pregnancy we'd talk about whether we would keep the baby or not. I was evasive, because just like when I was pregnant with Alice, I had a tiny but firm voice in my heart telling me this baby was mine and needed to be born. By the time we reached the clinic, as if sensing the tension between her two parents, Alice was bawling her head off.

'I'll wait out here,' muttered Dickie, after we'd signed in and found a spot in the waiting room. He was bouncing Alice on his hip as she continued to wail at the top of her lungs, trying to get her to calm down. 'Good luck, okay?'

In any other circumstances we probably wouldn't have brought Alice along, but that day we were due to see my dad for lunch. He was arriving at Euston on the train from Birmingham, so right after our appointment we were heading to central London to meet him. He adored his little granddaughter, and I just hoped that she'd have got over her grouchy mood in time for lots of cuddles with her devoted grandad.

'Natalie O'Rourke?' I followed the nurse who had called my name into the small treatment room, and lay down on the bed. She smeared my skin with cold gel and started moving the ultrasound probe over my belly. In between her checks, we were chatting away quite cheerfully – she was asking me about Alice, and I told her about our lunch plans with Dad – but then she fell silent.

'Ah,' she said eventually, and tilted away the screen which was showing blurry images of the inside of my womb. 'Okay. I'm just going to get my boss.'

She hurried out of the room, and I suddenly felt as cold as the squelchy gel on my stomach. All I could think was – there's something wrong with the baby. Oh god, oh god. I thought of Dickie outside in the waiting room, who already didn't want me to go through with a pregnancy – what would he say when he found out there was a problem?

The nurse returned with her boss, a sharp-faced woman with square glasses and dark hair pulled back in a loose bun. The two of them stood and stared at the screen for a long time, continuing to move the probe across my midriff, seeming to forget that I was in the room.

Unable to bear it any longer, I yelped: 'What is it? Is something wrong?'

The senior midwife turned to look at me, as if seeing me for the first time. 'We're not sure, but I'm afraid that yes, the scan does seem to be showing some abnormalities. I'm going to refer you to Queen Charlotte's – it's a maternity hospital, so they will be best placed to give you an accurate picture of what's happening here.'

'Okay,' I nodded. 'So will I get a letter? How long will it be until my appointment?'

The woman looked at me as if I was mad. 'Letter? No, you need to go right now. I'll call them so they know you're on your way.'

That was when I really started to panic. This was the overstretched NHS – if they were moving with this much urgency, I knew they must have some serious concerns. They called Dickie into the room and he listened gravely as they filled him in on the situation.

'You've got to try and stay calm,' said Dickie, as he helped me to the car afterwards. My whole body was shaking uncontrollably as I imagined all the danger this tiny little embryo of ours, which I realised I already loved, could be in. 'They're probably just being extra cautious.'

But I knew in my heart of hearts that wasn't the case. As Dickie drove us to Queen Charlotte's, I rang my dad to tell him we wouldn't be able to meet him as planned. Poor Dad hadn't even known I was pregnant, so it was a lot to take in.

'Listen, Nat, you are the strongest person I know,' he told me. 'So gather that strength and face this head on. You're going to need it. I'll be thinking of you.'

The next couple of hours at Queen Charlotte's went by in a blur. There was another ultrasound, then I was ushered into a smaller room for blood tests. Then there was what seemed like endless sitting in the waiting room, trying to keep Alice – and ourselves – calm. Finally, we were summoned into a consultation room where we perched on plastic chairs and waited to hear the verdict from a doctor with thinning hair and a mouth that turned down at the edges. Thankfully, Alice had finally fallen asleep in her pram.

'As you know, we have carried out a number of screening tests today,' Dr Shields began. 'We have established that you are eleven weeks pregnant. However, we have also detected a high risk of a health problem with your baby.'

Dickie's fingers found mine and squeezed them tight. I felt like I could hardly breathe.

'Based on the tests we have carried out,' continued the doctor, 'we believe your baby may have a genetic or chromosomal condition, such as Down's syndrome, Edwards' syndrome or Patau's syndrome.

'What we recommend doing now is a further test, called chorionic villus sampling, which you may have heard referred to as CVS. The test will be able to diagnose for certain which, if any, of these conditions your baby has. And after that you will be able to decide whether you continue or end the pregnancy.'

There was a silence as we digested these words. I felt almost as if I was drifting away from my body. In another life, I would be enjoying a noisy and carefree lunch in Pizza Express with Dad, toasting the prospect of a healthy new baby with glasses of orange juice.

'So, er, what would that test involve?' asked Dickie. I didn't say anything – I knew if I opened my mouth no sound would come out.

'In most cases, a needle is inserted into the stomach and

used to extract a sample of cells from the placenta,' the doctor explained, addressing himself to Dickie now, although it would be my stomach and my placenta which would face this horrifying needle. 'It takes about ten minutes and you will have the first results within three days. There is, however' – his glance flicked to me – 'a risk of miscarriage.'

I swallowed, then dug deep inside of me for my voice. 'How much?' I asked, hoarsely. 'How much risk?'

'About one in one hundred,' he replied.

'And do we have to do the test?' I said.

'We strongly recommend it,' said the doctor. 'We recommend that the test is carried out within fourteen weeks of the pregnancy. Although in some cases it can be done later.'

'And then what – we have until twenty-four weeks to decide if we want an abortion?' said Dickie.

I decided I couldn't listen to this any longer, and got abruptly to my feet. The room felt claustrophobic – some animal instinct was telling me to get out. I was already wheeling Alice's pram towards the door, but what I heard next stopped me dead in my tracks.

'Actually, no,' said the doctor. 'The twenty-four-week limit for abortion doesn't apply in these cases. If a baby has a disability such as Down's syndrome, abortion is legal right up until birth.'

My hands flew to my stomach, as if I could keep the growing bundle of cells safe in there with my touch alone. I knew in that moment that if I wanted this baby, I would have to fight for it.

Gather your strength, Nat – you're going to need it.

CHAPTER FIFTEEN

Welcome Woody

It's no exaggeration to say that the next few months were the hardest and darkest of my life.

First there was the agonising decision of whether to get the CVS test or not. Dickie was insistent we should – but I wasn't sure, because of the risk to the baby, and because of the further decision it would inevitably lead to.

I eventually agreed to have it, but things were still frosty between Dickie and me. Just like I had at every hard time in my life, I started to spend more and more time with the horses, just sitting by their stables and listening to them breathing and chewing their hay, which helped me to feel better. I'd fallen hard for Foxy, who was playful and cheeky and never failed to put a smile on my face, even on the toughest days.

I was leaning on his stable door cooing into his ears when I got the phone call from the hospital with the test results. Seeing the number flash up on screen, I hurried next door to the cottage to take it.

'Natalie O'Rourke?' said the expressionless voice at the end of the line.

'Yes, that's me.'

'I'm phoning with your results from the CVS test. I'm sorry to say your baby has Down's syndrome. You can book an appointment to discuss this further with Dr Shields.'

And that was it. Your life can change in three sentences, and then they hang up the phone. I sat there, trembling, letting the news sink in. It wasn't exactly a surprise – from that very first moment when the nurse at my ultrasound had fallen silent, I'd been expecting something like this. But hearing it in such stark terms was still something of a shock.

The phone rang again. Dazed, I reached to answer it, assuming it was the hospital ringing back with some more information.

'Hello?'

'Is this Ms O'Rourke? I'm phoning from the Reproductive Choices Clinic. Just wanted to confirm your appointment tomorrow at 2 p.m.'

I was confused. Reproductive Choices?

'I think you've got the wrong person,' I said. 'I haven't booked an appointment for tomorrow.'

'Oh, I think it was the hospital that rang on your behalf,' said the cheerful nurse at the end of the line. 'They've booked you in for a termination. Tomorrow – is that not what you were expecting?'

I felt so sick with anger that I felt like my jaw was clamped shut. So that was how little regard the hospital had for my baby – the moment they had found out it was 'faulty' they had booked me in for an abortion, without even asking if I wanted one.

'No, it is not what I was expecting,' I said through gritted teeth, trying to keep my voice level. 'Cancel the appointment. I don't need it.'

'Oh ...' said the nurse, confused. 'Well, I'll keep it open for you just in case you change your mind – just so you know it's—'

I didn't want to listen to any more of her explanation of why I could and should go for the abortion, so I hung up the phone and hurled the handset across the room.

That conversation set the tone for the following months of interaction with the medical profession. There were endless scans and appointments to attend with various doctors, who all started off by trying to convince me not to have the baby. Over time, I learned that Down's syndrome was caused by the child being born with an extra chromosome. This can cause physical and mental developmental delays and disabilities, some of them enough to shorten life expectancy. Many Down's syndrome pregnancies ended with miscarriage or stillbirth, and if your child lived they could still expect to face all sorts of serious health problems throughout their life.

So I was told that my baby's heart was no good, his brain wasn't forming right, he'd have issues with his spine, I should expect vision and hearing impairment. I was warned the baby would have poor muscle tone, and that meant he wouldn't be able to breastfeed, though that was just the start of the challenges I should expect. Every scan seemed to throw up a fresh problem. I listened calmly to each new litany of woe, but I refused to change my mind about the termination. The doctors seemed wrongfooted by my determination, and it made me wonder how many other scared and confused expectant mothers they had talked out of their babies.

Meanwhile, all Dickie and I seemed to do was fight. In hindsight I can see he was frightened – the prospect of looking after a child with a serious disability, when you feel totally inexperienced and ill-prepared, is terrifying. I could feel the baby inside me, and the deep and mysterious connection with it was what made me feel calm when I should have been afraid. But it wasn't that easy for Dickie. I think he was protecting his heart too. By saying he didn't want the baby, perhaps it would make it easier if we lost it – which was a real possibility, either before birth or shortly afterwards.

The stables were my anchor through all this uncertainty, and I continued to teach and care for the horses as I always had done. Teaching the riding lessons, brainstorming with Izabell and David, having a joke with Amelia, Liam and Rowena, or simply taking half an hour to rub down Prodney or fluff up the straw in the stables, were all welcome relief from the endless rows and discussions and questions that I was experiencing in the rest of my life.

It took a lot of heartache, but Dickie did come round to the idea of the baby I was determined to have. I knew he had when he asked me one night after we'd been told the baby was a little boy: 'Do you think we could call the baby Woody?' I knew Woody Guthrie was his favourite folk singer.

'Call the baby what you want,' I grinned. 'I'm just glad we're doing it together.'

Woody arrived in September 2012. The labour was so quick that he started to crest when I was still on a hospital trolley, and I'd barely made it to the bed when he arrived in the world, caught by a midwife who lifted his slippery pink body into the air. And then – he started to cry.

Dickie and I stared at each other, astonished. In all those meetings of doom with the doctors, we'd been told our boy would be born at the brink of death, unable to breathe well enough to cry. We'd been told he'd be taken from us straight away and whisked off to intensive care, where it would be touch and go whether he'd make it. And yet here he was, bawling at the top of his lungs, and the midwives were fussing around him as if everything was perfectly normal, cleaning him up and cutting the cord.

They wrapped Woody in a blanket and placed him into my arms. I could not have held him with more reverence if he'd been made of priceless crystal. My tiny miracle. I looked down at his face which was as open and beautiful as the moon, with wide-set almond eyes and a button nose.

'I fought for you,' I whispered, and as I said it I felt as strong and powerful as a lioness. The whole world had been against me and this child but he was here now, and we were a unit no one would ever be able to break apart.

I was suddenly aware that the midwife was staring at me. The labour had been so rushed, there hadn't been time for the medics to get my notes. So this was the first time that they were realising that Woody was not your average baby.

I caught her eye. 'Oh yes, my baby has Down's syndrome,' I said breezily.

'I'll just ... um ... get a doctor ... ' she said, and hurried out of the room.

Then it was just Dickie and I alone with Woody. He reached out a trembling hand to touch his son's head, and I could see tears were streaming down his face.

'You were right, Nat,' he said. 'And I'm so sorry I ever doubted you.'

I tried to hand Woody over to Dickie, but he was wriggling and I knew that he was hungry. We'd been told, of course, that he'd never be able to breastfeed, but hadn't we been told that he wouldn't cry either?

'Why don't you just try and feed him, before the doctor

gets here?' said Dickie, as if reading my mind. 'Can't do any harm, can it?'

So I did, and to our astonishment, Woody latched on with no problems at all. You should have seen the doctor's face when he arrived to find this surprise Down's syndrome baby defying all expectations and happily feeding at his mother's breast. I had to laugh then. After the terror and the stress and the pain of the pregnancy, it all just seemed so easy.

I had been so superstitious about Woody that I had refused to buy any new baby stuff at all, in case it tempted fate. It meant that when we got home the next evening, Dickie and I realised we had nothing for the baby to sleep in. It was late, and most of the shops were closed, so Dickie went to Tesco's and came back with the next best thing – a washing-up bowl. We padded it out with blankets and that's where our precious son spent his first night, until we could get to the baby shop the next day.

Although we were both exhausted, Dickie and I stayed up late that night, just watching our son sleep in his little nest. He was the Technicolor sunrise that follows a stormy night, the first snowdrop after a harsh winter. We leaned against each other and breathed him in, knowing our next big adventure was just beginning.

Part Two

CHAPTER SIXTEEN

Unlocking Eli

I stood at the stable yard door, watching the small boy on the other side of the road who was spinning and spinning as if his life depended on it. On every second spin, he would take his clenched fist and hit himself hard in his small, worried face.

I winced every time, feeling powerless as I watched this spectacle of uncontrollable emotion. Next to him, the boy's father barked angry words and tried to grab his hands, but the boy just spun out of his reach.

I could tell we had a hard task on our hands.

The boy was Eli Boateng, ten years old, and severely autistic. He had been referred to Park Lane by his social worker, who knew we had recently set up as a Riding for the Disabled centre in mid 2014. The notes she sent me said that Eli was non-verbal, extremely agitated, easily overwhelmed and besieged by debilitating repetitive behaviours. Even the teachers at his special school were struggling with him, and his parents were terrified that he was retreating further and further into himself. But the social worker thought we might be able to get through to Eli when nothing else had succeeded.

I took a deep breath, and tightened my blond ponytail. Time to get to work.

I crossed the road, beaming at Eli and his dad.

'You must be Eli!' I said cheerily. 'How lovely to meet you. My name's Natalie, and I think we're going to have a lot of fun together.'

Mr Boateng, a big man with hands shoved defensively into the pockets of his heavy coat, looked at me with barely concealed fury. 'Fun?' he raged. 'Bloody waste of time, more like.'

I'd been warned about this sort of situation when I was training as an instructor for the Riding for the Disabled Association (RDA). My tutor told me it was common to encounter doubtful parents, who had no experience of horses and were often at the end of their tether with their challenging children. The idea that a pony ride could make any kind of difference was baffling to them. But it was up to me to win them round.

I didn't let my smile waver. 'Hello, Mr Boateng. I hope you didn't have too bad a journey. I'm so glad you've brought Eli to see us today.'

Mr Boateng grunted and turned back to his son, who was still spinning anti-clockwise on the spot, even faster now, as if stressed by the situation. 'God knows what you think you'll be able to achieve,' he said.

'I think you'll be surprised,' I said, and I meant it.

Things had changed drastically at Park Lane since Woody was born. It's probably a cliché to say that having a disabled child puts things into perspective, but it is one that I had found to be true.

Having spent my pregnancy being warned of all the things

Woody wouldn't be able to do, since he'd been born, every day he amazed me with all the things he could. Yes, it took him longer than it had taken Alice, but whether it was rolling over, or picking up a toy, or learning to laugh, he had achieved all the milestones that babies are meant to reach. And he was also so happy, so charming, so uninhibited in his enjoyment of life. So many people look at disabled children and see only their limitations. I wanted to change that perspective – and help them see their potential instead.

It was this that had inspired me to transform Park Lane from an ordinary riding school into a Riding for the Disabled Association centre.

I knew of the RDA from school, when in lower sixth we'd all been required to spend one afternoon a week volunteering. Obviously I'd wanted to do something with horses – and that's how I found the RDA. A lovely lady called Faith would pick me up from college on Wednesdays and drive me over to Solihull where I'd lead the ponies for the disabled riders and help with grooming and horse care. I'd loved it there – seeing the happy faces of the participants and the way their fitness and skills developed week by week. It was a happy, inclusive place where I'd immediately felt at home.

Setting up an RDA centre of my own turned out to be a long and arduous process, taking almost two years. The practical side of things was the most straightforward; I started going to other RDA centres and learning alongside their qualified coaches, while Izabell and David covered the lessons back at the stables. I had lots of reading to do and exams to take, but I was used to that having previously got my qualifications as a regular riding instructor.

What really blew my mind was all the paperwork and

diligence involved in becoming a charity. It's complicated, and rightly so – because it's designed to stop fraud. Once a week I'd meet Diane, a volunteer with the RDA, at a café in Waterloo station, and we'd go through what I'd done. Nine times out of ten I'd have filled in something wrong and have to start again.

There were times I almost gave up – not least during a terrifying period in early 2014 when Woody ended up in hospital for nearly four months after a bad bout of flu sent him into a coma. We were warned that spending that long in a coma could leave him fundamentally changed, and when they first woke him up I remember him looking worryingly blank. But then my dad walked into the hospital room and Woody's little face split into the biggest smile – and we knew he was just the same.

When we were finally able to take Woody home, with all the requisite oxygen equipment plus twice-daily visits from district nurses, I knew it was more important than ever to press on with my RDA plan. We were lucky – with me, Dickie, Jenny Bear and Dad, Woody had a whole team around him. But for many parents of disabled children, every day can be a struggle – and it can be incredibly stressful and isolating.

Behind his gruff exterior, I guessed that Mr Boateng was a case in point. He was dealing with all the fear and anguish that comes from having a child locked in their own world, who you can barely communicate with but you can sense is desperately unhappy. I wanted to make things better for both of them – but it would be baby steps.

'He won't even cross the bloody road,' said Mr Boateng. 'Sat on a bus for an hour and just as I thought, it was totally pointless.'

I crouched down next to Eli, and while he continued spinning, he did slow a bit, as if taking me in. 'Hi, Eli,' I said softly. 'We don't need to go near the stables just now. Let's just smell them, shall we? Take a big breath in. Smells funny, doesn't it, but quite nice I think. That's what horses smell like.'

There is a very distinct smell that greets your nostrils as you come down Park Lane and towards the stables. It's that sweet grassy scent, mingled with leather tack and a sort of warm musk of living creatures. I've always loved it; to me, it's the smell of home. When Alice was a baby and I took her out in her pram, she'd always start crying as we walked away from the stables and she could no longer smell the horses. As soon as we turned around and she could catch that scent again, she'd stop.

For a kid like Eli, turning up at Park Lane was an assault on his senses. He was totally outside of his comfort zone, and for autistic children, it's important to create order among the confusion. I knew he'd have to get used to the place and its sounds and smell before we had any hope of getting him on a horse.

Eli kept spinning, but his clenched fists stayed by his waist now, and I heard him take in a big sniff of air.

'Well done,' I said, just as a horse whinnied in the stable. 'And can you hear that? I think that's Samson saying hello.'

Eli had his face turned away from me, but I saw him give a barely perceptible nod.

'Samson is one of my favourite horses,' I told Eli. 'He's a bay cob – that means he's brown with a black mane and tail and he's a bit hairy and chunky. Actually, if you stand still for a second, you might be able to see him.'

That morning we'd put Samson, a sweet-natured pony with an endless capacity for patience, in the front stable, where a half door allowed him to look out into the road. As if sensing he was needed, he had just at this moment positioned himself with his handsome, kind face over the door and looking directly at us.

Eli was spinning slowly now, and on his next circuit he stopped – just for a second. I saw his eyes flick furtively to Samson, who pricked his ears forward in welcome. Then Eli started spinning again.

'Oh for god's sake!' exploded Mr Boateng. 'He's not even going to look at the bloody thing. You'll never get him on one.'

I straightened up. 'You know, Mr Boateng, I think we will,' I said. 'We just need to go at Eli's pace. I think it will take a few weeks, but I hope you'll stick with me. Here,' I dug in my back pocket, and pulled out a picture of Samson that I'd had printed on a postcard. 'Please stick this on your fridge this week. Talk to Eli lots about the stables before you come back. We've got to get him comfortable with the idea of it, but I think this could be really good for him.'

Mr Boateng made a sound of incredulity, but I saw him looking at his son, who was already markedly calmer than when he had arrived. His spins had slowed into a gentle sway, and he'd lifted his head from his shoes so he could catch glimpses of Samson. The father folded the picture and put it in his pocket.

'We'll see,' he said, doubt heavy in his voice.

That was as far as we got with Eli that day. He didn't want to cross the road and get any closer to the stables. I wondered if we'd ever see him again.

But to my surprise, the next Wednesday afternoon, there was Eli and his dad again waiting on the other side of the road. Mr Boateng was in an even worse mood than the week before, having faced a delay on the bus which had in turn triggered Eli to cause a scene by hitting his head hard against one of the poles. But to give Mr Boateng his due, he stayed quiet as I ran through some communication exercises with his son. I could tell that however much he disapproved of us, there was something in him desperately hoping against his better judgement that this could work for Eli.

That second week, we managed to get Eli across the road to stand next to Samson's stable. He didn't want to touch the pony, but even getting him that close felt like a milestone. Gentle Samson seemed to sense that this was a child not to be spooked, and just quietly chewed his hay, making no sudden movements.

'So next week, is this riding lesson actually going to feature any riding?' Mr Boateng said, as they headed for the bus stop.

'Oh, I shouldn't think so,' I said cheerily. 'We need to get Eli used to wearing the hat first!'

Wearing a riding hat is a challenge in itself for some of our disabled riders. It's heavy and a strange sensation, and for Eli, who didn't like people invading his personal space, having me do up the strap under his chin was going to be a real ordeal. But as the weeks went by, I could sense him relaxing a bit in my presence.

As I had hoped, the sensory cues of the stable seemed to comfort him. Just as I'd taught him in week one, I often saw him take in a big breath when he first arrived. Eli never made eye contact with anyone, but he'd look directly at Samson, and hold his gaze. Even Mr Boateng reluctantly admitted that the bus journey over to Park Lane had become the one time in the week when Eli was remotely calm, and didn't hit himself.

Even so, the idea of getting Eli on to Samson's back still felt a long way off. After we'd got him used to wearing the riding hat, we presented him with his biggest challenge yet: practising what it would be like to get into the saddle.

For this we had Samson fully tacked up and standing next to a mounting block. With Izabell holding Samson's bridle, I'd then encourage Eli to go up the steps and stand at the top. Once he got used to that, I hoped that we'd eventually get to a point where he'd be able to swing over his leg and finally sit in the saddle. I imagined we'd have several weeks of practising the step first.

On his first go, I could see Eli shaking with the concentration required. To contain his physical tics and focus on a task at hand was a big effort for him. But he did it; got to the top, then with my encouragement, got back down again.

'Well done, Eli!' I said, as he took a couple of spins, which I knew he did as a way of self-soothing. 'That was amazing! I am so proud of you.'

Izabell was beaming; I knew she loved to see progress like this as much as me. Mr Boateng, who was sitting further down the stable fiddling with his phone, looked up with interest.

'Okay, let's try it again, shall we?' I said to Eli. 'Remember, it's just a practice. All you need to do is get to the top, then you can come back down again.'

Eli nodded. I stood close enough that he could rest his arm on my shoulder if he felt unbalanced, but I knew he preferred it if I didn't touch him. He tentatively climbed the first step, then more confidently the second. When he got to the top, instead of coming straight back down as I assumed he would, he paused for a second, then swung his leg over and plonked himself down in Samson's saddle!

You could have heard a pin drop in that stable as Izabell, Mr Boateng and I exchanged astonished but delighted glances. None of us could believe it. The frightened little boy who hadn't even wanted to cross the road a few weeks ago, had just mounted a horse all by himself. And then he did the most astonishing thing of all. He tilted his chin up, looked his father directly in the eye, and smiled.

I heard Mr Boateng take a sharp intake of breath. 'Look at you, son,' he said softly. 'You look magnificent.'

I could feel the tears welling, but I knew I had to hold it together. 'Samson is very happy to have you on board,' I told Eli. 'Can you feel him breathing? It's funny, isn't it, because you're you and he's him but now you're sort of together.'

It was a magical session that day, seeing Eli climb on and off Samson's back. I knew he wasn't ready to try moving on the horse yet, but that would come. Samson was as good and faithful as ever, and at the end, he rubbed his long nose against Eli's shoulder as he fed him a thank-you Polo.

Mr Boateng was overwhelmed. 'I never thought I'd see the day,' he said. 'You know, he never makes eye contact with me or his mother, or anyone for that matter? I take it all back – maybe you're miracle workers.'

I laughed. 'If anyone is, it's Samson.'

From that day forward, Eli went from strength to strength. He started making eye contact with not just his dad, but with all of us too. Mr Boateng told us how Eli's excitement would start to build as Wednesday afternoon approached, and it would make him strangely calm. Just looking at the picture of Samson on the fridge seemed capable of changing his mood.

The weeks went by, and we taught Eli to ride. Not just how to sit on the horse; but how to hold the reins, and how to signal to trot, how to rise and fall in the saddle. How to push his heels down and his toes up in the stirrups, and keep his core tight and his shoulders back. He absorbed it all silently, like a little sponge.

As I had hoped, the strides he was making at the stables filtered into the rest of his life. Mr Boateng told us that at home Eli's behaviour had become far more manageable, and his teachers at school said that at last he'd started to make some good progress. He had learned to engage with the world, and it was as if he'd discovered the key to escape his own internal frustrations.

But Eli still had one last surprise for us up his sleeve, and it came one December afternoon, like an unexpected Christmas gift. We'd just finished the lesson, and as had become his habit, Eli helped me untack Samson and put the saddle and bridle away. Once that was done, I gave Eli a chunk of carrot to give to his pony pal before it was time for him to go.

As Samson snaffled the treat out of his outstretched hand, Eli turned and looked at me. 'Horse,' he said simply. I almost dropped the bucket I was holding. It was his very first word.

CHAPTER SEVENTEEN

It's What You Can
Do That Counts

'It's what you can do that counts.'

I had those words carved on to a block of wood which we put above the stable door. I was so sick of people saying children with disabilities wouldn't be able to achieve certain things, because I knew that no matter their limitations, there were always things that they could do. We had many children like Eli, who the world had written off. But we had to find a way through to them.

There was nine-year-old Ryan, who could speak – but the only way he communicated was by reciting *The Gruffalo* word for word. Or sometimes he liked to have a conversation of opposites – so he would say white to me, and I'd say black. I would say up, he would say down, and so on. But a proper conversation – forget it. So you can only imagine how overwhelmed his parents were when I invited them to the park to watch Ryan riding independently, following my instructions to go round different-coloured obstacles, without a single fault. His dad was in tears. 'I never thought my son would be able to achieve anything,' he said.

As well as children with autism and learning difficulties, we had lots with physical disabilities – wheelchair users or with conditions like cerebral palsy or spina bifida.

From when Woody was just a toddler, I'd been doing back riding with him – which meant he sat in the saddle in front of me, while I controlled the reins. His Down's syndrome meant he was naturally weak and floppy, but I knew that riding would strengthen him. Some people told me it was unsafe, but I knew what was best for my boy. I'm convinced that one of the reasons he grew up strong and able was because of those early rides – and I was evangelical about passing on the benefits of riding to other people with physical disabilities.

I felt like Park Lane was achieving tiny miracles every day. And it wouldn't have been possible without the incredible team around me. Izabell and David followed me in qualifying to become RDA coaches, and in early 2015, I also took on a new stable hand – Rebekah.

When she pitched up at the stables looking lost and unhappy, I could tell Rebekah had been through a tough time. 'People don't like me,' she told me frankly, avoiding my eye contact. 'So you probably won't want to give me a job.' As job applications go, it was certainly unusual.

With some careful questions, I discovered that Rebekah was eighteen, absolutely horse mad, and had Asperger syndrome. She had grown up around horses and wanted to make a career in the equine world, but everywhere she went she found she simply didn't fit in. She said that people didn't like her – but I think a more accurate description would be that people didn't understand her. People on the autism spectrum can face harsh judgement simply because they need to learn the things that come naturally to others.

'All right then,' I told her. 'How about you do a day's work with me today, and we'll take it from there?'

Rebekah worked like an absolute Trojan that day, and although there were certain things she was uncomfortable with – the idea of wet mixed with dry disgusted her, so making up feed buckets was a no-no, and greeting clients made her anxious – she clearly had a solid work ethic, a natural affinity with horses and an incredibly organised mind. I gave her a job on the spot – promising her that her differences would not be tolerated, but celebrated.

Two more amazing additions to the Park Lane community were our physios, Julie and Sally. Together we would work on learning plans for the children with physical disabilities which would help with their mobility or getting their core stronger.

For some, the challenge would be as simple as learning to sit up in the saddle unaided. For others, even that was out of reach.

Julie and Sally were both trained in hippotherapy, which meant Park Lane was able to take on even the most severely disabled riders who couldn't hold their heads up unaided. The best way to describe this unique therapy is that the horse becomes an instrument. Under the direction of a physio, we use the horse's natural gait and movement to work the muscles of the rider, who may be lying across the horse or sitting up with our support. The warmth of the horse, the sensory feedback of the sounds and smells, and that soothing movement can have an astonishing effect on the people who try it. I will never forget the day that Abi, who had used a wheelchair all her life, stood up on her own for the first time after a year of hippotherapy sessions.

A lot of the children who came to Park Lane were non-verbal.

I can sign thanks to Woody, who also has trouble with his speech. Some parents don't like it when people sign to their children, thinking that it's slowing down their child's ability to speak. I remember one little girl, Frankie, turning up, and she was so shy and downcast-looking. I crouched down to her level and started to sign. Her whole face lit up – she couldn't believe there was someone here speaking her language.

'Oh no, we don't do signing,' said her mother. 'She needs to work on her speech.'

'You might not do signing, but I do,' I told her firmly. And that was the end of that. Some parents don't want to admit their child needs that intervention, which I totally get – it can be a hard thing to admit to yourself when all you want is for your child to face as few difficulties as possible. But actually, we all just want to feel understood. If the best way to do that is through signing, then that's what I will do.

I always made sure that the lessons were about so much more than riding. It frustrates me that people think RDA is little more than a donkey ride. It's really not – we listen to the child's needs and based on that we set targets and goals that we can work towards. If we don't achieve that, then we think of something else we can do. It's not always about pushing and pushing; but I do want the children to be the best they can be.

I started to see that riding was part of a much bigger picture. I began working in tandem with the local special schools, speech therapists and social workers who knew the children who rode with me, to make sure that we were carrying their learning through. My first mission was to make sure that every rider left happier than when they arrived. But more often than not, there was also a knock-on benefit in the rest of their life too, which made me so proud.

It wasn't only people with disabilities that we catered to either. Now that we were operating as a charity, we had even more capacity to take on children with a social or emotional 'need'. In care, grieving, troubled by mental health issues or simply disadvantaged, some would get referred to me by social workers, others would just find their way there by word of mouth as they always had done.

One of my toughest cases was little Connor, who started coming to the stables when he was just three years old. I had only the haziest details on his early years, but suffice to say that they had been filled with the sort of violence, abuse and horror that no child should face. But he'd now been adopted by a lovely couple in the local area, who were desperate for him to find an outlet for the hurt and anguish inside.

Connor looked like a little angel – big blue eyes, white blond curls, cherubic cheeks. However, he didn't speak like an angel. The first words he said to me were: 'I f—ing hate you.' Remember, he was three.

Being with Connor would break my heart. One minute he'd be as cheerful and sweet as any toddler, then the next he'd be in a rage so painful and powerful it seemed to rip him apart. It made me so sad to think of what he had endured that even at this age, this was the only way he knew how to interact with other people.

Then one afternoon, he attacked me. It was my fault; there was a stick of old fencing leaning against the stable wall, which I hadn't had time to tidy away. I told Connor it was time to take his riding hat off, which he didn't like, and he grabbed the fencing and smacked me in the face with it, using all his strength. I couldn't believe what had happened and just stood there, blood dripping from my nose.

Connor stood stock still and we regarded each other, as if in a Mexican standoff. He was in as much shock as me, because he couldn't understand why I wasn't retaliating.

'Oh, that really hurt, Connor,' I said eventually. 'It's not very nice, is it? Shall we put the stick down and be friends again?'

It proved to be a turning point for him. He didn't get over his issues overnight – far from it – but as if reassured that I wasn't going to hurt him he stopped looking for ways to hurt me. He started talking nicely and not trying to hit or kick. Most of all, he started to calm down. He was in love with Barney, a little Shetland I'd named after my old friend from the pub. If Barney was in the vicinity, Connor would always be on his best behaviour. It was like he didn't want to let Barney down.

As much as the riding was important for the children, I knew it was vital for their parents too. The short time the kids spent with us could provide their mums and dads with some vital downtime. And I knew part of the reason they trusted me was they knew I got it – because of Woody. My gorgeous baby grew into a noisy, extroverted little boy, who wanted to be friends with everybody and lived his life out loud. Ask anyone who knows him and they'll tell you that Woody is a life enhancer – he just makes everything better. But being the parent of a disabled child is a unique experience, and one that undoubtedly has its challenges.

Woody is up like a lark at 5 a.m. every day, and from then on it's a barrage of trying to manage his boisterous energy, his fluctuating moods and his various health needs. He doesn't understand the world in the same way as other people – everything is literal, which means that he can get easily confused and upset. Routine is vital, and it ends up governing your life – that and the worry about what might happen to your precious child, what social or medical problems might befall them that you're not able to protect them from. Being Woody's mum was wonderful and exhausting and exhilarating and scary and tough and perfect, all at the same time.

The parents who entrusted me with their children knew I understood this strange cocktail of emotions. We were all on the same side.

CHAPTER EIGHTEEN

Friends Old and New

Although the work we were doing with the disabled was increasing, I never wanted Park Lane to be 'just' an RDA centre. In fact, it wasn't 'just' anything – it was totally unique. I saw Park Lane as a community stables, which means that much like the library or the swimming pool, we were there for anyone that needed us.

We still had a thriving Pony Club, for young people who wanted to ride and learn about horses and build their character at the same time. But I made sure there was no 'us and them' mentality, and the Pony Clubbers and the RDA participants all shared a love of ponies which transcended any other differences. It was lovely seeing them develop friendships with each other and with the horses – never more in evidence than during the regular open days we held at the stables.

With more than twenty horsey mouths to feed plus the frequent necessity for new equipment and training, Park Lane was in constant need of money. We relied on the ever-generous Teddington community, who over the years had really taken the stables to their hearts. At our open days we sold delicious cakes made by parents and horseshoes painted by the Pony Clubbers, we'd have a bouncy castle and face painting and always lots and lots of pony rides. Our marketing guru Richard Sharp could always be relied on to get the word out – especially if we were raising money for a particular cause, like the party we threw to raise funds for ageing grey gelding Trigger's knee surgery, or the odd sock parade we held in honour of World Down's Syndrome Day.

The local people were always so generous with us, so we liked to make sure we always did what we could for Teddington too – whether it was decking out the ponies in poppies for the Remembrance Sunday service, or providing horsey comfort where we could. For example, when in late 2015 a local care home phoned me up and asked whether I'd consider bringing a pony to visit the residents, I didn't hesitate to say yes. I had just the pony too – a little cuddly grey called Caesar, with a big appetite and the most open, friendly nature.

When I arrived at the imposing Victorian building, with its dormer windows, ivy-clad walls and big sweep of lawn at the front, I assumed that the staff would be ready with some of the residents in the garden. But the smiling carer waiting for me on the front steps dressed in bright pink trainers and a jazzy tabard, who introduced herself as Flora, beckoned me to follow her.

'What, you mean … inside?' I said, looking doubtfully at Caesar, who was standing patiently next to me at the end of his lead rope.

'Absolutely!' she answered, still beaming. 'He's only little, isn't he?'

'All right then,' I said, then leaning closer to Caesar, I whispered in his ear: 'Best behaviour, okay?'

I followed Flora through the glass doors and down a magnolia corridor, worried that Caesar might take a dump right there and then on the linoleum. But he didn't – and he seemed remarkably pleased about getting to see these new surroundings. Flora led us into a large lounge, where about eighteen grey-haired residents were sitting on various armchairs and wheelchairs, loosely arranged around a large TV.

'Oh, get that bloody horse out of here,' one elderly gentleman said, craning past us to see whatever game show was on the screen.

'Don't mind Keith,' Flora said, raising an eyebrow. 'You'll have made his day by giving him something to moan about.' I had to giggle.

Keith might not have been happy, but he was the only one. The lethargic mood in the room instantly lifted, and the delight among the older people was palpable.

'Isn't he beautiful!' said a lady with tight-set curls to my right.

'Touch him!' I encouraged. 'Caesar loves cuddles.' She happily reached out and stroked him, and her face went misty and quiet as she enjoyed that brief moment of companionship with the pony.

We did the rounds of the room, stopping to chat with individual residents, and I could tell Caesar was in his element. It had evidently just been tea time, and some of the older people had half-eaten custard creams on their plates which they gingerly offered to him in return for a cuddle. Caesar hoovered them all up with gusto.

We'd been round almost the whole room when we got to a tiny, birdlike lady with white hair who was sitting by herself in a corner, covered in a tartan blanket. As we approached, Flora whispered to me: 'This is Mary. She has very severe dementia, so don't worry if we don't get much out of her.'

The lady had a faraway expression, and I could tell that her mind wasn't really with us in the room. But as we got nearer, her face changed. She took a deep breath in, as if inhaling Caesar's scent. And then, she started to cry.

'Is it Beauty?' she asked. 'Such a lovely horse . . . We'll go for a ride later with Winnie, she'll take Patch, let's go down the lane and across to the river.'

'Winnie, your sister Winnie – you remember her?' Flora asked Mary, with evident excitement.

'Oh yes, my best friend in the world, is Winnie,' smiled Mary. We were close enough now for her to touch Caesar, and she buried her hands in his mane, taking in the sound of him chomping on the most recent biscuit he'd pinched and his gentle breathing.

'Except for maybe Beauty – did I tell you how my father won Beauty in a fair? Oh, how happy we were that day to see him coming up the street with this perfect little brown pony in tow . . . it was like all our Christmases had come at once.' Mary continued to speak of Beauty, the pony she'd loved as a child, and Flora and I crouched down to listen to her, while Caesar snuffled happily around her open hands.

Eventually, Mary seemed to tire herself out. Flora gestured subtly that it was time to go. As she showed us out, the residents all waving happily to Caesar, I could tell Flora was bursting with excitement.

'I've never seen Mary like that,' she said giddily, when we reached the corridor. 'Her sister Winnie visits every week and she never recognises her. And she hasn't spoken about her memories in, well, years. It's like . . . you've unlocked something in her.'

'It's all down to Caesar,' I said, rubbing his little neck as we finally reached fresh air – with no accidents! 'The smell and the sound of him probably takes her all the way back.'

'Yes, I'm sure that's true,' nodded Flora. 'The senses are so powerful. You will come back, won't you?'

Of course I did – we went back every week for years after that. Caesar loved it – he'd march straight in there with an expression on his face which said: 'Where are my biscuits?'

As our role in the community grew, so did the Park Lane family. It was funny to think that it had once just been me, calling on Jenny Bear and Lou to help when I ran out of hands. 'Well, I'm certainly glad that changed,' Lou joked with a raised eyebrow, during one of our regular meet-ups at the pub.

Jenny Bear still liked to pitch in on the summer camps which saw me take a group of kids down to Pachesham in Surrey once a year to have a solid week of riding and horse care, but that was just because she loved it. 'Well, I do love it, but also you're technologically challenged, aren't you, so you couldn't cope without me,' she said, giving me a friendly nudge. That was true – anything to do with computers was beyond me, so it was always down to Jenny to make a digital presentation I'd show to the kids on the first day, or design a picture quiz, or create worksheets or whatever else.

I always appreciated her help, but I also had a veritable army of volunteers I could call on now. More than ever, of course – now that we were offering riding for the disabled – I needed people who could do leading and sidewalking; that means walking alongside the pony and supporting the rider. And with so many new ponies, there was lots of work to be done getting them groomed and tacked up ready for the lessons – as well as all the feeding, cleaning, sweeping, mucking out and poo-picking to be done around the stables and up at the field.

Lots of my volunteers were young – first among them Amelia, who had grown into a level-headed teenager who never lost her love for riding, and Rowena, who would have slept in a stable if she could. Philippa, who in some ways had been our first RDA participant before we were an RDA centre, had a really important role inspiring the younger disabled children and organising social activities. Then there were volunteers who had retired – like Joy, an artist whose name couldn't have been more appropriate, and Nicola, who had recently left her job as a school administrator and was relishing spending more time outside with the ponies. But we didn't have loads of volunteers in the ages in between – so Verity was a little unusual.

Verity, who at about thirty was a few years younger than me, burst into our lives in the autumn of 2015. I'd been up at the field swapping horses around, and when I arrived back at the stables with one of our newest additions, Dougie, expecting to see the usual coming and going, I found the street outside deserted. I could, however, hear raucous laughter coming from inside the stable block.

It was one of those short October days when you know there is going to be a frost that night, and the dark was already drawing in. I followed the noise of the laughter through the gloom and found Izabell, Rebekah, Amy and Rowena all gathered around Trigger's stable, chatting with a young woman I didn't recognise.

'Oh, this is Natalie we've been telling you about!' said Izabell brightly, as she saw me coming. 'Natalie, this is Verity.'

The woman turned around, and gave me the most dazzling wide smile. Her long hair was twisted on top of her head in a messy bun, her long legs in spotless skinny jeans.

'Hi, Natalie, I'm so pleased to meet you!' she said. 'I was just telling the girls here, I'd love to get involved with what you do. I just think, wow, if I was a kid right now, with all that's going on in the world, a pony would really help me, and that you try and do that for all sorts of people – it's brilliant, and I can imagine it's a total privilege to work here, and I love horses too, so I can't imagine anything better than being here and doing that – oh god, I'm babbling.' She stopped, and hit me with another knock-out smile. 'Sorry, I'm nervous . . . from everything Izabell and the girls have told me, you're an absolute hero, and well, I'm between jobs, and if there's any way – any way at all – that I could be useful around here, then I'll do it. No matter how big or small the task.'

There was something about Verity's openness that I found almost unnerving – she was simply the friendliest person I'd ever met. The shining faces of the girls told me they'd been charmed by her right away. But was she too good to be true?

Well, that was unnecessarily cynical of me – because over the next few years, I found out that yes, Verity really was that nice. She was like sunshine in human form – someone who never seemed to have an off day, who was always patient, and could put even the most anxious and nervous rider or parent at ease. She started at the stables as a volunteer, but she was so brilliant I urged her to take her exams and before long she joined the staff team as a coach. As well as teaching, I put her in a sort of front-of-house role – after all, I'd wanted Park Lane to be the friendliest stables in London, so what better than having the friendliest face in London to greet you?

Verity joined the team just in time, because the clients just kept coming – and we had to keep pace with demand. We developed a reputation for taking riders that other stables couldn't manage. They came not because we were particularly gifted, but because we were open minded.

If someone was scared or sad or lonely, David would be there, to talk and listen and never judge. A child with lots of physical needs had the expertise of Julie and Sally, who thought of the most innovative solutions for an enormous range of impairments. If you were nervous or shy, Verity would take away your worries without you even noticing. Need a friend? Join Amelia, Rowena, Amy, Lexi, Philippa and all the rest – they would tell you which ponies liked their ears scratching just so, and who had a penchant for carrots. If you wanted to push yourself, achieve things you didn't know were possible, then Izabell was your girl – she'd take you to your limits and cheer you all the way.

And none of us saw differences as drawbacks – whatever someone's situation or capabilities, I always just thought: okay, how can we get this person on a horse?

CHAPTER NINETEEN

Driving Lessons

I hate saying no. And saying no to Colin broke my heart.

At thirteen, Colin had already had a tough life. He had muscular dystrophy, a degenerative condition which causes the muscles to weaken over time until eventually it affects the whole body.

He was mad about sport, but while other boys his age were chasing around after footballs, he had to watch from the sidelines. His life was a monotonous routine of physiotherapy, hospital appointments and stretching rituals at home with his parents. Shortly before he was referred to Park Lane in 2015, he had taken the difficult step of swapping his walking frame for a wheelchair. Despite the challenges he faced, Colin was as cheerful and polite a teenager as you could hope to meet.

The move to the wheelchair had been more difficult for his parents than for him, I think. He saw only the benefits; he was more independent, and less likely to fall. But his mum and dad found it hard to accept that he needed the assistance, and perhaps it was too harsh a signpost on the tragic journey they were on. I knew that most boys with Colin's particular form of MD were not expected to live past their early thirties.

So that was the situation when Colin first arrived at Park Lane. He'd been advised that riding might be a good way to complement his physiotherapy. I don't think his family expected that Colin would find what he did – which was freedom. From the moment he got into the saddle, he loved it. Here was a sport that he could do, and he could do it on his own – he was still able to sit up and hold the reins and control the horse. He told me how good it felt to move his wasting muscles with the rhythm of Eddy's jaunty pace. He adored that pony – and I think the feeling was mutual. The once naughty dapple-grey Highland pony was now as steady and reliable as they come, and would always whinny in delight when he saw it was Colin arriving for a lesson. The pair of them had a special bond that came from Colin finally feeling like he was part of a team, something he had longed for his entire life.

Colin had weekly lessons with us for just under two years, and during that time I witnessed the true and tragic meaning of the word 'degenerative'. As the months went by he needed more and more help to get into the saddle, stopped being able to sit up unaided, and his hands would no longer grip the reins effectively. He was on powerful steroids to slow the rate of his decline, but these in turn caused him to gain excessive weight. Eventually, after one lesson which had seen three of us struggle to get him into the saddle, Julie the physio said that we'd have to stop.

'It's just not safe any more, Natalie,' she told me, as we had a cup of tea back at my cottage. 'Colin's too big for us to be certain that we won't hurt him or ourselves. And he's probably too heavy for Eddy now too.'

I knew she was right – and I had to put Eddy first. It wouldn't be fair to anyone to continue. But how was I going to break that to Colin and his family?

It was a conversation that could only be had in person, so the next day I clipped Murphy on his lead and walked the hour's route through the Hounslow streets until I got to their house.

Colin's mum answered the door, and she seemed to know immediately why I had come. She crossed her arms and didn't invite me in. I found myself getting emotional as I tried to explain as sympathetically as possible why it wouldn't be possible for Colin to continue at Park Lane. She listened in stony silence.

'You know, it's the one good thing he has in his life. The one time he is happy,' his mum said when I had finished, her voice quietly furious. 'And now you've taken that away.'

I opened my mouth to protest, to tell her he would still be very welcome to come and see Eddy, that just spending time with the ponies could be valuable too, but she was already closing the door. Just before she did, I glimpsed Colin's stricken face, peeping round from a doorway at the end of the hallway.

The guilt felt like a dead weight on my shoulders as Murphy and I walked slowly back to Park Lane. I knew how important riding was to Colin, and how special was his friendship with Eddy. I'd let Colin into the secret that Eddy's favourite thing in the whole world was a custard cream biscuit, and he always came with one in his pocket to give him after the lesson. And he'd laugh hysterically as Eddy pulled his famous dunking trick – taking a mouthful of hay then immediately dunking it in water before he ate it.

I sensed that Colin's mum's anger would mean we wouldn't be seeing him any time soon. I just wished there was a way we could still give him all the amazing benefits of riding – the movement, the teamwork and the fun – without putting anyone at risk.

Later in the cottage, as we watched Alice and Woody play an elaborate but confusing game that involved them putting pants on their heads, Dickie gave me a nudge.

'What's up with you today? You've hardly said a word this evening,' he said.

I sighed. 'Just a lot on my mind,' I said. 'Remember Colin? I had to tell his mum he can't come riding any more because he's too big. I just wish there was another way.'

I was also thinking of other very disabled children for whom even hippotherapy wasn't an option. A girl called Bolu, who had come to us a few months ago, but had cerebral palsy so severe she couldn't move her hips apart at all. We'd had to turn her away too. And she wasn't the only one.

'What if there was a way that he could have a horse ride, without actually riding a horse?' said Dickie. I rolled my eyes at him thinking he was trying to be funny, but he looked seriously back.

'What do you mean?'

He said, 'I mean – what about a carriage?'

It felt like a light bulb going on in my head. Of course – this was the answer! If we could get a wheelchair into a carriage, then the child would be able to enjoy the thrill of movement and all the sensory feedback from the horse without actually having to get out of the wheelchair. This could be the solution I was looking for.

'You're a genius, Dickie!' I said, giving him a quick kiss.

'I have my moments,' he smiled.

I didn't waste a minute – grabbing my laptop and punching 'wheelchair carriage driving' into Google. I found that some other RDA centres offered it as an alternative to riding, with specially adapted carriages that enabled the wheelchair to easily get on and off.

'This is brilliant, Dickie!' I said, scrolling through testimonials from parents who said the carriage driving had changed their child's life. Some children might have enough upper body strength to learn how to drive the carriage themselves, others would simply enjoy the ride and the chance to be that close to a horse. I could already imagine Colin, sitting smiling and proud in a carriage, the wind in his hair and joy in his heart.

'So I guess we'll need to do some training, and get one of these carriages ... ah.'

I stopped short, feeling the cold hand of reality halt my racing daydreams in their tracks. I'd just clicked on a link to where you could buy an adapted carriage, and discovered it cost £15,000 – money we certainly didn't have.

I spun the laptop round so Dickie could see. 'I see the problem,' he said slowly. 'But you've never let practicalities get in the way of a good plan before, have you?'

He was right – and I wasn't about to start now. The next morning, I told Izabell I needed her help.

'We've got to raise £15,000, as soon as possible,' I told her excitedly, as we loaded horses for that day's riding lessons into the lorry.

'Why don't you just ask for it?' she shrugged. 'Someone local. That's not much money to, say, a businessman.'

I loved how general her concept of a 'businessman' was, but she had a point. Local businesses were always generous in their support of Park Lane, whenever we held a summer fete or Christmas party. I was often being told how much everyone loved having us as part of the local community. Maybe it was time to cash in on some of those compliments?

I was in the tiny room we used as a tack room and office,

making a list of places I should approach, when David came in, carrying some hats to put away.

'Hiya, what you up to?' he asked pleasantly, as he put the equipment in the cupboard.

'Just deciding who I should tap up for a £15,000 carriage,' I said wryly.

David paused, and I could tell he was thinking. 'I'd start with someone with a connection to wheels,' he said, then turned and headed down the stairs.

It sounded a bit mad – but I totally got where he was coming from. It's like when a betting company sponsors a football team, or a sugar maker advertises during *The Great British Bake Off*. We needed someone with a connection. I glanced down at my list.

'What about H&L Motors?' I called after David's retreating back.

'Got to be worth a try!' he called back.

That's how me and a bunch of kids – Philippa, Hannah, who was visually impaired, and Connor, who had promised to be on his best behaviour, ended up going for a meeting with the boss of H&L Motors, Peter Laney. I got the children to each tell him what horses meant to them, and to hold up pictures they'd drawn of themselves at their riding lessons.

'But you see, not everyone can have the wonderful experience these children have,' I told Peter, who wore a sharp suit but had a kind face. 'And that's why we need your help, to buy a carriage and ensure horses are accessible for all.'

Peter smiled, and leaned forward on to his oak desk. 'And how much does a carriage cost?'

'It's £15,000,' I said, and he sat back in his chair, letting the air out of his cheeks. 'But even if you could just contribute some of that money,' I added quickly, suddenly fearing I'd been too bold. 'That would really help us.'

Peter reached into his desk drawer and pulled out a cheque book. 'Don't be silly,' he said, and my heart sank. But then he added: 'I'll give you the whole lot!'

I couldn't stop staring at the cheque as we walked out of his office, the children whooping over our success. We'd done it! Thanks to the incredible generosity of a stranger, I'd be able to change countless lives.

Obviously, we still had no knowledge or experience of coach driving, so the next step was to get some training, which both David and Dickie were keen to do too. It's just as well they did, because during our training sessions it quickly became apparent that I was rubbish. RDA guidelines say you have to drive the carriage one handed, so your other hand is free to help the child. But because I was such an experienced rider, I found it very unnatural to hold the reins with only one hand. Our RDA coach, Judi, agreed that it was probably best for me to bow out – something Dickie certainly enjoyed teasing me about once he was a fully qualified carriage-driving instructor.

Finally, we needed a horse to pull the carriage. And getting one that was trained to do that and licensed by the RDA was probably even harder than getting the £15,000 had been. Eventually, Judi told me about Sam, a black cart horse with white feathers and a white blaze down his nose, who was working at an RDA centre in Wales. We bought him unseen – and thank god we did, because he was every bit as sweet and reliable and strong as I'd hoped he would be.

People in the area or with connections to the stable were aware that we were getting ready to start carriage driving, and before Sam even arrived I found I had a waiting list. So many children can't ride for one reason or another, and those are usually the same kids who can't do any other activities either. No wonder there was so much demand.

But there was one person I knew had to be top of the list. It had been a full nine months since Colin's mum had slammed the door in my face, but I hoped she would give me a chance.

I rang her one evening, explained what we'd done and how I wanted Colin to be one of the first people to try out our new carriage, if she would agree. She sniffed, then said: 'You better talk to Colin about it.' There was a rustling as she handed the phone over, and Colin came on the line.

'Hi, Colin,' I said. 'We've missed you so much at Park Lane.'

'I've missed you too,' Colin said, with difficulty. His speech seemed to have become even slower and more slurred since we last spoke, which I knew would be a result of his condition worsening.

'I have something I want to ask you,' I said. 'We've got a carriage now at Park Lane, and it's really easy for us to put a wheelchair on it. So I was wondering if you'd like to come and try it out for me – could be fun, do you think?'

I could hear Colin breathing heavily as he struggled to find the words. Eventually, he said: 'Will Eddy pull it?'

'No, sorry, Colin. It's a new horse, called Sam, but he's very friendly and I think you'll like him. And Eddy will be there, you can give him an apple afterwards.'

'Okay,' said Colin.

'Okay, you'll give it a go?' I asked.

'Yes please,' said Colin, and hung up the phone.

The day that Colin came for his first carriage ride, I was determined everything had to be perfect. I got up extra early to groom Sam and put bows in his plaited mane, then I put a few in Eddy's too. David had polished the wheels of the carriage until they shone. We were in Bushy Park waiting for Colin and his mum well before they were due to arrive, and I couldn't help but feel a little nervous as the minutes inched by.

Finally, they arrived. I could see Colin's mum hurrying to keep up with him as he put his electric wheelchair into fast mode, eager to get to Sam and Eddy, who Izabell had on a rope. His smile was so big it looked like it might crack his face in half.

After a fond reunion with Eddy, Dickie and David helped manoeuvre Colin's wheelchair into the bespoke space at the front of the carriage. I couldn't believe how wonderful he looked up there next to Dickie, who had dressed for the occasion in a jacket and tie.

'Ready to go?' Dickie asked Colin, who nodded fervently. And they were off! We cheered as the carriage trundled away down the park's pathway, Sam trotting obediently in front.

'I owe you an apology,' Colin's mum said to me, once her son was out of earshot. 'I know you were doing the right thing. I was just frustrated and sad for Colin, but I shouldn't have taken it out on you.'

'It's okay,' I told her, putting a hand on her arm. 'You were right to say what you did. It gave me the kick up the bum I needed – it's not good enough to be turning people away.'

The sound of a jangling harness indicated that the carriage was coming back towards us. Watching Colin, I could imagine how much sensory feedback he was getting up there: the familiar smells of the horse, the sounds of the hooves, and the feel of that wonderful rolling gait. He seemed higher up than I had imagined he'd be too, at one with a world which had been closed off from him for so long.

'You look amazing, Colin!' I called out to him. 'How do you feel up there?'

Colin grinned and waved. 'I feel free!' he said.

His mum made a muffled little sound, and gripped my arm back. I could feel myself welling up, and if I wasn't much mistaken, even Dickie was holding back a few tears.

Now, thanks to Colin, we don't say no to anyone.

CHAPTER TWENTY

By Royal Appointment

I lived for moments like Colin's first carriage ride. That's what my horses and my team were here for – to empower people no matter the obstacles life had thrown at them. At Park Lane, we did this in a million tiny ways every day.

Now that we were offering carriage driving, we had a whole new crop of participants – like Dominic, who had severe cerebral palsy and had become socially isolated, and Lucy, who had spent her life in a wheelchair but had always adored horses. Kids like them had spent their lives being turned away from sports and activities, being told that they simply couldn't do it. But with carriage driving, they discovered that yes, they can.

I couldn't have been prouder of what we were achieving at the stables, but behind the scenes, we were facing a battle to survive. In the summer of 2014, when I had tried to renew my operating licence with the council, they had carried out an inspection and discovered that the roof of the stables was badly damaged. They gave me an ultimatum: repair it, or I'd have to find new premises.

For me, it wasn't even a decision. There was no way we could move – not when we'd already become a lifeline for so many local people. Park Lane's location was unique – easily accessible by public transport, which was particularly important for disabled and socially disadvantaged participants, and right in the heart of the Teddington community, which had defined the spirit of the stables.

Under the terms of my lease, it was me, not the landlord, who was responsible for the repairs. That meant it was up to me to find the money – and fast.

I got everything priced up – and even with local architects Astronaut Kawada offering to work on the project on a pro bono basis, and construction firm Reed, whose director, Simon, was the dad of one of our Pony Clubbers, saying they'd do it for mates' rates, it was still going to cost a whopping £70,000.

'That's a hell of a lot of money,' whistled Izabell, when I told the team. 'How are we going to get that together?'

'Well, I've spoken to the bank, and they'll give me a £30,000 loan,' I said. 'But that still leaves a £40,000 shortfall. So – you know what that means. Fundraising!'

Over the next nine months, we raised that money practically in 10p instalments. We held quizzes and cake sales and sponsored rides, but once they knew of our fate, the Teddington people came through as always. A local Italian restaurant, Il Casale, threw us a pizza party, while a local artist, Liz, created a painting of the stables and gave us the prints to sell. Then there was an incredibly generous donation of £5,000 from the Rugby Football Union who were based nearby at Twickenham.

It was a long slog, but by the following summer we were in a position to start the necessary works. Seeing as we had to do the roof anyway, Dean, the architect, had suggested we take the opportunity to make better use of Park Lane's limited space. His design reconfigured the stables so there would be room for two more horses, and created a loft room that could be a social space or classroom. I loved the idea – at the moment, RDA participants had to go home after their lessons, but I liked the thought of them being able to stay for a cup of tea and a chat.

Having builders on site just added to the general chaos at Park Lane. The horses had to be moved out, and we leased some stables down the road in Hampton, which was where we already rented an arena for hippotherapy sessions.

With the help of my incredible team we managed to keep on operating anyway. Nicola, the former school administrator turned volunteer, offered to help me with the paperwork that was bogging me down, which I gratefully accepted. To me, keeping track of all the admin was the hardest part of running the stables, and especially with the fundraising effort and the works that were going on, I needed help more desperately than ever.

Shortly before Christmas 2015, Nicola and another helper, Kath, called by the cottage with a load of papers for me to sign. I made us a cup of tea, and we sat at the kitchen table while I went through the documents, with Kath jiggling Woody on her lap.

'Oh, just another thing,' Kath said, as I signed the last sheet. 'We've had a letter from the RDA. Their patron, Princess Anne, is going to be visiting some of the centres next year, and they're inviting applications from ones which have something to celebrate. I thought, wouldn't it be a good idea to have her open the stables once the works are done? What do you think?'

'I think that's an absolutely brilliant thought, Kath,' I said, grinning. 'I love it. Although I guess they must get tons of applications, and we're only small.'

Kath smiled. 'Got to be in it to win it,' she said. 'Leave it with me.'

A few days later, Kath emailed me the application for the

Princess Anne visit – I made a few amends and sent it off, and then to be honest, forgot all about it.

Christmas was always mad at Park Lane, and 2015 was no different. The kids always worked themselves up into fever pitch at that time of year, and there were school concerts and nativity plays and Christmas bazaars to attend, where we'd often take Caesar or Diana in lieu of a donkey. On the day itself, the cottage was heaving at the seams, with Jenny Bear, Lou, Liam, Amy, and Anwar from the flats across the road all joining Dickie, the kids and me for Christmas dinner. Then it was New Year's Eve, and my annual drinks with Barney, Sam and Pasty, which we still held every year all together still for old times' sake. With all that merry-making – plus the demands of looking after more than twenty horses in the dead of winter – the royal visit had gone completely out of my mind.

So imagine my surprise when in the first week of January, I got a phone call from the RDA. They were ringing to say we'd been chosen for a visit from Princess Anne – and that she'd be coming to us on 16 February.

'Wow, that's amazing news!' I said, trying to keep the panic out of my voice. I was standing by the cottage window, looking out into the street which was still very much a building site. I flipped open the battered diary I kept on the kitchen counter – 16 February was just over six weeks away.

'So shall I tell them that it will be an opening ceremony?' the RDA lady asked me. 'The works are finished, aren't they?'

'Very nearly!!' I said, trying to sound as bright as possible. 'We'll be ready for her, don't you worry!'

I hung up the phone and flung on my jacket, hurrying round to the stables where Simon and his team were busy drilling and sanding and banging planks of wood together.

'Simon, Simon!' I shouted, trying to make myself heard above the din. I waved furiously and he suddenly noticed me, and flicked off his drill.

'All right, Nat?' he said, taking off his plastic goggles. 'What's up?'

'So, I've got some news and I'm not sure you're going to like it,' I said, with a grimace.

'Don't tell me – you've run out of tea,' joked Simon.

'Worse than that I'm afraid. Well, actually, it's not really bad news. Princess Anne is coming to visit us – to open the stables.'

'That's not bad news!' exclaimed Simon, looking baffled. 'What's bad about that?'

'Well, it's on 16 February.'

'Ah,' said Simon, and I could see he was running calculations in his head. 'No chance of moving that, I suppose? Because really, we're a good ten weeks off being done here.'

I shook my head. 'I'm afraid not,' I said. 'So I guess, I'm here to ask – can you do what you can?'

The other four builders had laid down their tools by now and were listening to our conversation. 'We'll do our very best, won't we, lads?' said Simon, looking round at them. 'You just keep the tea coming,' he said to me, with a wink.

Simon and his team were as good as their word. Despite the freezing cold weather and the short, dark days, they worked round the clock on the stables. They were there at first light as I drove off to Oxshott to see to the horses, and they were there in the gathering dusk as I waved goodbye to the last riders of the day. The new-look stables were coming together – but there was still a lot to do.

A week before the visit, Princess Anne's security team came to do a recce of the stables, so we could discuss how the day would progress. One of the bodyguards raised an eyebrow as he peered into the stable block, to be greeted with a cloud of sawdust. 'Just some last-minute finishing touches!' I said quickly. 'Now, let me show you to Bushy Park where I thought we could greet Her Royal Highness ...'

I didn't know quite what would happen if we weren't ready in time, but I wasn't going to waste any time worrying about it. There was too much to do. All sorts of people – from old friends like Pasty to parents of our riders like Eli's dad – turned up to pitch in during that last frantic week. We were still painting the loft room on the night before the Princess arrived, while my team of volunteers were hard at work bathing and grooming the ponies to within an inch of their lives. Everything had to look its best.

I barely slept at all that night, I was so nervous. I'd tried to arrange things so as many of our volunteers as possible, as well as the incredibly hardworking builders and roofers, would get a chance to meet the Princess, but I realised it would be on me to make sure everything went smoothly. 'Try not to worry, Nat,' said Dickie sleepily, as I tossed and turned. 'I know she's a princess, but she's also just a woman who's really, really into horses – and you know how to talk to people like that, don't you?'

Finally, the morning of our royal visit arrived. The plan was that we'd greet Princess Anne up at Bushy Park. So that's where the team and I headed, with ten of the horses, and two volunteers to each horse. We helped the RDA participants up into the saddles and got them all lined up to wait for our royal visitor. Seeing the gleaming tack, the volunteers in their spotless jodhpurs, the horses waiting patiently and the big smiles of the riders, I felt quite overwhelmed.

'I think I might cry, you know,' I said to the royal bodyguard who'd come on ahead. He looked at me sternly.

'Well, if you do, it will be the first time that's ever happened.'

Chastened, I practised my curtsy one more time.

Suddenly, a convoy of black cars was pulling into the car park ahead.

'She's here!' I whispered excitedly to my friendly volunteer turned coach, Verity, who squeezed my hand, looking just as giddy as me. Everyone was craning their necks to get a first glimpse of the Princess. She was walking at a stately pace towards us, dressed in a long camel coat. I prepared myself – it was time to curtsy.

The rest of the day went so quickly, I had to pinch myself and ask – did that actually happen? It was like a real-life fairy tale. The Princess was genuinely fascinated by watching our RDA participants go through their paces, and as Dickie had predicted, it was clear that she had a deep affection for the horses. After she'd seen a little taster of one of our lessons, it was time to walk back from the park to the stables.

Now, that really was surreal – walking down the street with my new mate Anne, chatting about horses. She couldn't believe that we lorried them every day between Oxshott and Teddington.

'Well, the horses have to be happy or none of this would work,' I said. 'So even if that means a bit more hassle for the humans, we have to do it.'

Princess Anne nodded sagely. 'I quite agree,' she said.

As the stables came into view, so did the sound of cheering. The police had closed off the road and about a hundred people had gathered, some waving Union Jacks. I showed the Princess into the stables to meet a few more of the ponies, and she made lots of fuss of friendly piebald Doris. And she took the time to chat to the young volunteers, and then we went up into the new loft, where she met the incredible workmen who had made the new stables a reality.

Finally, it was time to unveil the royal plaque marking that our new home was officially open. Flanked by Dotty, our little spotty Shetland pony, the Princess removed the velvet curtain and that was it – Park Lane 2.0 was in business!

One of our carriage drivers, Lucy, had been waiting outside the stables in her wheelchair the whole time, holding a bouquet of flowers we were presenting to the Princess in thanks. After she'd done the honours with the plaque, Princess Anne headed directly to her, and started to talk to her about her experience of carriage driving. It was freezing, so I went to rub Lucy's hands warm – until a sharp look from the lady from RDA's head office told me that wasn't the done thing when the Princess was talking!

As the Princess waved goodbye and was escorted back to her car, those tears that had been threatening since the morning finally came. We were just a scruffy, oddball little stables, held together with kindness, but today we'd had some royal fairy dust sprinkled over us. I knew it was a day that would live in my mind – and the minds of so many of the people I cared about most – for a very long time. None of it would have been possible without the generosity of friends and strangers, and the hard work of people who believed in what we did. Raising £40,000 in nine months had felt like an epic feat. Little did I know that within a few years, something would happen that would make that effort seem like child's play.

CHAPTER TWENTY-ONE

Team Spirit

The new loft lounge proved to be the brilliant addition I'd hoped it would be. Park Lane had always been a very sociable stables, but now we had a place where people could gather which wasn't just an empty stable or the tack room. We decorated the walls with photographs of pony camps and competitions, and always had an urn of tea on the go. It became a classroom, a café, and a party room – with Philippa always thinking of some new activity that we could try up there.

The years ticked by and some kids came and went, but there were always certain stalwarts who never had enough of us – like Philippa herself. Remember Amelia, the little girl who took the first pony ride at my first school fete all those years ago? Well, she stayed with us as a volunteer all through her teens and, after she finished college, I offered her a job. She was so patient and hardworking and could turn her hand to just about anything around the stables. And she was determined to take her British Horse Society exams, and progress to being a coach.

Amelia joined the team as a staff member in 2018 – just after

Izabell went back to Cyprus. Saying goodbye to my right-hand woman after all those years was a real wrench; we'd worked together for so long by then, and sometimes it felt like we shared one mind. But she had her own life to live and adventures to have, and I knew the impact she'd made on Park Lane would last.

'You'll be okay, won't you?' said Izabell, wiping my tears away as I gave her one last hug at the airport. 'Make sure you send me pictures all the time – I'm going to miss you so much!'

Words couldn't describe how much I'd miss her too – but along with Amelia, Verity, Rebekah and David, we had a thriving team at Park Lane. We needed it – because by then we had grown so much we were providing three thousand sessions of therapeutic riding every year for adults and children with disabilities and mental health challenges.

To help with the load, I'd offered Nicola a proper job doing admin, and I'd taken on Daisy, a glamorous twenty-something who always had immaculate nails and lashes, but nevertheless got stuck into the dirtiest jobs around the yard. And I'd also started to offer opportunities to people with additional needs.

So by 2018, we had Hannah, who had graduated from rider to apprentice to assistant, working with us despite her visual impairment. Someone in the horse world had once said to me that Hannah would never be able to pass her British Horse Society exams, and you better believe that meant I was determined she would. I helped Hannah study, but she took herself off for her examination and passed with flying colours all on her own. I told her often that she was an inspiration to us all.

Also on the team were Daniel and Arthur, who like Rebekah were both on the autistic spectrum. It didn't bother me that they all had little quirks – like Arthur was terrified of thunder, so I said it was fine for him to always stay home if the weather looked bad. Instead, I liked to celebrate what they could do. Rebekah was an incredibly hard worker, who thrived on routine – she made sure the yard was always running with military precision. Arthur had a remarkable memory and was brilliant at helping me sort out riding schedules and timetables. Daniel was super funny and could always be relied upon to liven up the team. All they needed was an opportunity and they proved their worth ten times over.

Working with people with additional needs was further proof – as if I needed it – of the value of an open mind. That's why I also got involved in a scheme that offered volunteer placements to people recently released from prison. The idea was that if they completed it successfully, I'd then give them a reference which they could take to a future employer.

As far as I'm concerned, everyone deserves a second chance, and if you've served your time in prison then your punishment should be considered over. I met all sorts of fascinating blokes, many of whom had ended up in jail thanks to some bad choices and a lack of guidance when they were young, and genuinely wanted a fresh start. More often than not they'd work hard, turn up on time and behave well.

One, however, raised even my eyebrows. When his DBS check, which provides a person's criminal record, came back in late 2018, I saw that the crime he'd been convicted of was attempted murder. At first, my reaction was one of alarm – but then I told myself sharply to stop being so stupid. If the probation service thought there was nothing to worry about, then I had to trust them.

Even so, I arranged for the guy, Patrick, to come early in the morning when there was no one around but me. He mucked out stables, moved heavy bags of feed, did general odd jobs around the yard and was gone before anyone else arrived. He was professional, polite and reliable. I couldn't fault him.

Dad visited often and would always spend time chatting to the young people and volunteers I'd taken on. He always said that I reminded him of Mum. 'She liked to collect people too,' he said, smiling. 'She'd be very proud of what you've built here.'

'It's not just me you know!' I'd always say to Dad, slightly embarrassed. And that was true. The lifeblood of Park Lane was the volunteers – without whom it simply wouldn't be possible to operate. There are too many to name them all, but just to give you an example of a few – there were Toni and Dannii, mother and daughter, who turned up no matter what the weather to help up at the fields. There was Peter, who trained our new volunteers and gave talks to prospective funders, and there was Marnie, who lived close by and would often drop everything at a moment's notice when we needed an extra pair of hands.

And then there was Nina. She was more than a volunteer – she also became one of my very best friends, and kept me sane. Nina had kids at the same school as Alice, and I'd seen her around when I first started doing the school run in 2015. Tall, beautiful, immaculately dressed and with an air of proficiency about her, Nina ran the school cake sale every Thursday. Her three kids were a bit older than Alice, so we'd never been introduced, but when I mentioned to some of the other parents that I was keen to get back into running and wanted a buddy to run with, they suggested Nina. I had no idea if she'd go for it, but I bowled over to her one Thursday cake sale and introduced myself all the same. To my surprise, Nina said yes – and just like that a friendship was born. We were like a double Forrest Gump, literally running thousands of miles together over the years – ironing out our problems as we pounded the streets, sharing good times and bad, ideas, hopes and dreams, tears and laughter. Nina and her daughter Olivia, who was six years older than Alice, quickly became stalwarts of the stables too – volunteering to help with challenging RDA classes and always being there for moral support when I needed it.

My army of helpers were the ones who kept the stables running year after year. The months had their own rhythm – April was our open day, May was Chestnut Sunday in Bushy Park, a celebration that had been held since Victorian times, June was the Royal Windsor Show where our Pony Clubbers got to show off their skills and the rest of us got to show off our fancy dress, and August was the pony camp. All this was punctuated by creative writing and arts and crafts competitions for the RDA, riding proficiency tests for the Pony Club, Own Your Own Pony days for those who wanted to know what it was really all about, and of course, lots and lots of fundraising.

We were always just about surviving when it came to money – so I was always running marathons with Nina or staging fundraisers or begging H&L to sponsor another event (they always did) so that we could keep the horses happy and healthy and our RDA activities going.

Dickie said things would be a lot easier if we didn't keep making life more complicated for ourselves – but I knew he was only joking. He was referring to the fact that as well as running the stables, we had become foster carers once Jenny Bear got her own place and moved out.

Having had a couple of kids stay with us over the years – like Ruby, whose mum went on holiday without her, and Liam, who was sleeping rough – Dickie and I decided to formalise things. We became an emergency placement for teenagers, who are often the hardest to place in foster homes because people think they are going to be difficult. And often, they are. A teenager who has experienced family breakdown and is in and out of care will be angry, bruised and sometimes unable to control their own behaviour. But I worked with teenagers every day so I was used to it, and Dickie – well, he is just the calmest person you could ever meet. A kid could be literally having a meltdown, smashing things up, and Dickie will barely raise an eyebrow. His supreme coolness seems to work – once the kid realises they're not going to get a rise from him, you can see a mutual respect start to form.

Children ended up staying with us for anything from a few nights to several months. But one girl stayed so long she became part of the family, and Alice and Woody still call her their 'sister'. That girl was Rowena – the girl who had always so loved the stables. When she was fifteen, the unthinkable happened. Her father was knocked off his bike on his way to work and killed.

I remember her calling me in floods and floods of tears just after the police had informed the family. It broke my heart to hear her distress, and I had a bad feeling in the pit of my stomach as I wondered how on earth she would ever get through such a terrible tragedy.

I was right to be worried. The fallout from Rowena's father's death was terrible. The family struggled, and Rowena really lost her way. She was often in trouble and everything that could go wrong, did. Eventually, after lots of discussion with her family and the relevant authorities, it was decided that she would come and live with us. Having lost my own mum at a similar age, there was no way I could refuse.

Once she was with us at the cottage, Dickie and I gave her the things she really needed: time, space and love. If I know anything about grieving children, it's that you've got to let them deal with things in their own way. So if Rowena skipped a few days of school, we didn't say anything. But we tried to gently encourage her away from the things that were really bad for her – certain friends, certain activities and behaviours – and towards a healthier life balance.

Having Woody and Alice around certainly helped. Any kid that comes to live with us has to slot immediately into the cottage's routine, which is very much dictated by Woody's needs. That means eating what you're given, helping with the chores and accepting that you won't always be the centre of attention. For Rowena, who was so lost, the new dynamic seemed to ground her. She adored Woody, and the motivation of not wanting to upset him had an enormous effect on her behaviour.

Rowena ended up staying with us for the best part of three years, and in that time I saw her transform from wild child to a driven, sensitive and caring young woman. She won a place at Newcastle University, and Dickie drove her up there, believing she was about to have the time of her life for three years. So imagine my surprise when a few weeks later, I let myself into the cottage after a long day's teaching to find Rowena sitting on the sofa watching telly.

'What are you doing here?' I asked her, incredulous.

'Uni wasn't for me,' she said, not taking her eyes off the silly game show on the TV.

'Right then,' I said, and left her to it.

There was no point arguing with Rowena – she was as stubborn as anything, and anyway, I knew it was important she figured it out for herself. (Secretly, of course, I liked having her back home. She'd become like a daughter to me.)

Alice and Woody were over the moon when they found their 'sister' had returned too. It wasn't just them that had a positive effect on Rowena – having her around, as well as the other kids we'd fostered, had helped them develop into confident, sociable, tolerant and accepting children.

After a few weeks of moping around at home, Rowena announced she was going to apply to Sandhurst for army officer training. I was surprised – she hadn't been able to stick out a few weeks at uni, so how would she cope with the demands of such a tough environment? But I knew better than to question her.

Against the odds, Rowena got a place. Not only that, she thrived there. I remember going to visit her eight weeks into the course – during which time she had not been allowed to call or email home. In her dress uniform, she looked like a different person. And she was so happy – having made friends for life and found a job she loved. She had found herself at last.

It felt like things had come full circle. When I was a teenager myself, I'd been lost and lonely too, but now through my work at Park Lane and my new role as a foster carer, I got to ease the pain of other kids who felt as hurt and confused as I did. I'd come so far, and learned so much – and my hope for the children in my life was that they'd find a passion, like I had for horses, which would drive and sustain them for the rest of their lives. Anything I could do to help them find it, I would.

CHAPTER TWENTY-TWO

Prize Before the Fall

By 2017, Rowena had become a captain – and not only that, she'd been selected for the Army's luge team. Luge is that sport you've probably seen at the Winter Olympics, where the athletes hurtle feet first down a steep icy track. I couldn't be prouder of her, and I was always telling anyone who would listen about her achievements, as if she was my own daughter.

That year turned out to be quite a momentous one for our family and the stables, one way or another. Alice turned six, and had grown into an incredibly caring girl, a little firecracker who knew her own mind, but always put others first. At five, Woody was the life and soul of the party; mischievous, funny and outgoing. They were best friends – Alice had a sixth sense for what Woody needed and was fluent in the Makaton sign language he used to communicate. Meanwhile Woody helped Alice push past her natural shyness – Woody simply does not do hanging back.

But the reason I say it was a big year for the family was because in 2017 Woody discovered football. A passion that has dominated his life – and ours – ever since.

Having had heart surgery at the beginning of the year to finally repair the little hole he'd had in it since he was born, by the summer, Woody had a new lease of life and bags of energy. He was desperate to join a football team, so I found a local one and drove him down there one Saturday morning to sign up. But when we got there, the coach took one look at Woody and turned us away.

'Sorry, this club's not for kids like him,' he said gruffly. 'Look online – there's probably somewhere that will take his type, but that ain't us.'

I was very upset – my whole career is dedicated to inclusivity, so encountering the opposite felt like a slap in the face. On the drive back to Park Lane, Woody was uncharacteristically quiet, so I knew he could understand something unkind had happened. I had to fight back tears and tried to chatter away to him like normal – I couldn't bear the thought of him thinking there was something wrong with him.

That night, I was still so worked up that I wrote a post on Facebook about what had happened, and how I felt sorry for the coach because he would never experience the joy that Woody could bring. Then I went to bed.

The next morning I woke up to find my post had been shared hundreds of times. Not only that, but someone had forwarded our details to Brentford, our local Championship football club, who had invited Woody to be a mascot at that weekend's match.

Reading through all the lovely posts on social media, I called through to Woody in the next room. He came and climbed into bed with me, and I read some of the nice things people were saying.

'And now Brentford want you to go on the pitch with the

proper footballers, and wish them good luck,' I explained, giving his little shoulders a squeeze. 'Would you like that?' He nodded slowly, a shy contentment spreading across his face.

Leading out the Brentford team that weekend proved to be an overwhelming and life-changing experience for Woody. His smile was wider and more infectious than I'd ever seen it, and afterwards he signed that it had been the best day of his life. After that everything was Brentford, Brentford, Brentford. He wanted to go to every game we could, and if he wasn't there he just wanted to kick a ball against the wall or watch Brentford videos on YouTube, and he wouldn't wear anything except for the team's signature red and white.

Going to Brentford to watch his beloved team play, which we did as often as we could, always felt like having a big set of arms round us, giving us a hug. The club went out of their way to make us welcome, and other fans started to recognise us and give Woody a high five. And cheering the team on from the stands at Griffin Park did more for Woody's speech than hours of speech therapy – he started to pick up on the words and phrases used by the supporters around him, and use them too.

That's the thing – if you only ever look for what someone can't do, you never see all the amazing things they can.

Football brought out the best in Woody, and as the years passed at the stables, I could see horses do the same for my amazing students. I adored seeing them thrive – whether it was riding off the lead rope for the first time, passing a grooming proficiency test or competing at RDA championships. Even better than that was seeing how being around the horses could improve their communication, physical ability and relationships.

The horse world often measures the wrong things, I think; too focused on how high you can jump and how perfect you can be.

Well, Park Lane thrived on imperfection. To us, the real prizes were kindness and community.

That's why, for Christmas 2019, I decided to throw a prizegiving with a difference. I got the idea from Peter Laney actually, of H&L Motors, who'd called by the stables in early November with a cheque that nearly made my eyes pop out of my head when I saw the number written on it.

'This is too generous,' I said to him, trying to press it back into his hands. 'You do so much for us – you don't need to do this too.'

'I want to, Nat,' he laughed, lifting his hands up. 'I've seen how hard all those kids have worked this year. Give them a really good Christmas treat – celebrate their achievements.'

Peter was right – 2019 had been an incredible year for the stables. It was the first time we'd ever qualified for the RDA National Championships, and we'd come home with a sack full of rosettes including a first prize in the Countryside Challenge, a fifth in the Dressage, and a fourth in the Carriage Driving.

Our participants had also taken part in the newly created RDA grassroots endurance league, which sees riders record their time and distance riding out over the year in competition with RDA members all over the country. Incredibly, Philippa had won the league and seven out of the top ten riders came from Park Lane Stables. We'd even won first prize at the Royal Windsor fancy dress parade.

The Pony Clubbers had also had incredible success, passing grade tests and competing in everything from cross country to dressage. But it wasn't just the prizes that stuck in my mind. It was the enthusiasm of kids like Annie, a Pony Clubber who made the epic trip from Croydon every Saturday and would turn up with a wide smile on her face every week, no matter about the cold, wind and rain. It was the bravery of RDA participants like Daniel, who pushed himself outside of his comfort zone every day. It was the care with which Julie and Sally had settled our new hippotherapy pony, Eliot, and the bond he had already formed with the RDA participants he was helping. And it was the support the kids had shown each other and me, when we'd had to say a sad goodbye to Caesar. The little pony had finally lost a long battle with illness, but we'd been inundated with hand-drawn pictures and cards of condolence, which now plastered the loft room walls.

So that year, our Christmas party celebrated everyone at Park Lane and the things they'd achieved, big and small. With Peter's kind donation, I bought prizes for awards like Progression, Helpfulness, being a Park Lane Ambassador and Going the Extra Mile.

I think I'll probably remember that party for ever. We didn't know it then, but it was one of the last times we'd all be together in a noisy, friendly, carefree environment for a long time. I booked the Teddington Royal Legion, and two of our lovely volunteers, Christine and Liz, turned up early to deck it out with extra fairy lights and tinsel, while Nina and Daisy helped me make up little party bags for all the children. So many of our friends and supporters came, and I remember looking round the room and thinking how lucky I was to have each and every one of them. We even FaceTimed Izabell, so she could be there in spirit.

After the prizegiving Dickie appointed himself DJ and I can remember spinning and spinning with Philippa around the dance floor, belting out Mariah Carey's 'All I Want For Christmas Is You'. It really had been a magnificent year, and at that party, it seemed impossible that next year wouldn't be even better.

None of us could have predicted what was to come.

Part Three

Part Three

CHAPTER TWENTY-THREE

Our Annie

It was early February when I started to get a little worried by reports of a strange virus that was sweeping through China. Alarming pictures on the news bulletins showed Chinese officials in Hazmat suits disinfecting the streets, alongside reports of a spiralling death toll and citizens locked in their houses.

It was easy to dismiss it as a distant foreign story, until it started to cause chaos in Italy too. There were reports of people choking to death in hospital corridors because there weren't enough beds, while the Italian government imposed a draconian lockdown. Was that coming our way too?

'I think we'll be all right,' said David, as I discussed my concerns with him ahead of one of our lessons. I was worried that a lot of the people we worked with were vulnerable and I wondered if we were doing the right thing by carrying on.

'You know how important the lessons are,' David continued. 'I wouldn't stop them until you have to. You know, the Cheltenham Festival is still going ahead. If that's okay, then this' – he gestured around the windswept Hampton arena – 'definitely is.'

If the government thought it was safe for a quarter of a million people to pile into the races together, then David was right – we had to carry on. But I still didn't like what I was hearing.

I was still stewing on the threat posed by this so-called coronavirus as the children arrived for their lesson.

'Natalie, pleeeease can I ride Eliot this week? Pretty please?' It was Annie, all four foot three of her, tugging at the bottom of my coat. She was the first to arrive, even though, as I mentioned before, she lived in Croydon and her dad had to get up at the crack of dawn to take her on an arduous journey of tram, train and bus to get her to Teddington. But then, Annie's enthusiasm for horses couldn't be contained. Eliot was the black cob with a white blaze who she adored. When she'd come on our pony camp last year, the two of them couldn't be separated.

'Go on then,' I said, unable to resist that cheerful round face.

'Are you okay, Natalie?' she asked, frowning slightly. Although she was only ten, Annie had quite an adult way about her. She could tell something was wrong.

'Oh, I'm fine sweetheart, nothing to worry about,' I said as we walked towards Eliot, who was tied up at the side of the arena.

'Gosh, aren't we so lucky about the weather when it's only February?' said Annie, gesturing up at the bright blue sky, and flicking her long brunette ponytail over her shoulder. I had to laugh at that – she was not your average child. And her disposition was as sunny as the day, which made it impossible to stay gloomy. The lesson turned into a lot of fun, with my five little pupils cheering each other on as they all took turns cantering around the ring.

I forgot about coronavirus for that happy hour, but the next day, it was once again the only topic of conversation. Driving back from dropping the horses up at the fields with Rebekah in the passenger seat beside me, I turned up the radio to listen to a news report about how non-urgent NHS operations were being cancelled to free up extra hospital beds.

'Not sounding good, is it, Bex?' I sad. 'I guess the trustees will want to come up with an action plan, if things are going to get any worse ... will you check in my diary to see if there's a meeting this week, please?'

Rebekah picked up my phone to get to my iCalendar, then paused. 'You've got a missed call from Annie's dad.'

'That's weird,' I said. 'She doesn't have another lesson until next weekend. I'll call him back later.'

David was as devoted to Annie as my dad had been to me. After her lesson she liked to spend another three hours at the stables, helping with the horses and having fun with her friends. Her dad would sit in a nearby café waiting, never complaining, and always supportive of his daughter's passion.

Rebekah started tapping on my phone, then stopped as it started to vibrate. 'It's him again,' she said. 'Maybe he really wants to talk to you?'

'Pop it on speaker then,' I said, assuming it would be a quick conversation about a lost jacket or similar.

'Hiya, David!' I said cheerily. 'What can I do for you?'

'Natalie.' I knew immediately something was wrong. David's voice sounded hoarse and terrified.

'Whatever's happened?' I said.

'It's Annie. She's really sick. She's in hospital ... they think she's going to die.'

My hands were shaking as I hurriedly pulled over and killed the engine.

'What do you mean? She's fine isn't she ... I only saw her recently!' My voice didn't sound like mine, and I knew I wasn't making any sense. I looked over at Rebekah, whose eyes were wide in horror.

'She ... she had a headache. We thought she'd sleep it off but ... she got worse. We took her to hospital – Nat, it's meningitis. She's in a coma. They don't think she's going to make it.'

I felt as if the whole van had been plunged into an icy lake, and I was drowning, struggling to breathe. What David was telling me sounded so alien, so wrong – how could that happy, healthy girl, so full of life, suddenly be in such peril?

'What can I do?' I said, the practical side of my brain springing into action while the rest of me floundered. 'Anything, David. Tell me what would help.'

'I don't know what to do, Nat—'

'Why don't I come to the hospital with something that might remind her of the stables? Maybe if we surround her with familiar things, things she loves, she might' – my voice cracked – 'wake up.'

There was a pause, then David said: 'Yes please, I think she'd like that.'

'I'm on my way,' I said. I fired up the engine and put my foot down.

'We need some of Eliot's hair,' I said to Rebekah. She nodded, her face pale and set.

I must have broken every speed limit on the way back to Teddington, where Eliot was still in his stable. I clipped off a lock of his mane and held it briefly to my nose. It smelt of carefree rides and unconditional love and childish happiness.

Wrapping it carefully in a handkerchief, I stashed the hair in my pocket and got back into the van. I don't believe in God, but I said a prayer for Annie just in case.

Traffic was mercifully quiet, and in good time St George's

Hospital loomed into view. I was just indicating to pull into the car park when the phone rang.

'Hi, David, I'm minutes away, just parking!' I said hurriedly.

Then came the words I'd been dreading to hear.

'She's gone, Natalie,' said David, his voice thick with grief. 'Thank you so much for trying – but it's too late.'

How can you describe a pain like that? I felt like I was standing on a railway track, wheeling around just in time to see the blinding lights of a train before it smashed into me. I had to fight the urge to tell David to check again, get a second opinion, because surely his beautiful daughter couldn't really be gone? It must all be a cruel mistake.

Instead, I said the only thing there is to say. 'I'm so sorry,' I whispered. 'I am so, so sorry.'

They buried Annie on 20 March. By then the pubs were shut and children had been sent home from school. The funeral was sparsely attended, with many staying away out of fear of a virus which had made it plain it was here to spread death and terror. I could hardly bear to look at the unnaturally tiny coffin, or at the stricken faces of Annie's parents who looked crushed by the magnitude of their loss. Afterwards, I simply hugged them close on the steps of the crematorium and promised that if there was anything I could do to help, I would do it in a heartbeat.

Three days later, the Prime Minister delivered an unprecedented televised address, telling the country that we must all stay at home – except for essential shopping and an hour's exercise a day. Vulnerable people must strictly shield, and everyone should work from home. I felt numb as I watched it, barely able to comprehend the new world we stood on the precipice of. An invisible killer in our midst, and now everyone must shut their doors, retreat from family and friends, and wait.

The next day, I knew the worry would come. For what would become of the stables, and how would the people who relied on us cope? How could they bear this isolation, and would they be safe from the virus which so cruelly stalked our most vulnerable?

But for now, there was stillness. It felt like the whole world had stopped for Annie.

CHAPTER TWENTY-FOUR

Lockdown Blues

You must stay at home.

You should not be meeting friends.

You should not be meeting family members.

You should not go to work, unless it is absolutely necessary.

You should not be going shopping, unless for essentials like food and medicine.

Only one hour's exercise a day is permitted, alone or with members of your household.

You must stay at home.

These words, so simple and yet so devastating, were rattling around my restless mind that night as I tossed and turned, unable to sleep. The people who came to the stables didn't just enjoy being with the ponies, they needed them. How would they cope without them?

I thought about our autistic riders, who thrived on routine, who would feel as if everything they felt sure about had been turned upside down.

I thought about the most severely vulnerable children, who had the kind of health conditions that meant that they and their families would have to shield inside, without even the brief relief of feeling the sun on their face during an hour a day's exercise or trip to the shops.

I thought about the parents of the very disabled children, many of whom went to residential schools during the week where they had a whole team of carers to look after them. They were now completely on their own. I could almost taste their fear, as the stress and pressure and loneliness of that isolation loomed on the horizon.

And what about my own precious Woody? I knew he would struggle to comprehend what was happening. In his world, the things that mattered were things you could touch – footballs, people, chips. Trying to explain that all his routine was going to be taken away because of an illness no one could see would be like trying to talk to him in a foreign language. I knew he'd be devastated about not being able to go to school, bewildered by not being able to see his friends, and totally heartbroken by the lack of trips to see his beloved Brentford FC at the weekend.

'It's okay, Nat,' Dickie murmured, rolling over and pulling me close. 'We'll get through it together.' Even half asleep he could sense my agitation, and I felt so grateful for his calm and dependable presence.

The next morning dawned bright and blue, the sky cloudless and silent. The glorious weather felt out of place in March, but then everything else was topsy turvy, so why not this as well? For us, it was a small mercy. It meant that we could turn out most of the horses to run free in the fields, which would mean they would be okay without the exercise of regular riding lessons. It would also save us a lot of money – if it had been winter with no grass for the horses to eat, Park Lane could have been facing financial ruin.

I spent the morning ferrying horses from Park Lane to Oxshott, and making as many FaceTime calls as possible to the people who relied on the stables. Most looked shell-shocked, their faces pale and frightened, but when they saw that it was me – and a pony or two – they started to smile.

I had a long chat with my friend Stacey, the mum of Dominic, one of our most enthusiastic carriage-driving participants. 'Don't worry too much about us,' she said, but her eyes looked red and watery. 'I know this will be hard for you too.'

Eli's dad told me his son had been so worried that something had happened to Samson he'd been crying all morning – so it was a relief to see him alive and well on his phone screen. I made a mental note to check in with Eli every day – with Samson's help, of course.

My call to Rebekah was one of the hardest I had to make. She desperately wanted to keep coming to work, but I had to gently tell her that unfortunately it wasn't 'essential' and she would have to stay at home, as I'd be putting her on furlough. Rebekah had spent her morning researching coronavirus and because of her autism, she was scared and angry about not being able to find clear answers. It was awful to hear her so upset, and although I knew it wasn't my fault, I felt like I was letting her down.

I didn't sleep any easier over the following week, the needs of the Park Lane community weighing heavy on my mind. But as well as that, I had plenty to contend with in my own immediate family. As I'd suspected, what had started out as a novelty for Woody had turned into something that confused and infuriated him in equal measure. Dickie and I spent our days attempting to deliver some semblance of home-schooling to Alice, while trying to contain Woody's increasingly violent temper tantrums.

Coronavirus is not something you can see or touch, it is something abstract – so for Woody, and other people with similar learning disabilities, it is near impossible to understand. His conclusion was that he must have been naughty, and that he alone was being punished by being locked inside. His behaviour became increasingly unmanageable, especially as the one thing that always made him feel better was also taken away. The roar of the crowd at Brentford, the sea of red-and-white shirts, and that feeling of togetherness was not something we could recreate at home.

Just like some people need ponies, Woody needed football. Every morning, he would sign 'Brentford?' with his hands, his little face flickering with hope. And every morning, I'd have to sadly shake my head no. Then the fury would begin – and another long day of fighting to keep him (relatively) calm and stop him hurting himself.

It was tough, but I was so lucky to have Dickie, who is brilliant with Woody and the best possible team-mate. But I knew that for parents on their own, every day that went by was making the situation even more untenable.

Angie, a mum I knew whose teenage daughter Sarah had complex physical and emotional needs, phoned me in tears one day. Before lockdown, Sarah had two wonderful carers who came to their flat to help her, and a place at a fantastic school which provided all sorts of therapeutic support. But now Angie and Sarah were on their own. Sarah's condition meant she needed assistance for everything – even going to the toilet – and it was more than a one-person job. And yet Angie had been left to cope on her own; and she felt like she was barely coping at all.

Another day I got a long, frightened email from a parent, Yewande, who was terrified because her husband Michael had gone down with Covid. He was isolating in their spare bedroom but in their small terraced house she was convinced the infection would spread. What would happen, she asked me, if both she and Michael got so ill that they could not care for their visually impaired daughter Destiny? Would it mean Destiny would be taken into care? It was something I hadn't thought about before – but her fear made perfect sense. Again, it was a question that I had no answers to but I emailed her back promising that if the worst happened I would move heaven and earth to help.

Finally, there was a knock at the cottage door one evening. I opened it to find a man I only vaguely recognised, with his daughter in a wheelchair. I knew she wasn't one of our regular riders, but I thought she had perhaps attended another child's birthday party at the stables because her face was familiar.

'I'm sorry,' said the man, registering the shock on my face. 'I didn't know where else to go.' I realised there were tears in his eyes.

The man told me his name was Aleksy, and he and his daughter Zosia lived in a flat with no garden. She was unhappy and coping badly with the isolation, but he didn't know how to help her. He'd remembered that I worked with disabled children and knew where I lived, so thought maybe I'd be able to help.

It broke my heart to hear his story, and it was even harder to offer him such meagre support in return. I fetched him some playdough and colouring books that I had in the cottage, and recommended some activities that would give Zosia good sensory feedback, like popping bubble wrap. It wasn't much but Aleksy seemed lighter, as if even just talking to another adult had unburdened him. Before they left, I urged them to go and see our 'cuddle horse', who that day was Rusty. We had one stable where the pony inside could look out on to the road, and during lockdown we were making sure there was always one in there. We had noticed a steady stream of visitors during their daily walks, for whom the small pleasure of stroking a pony's velvet nose had become the highlight of their day.

I kept my distance but smiled as I watched Zosia reach out a tentative hand to Rusty's face, and giggle as she felt his warm breath on her palm. They stood like that for some time, Aleksy talking softly to his daughter who was transfixed by the gentle animal. Eventually, they waved goodbye, Aleksy promising Zosia they could come back again the next day.

I felt exhausted. I went back inside the cottage, where Alice and Woody were playing nicely and quietly for a change.

'Mum needs a hug,' I told them, sinking on to the sofa and opening my arms. They grinned and clambered on to me like puppies. I held them close, wishing I could make things better for them, and for all the children like Zosia too. Woody's hair had started falling out in big clumps; the doctor I spoke to on the phone had told me it was probably stress-induced alopecia, and I shouldn't expect it to grow back. Just another tiny war wound of this evil pandemic.

'Right, I'll start dinner!' said Dickie, opening the fridge and surveying the uninspiring selection I'd managed to grab during my most recent trudge around the supermarket, where the shelves had been stripped almost bare. 'How about chilli con carne – without the chilli or the carne?'

I smiled, and extracting myself from the children, gave him a quick kiss. 'Sounds delicious, Gordon Ramsay,' I said. 'Have I got time to walk the pony, do you think?'

'Go for it,' he replied. 'Food will be about an hour.'

Even though most of the horses were out in the field, we still had four ponies with us at Park Lane. They were Rusty, who was lame, and Red, who was recovering from recent surgery. Then there was Mini, unable to travel in a horse box, and Whizz, a diminutive new arrival who we'd bought just before lockdown with a grant from the RDA, to replace Caesar as a pony the smallest participants could ride. Whizz was predisposed to a painful condition called laminitis if he ate too much grass. That meant, like the others, we had to keep him inside unless they were under our watchful gaze. All four were too small for me to exercise them by riding. Instead, I was taking them for walks as if they were dogs. Mini had been out that morning, so it was the turn of Whizz this evening. Even though you were only meant to have one hour's exercise a day, I figured that exercising the horses fell into the category of essential work.

'Come on then, boy,' I said to Whizz, clipping a rope on to his red head collar. 'Let's get you some fresh air.'

The sight of the gentle little grey Welsh Mountain pony clopping along beside me, and the memory of my two gorgeous children pressed into my side on the sofa, vibrant with life, made me think of Annie's parents. How wretched they must feel now, cut off from the people they loved when they needed them most. I was calling them every day, but I wondered how many people were checking in on them, now that we all felt like we had problems of our own.

On the spur of the moment, I reached my phone from my pocket and FaceTimed David, stopping so I could position my face alongside Whizz's in the frame.

'Nat! Hi! Oh my god, did a pony just call us?' David's face was thinner than I remembered, but he was grinning at the sight of Whizz. 'Tracey!' he called to his wife. 'There's a pony on the phone for us.'

Tracey appeared on the screen; she had the look of someone who had forgotten how to smile, but was trying to anyway.

'I just wanted to let you know that we're thinking of you,' I said. 'We all are. I thought how much Annie would have loved to see a pony at a time like this and thought maybe you would too.'

'Thanks, Nat,' said David softly. 'We're always grateful for anything that reminds us of Annie.'

'I know I said to you at the funeral that if there's anything we can do to help, then we will,' I continued. 'But I know sometimes it seems like people say those things without intending to follow through. So I just wanted to put it back out there, I guess.'

David and Tracey exchanged a look. 'Well, there is something we thought of, actually,' said David. 'What do you think about naming a pony after Annie? When you get a new one, of course. She loved the stables so much, and it would be a lovely way to keep her memory alive.'

'That's perfect,' I beamed. 'And you know what, this little fella arrived just last week. His previous owners called him Whizz, but it doesn't really suit him because he's actually pretty slow. So how about we call him Annie's-Whizz?'

Tracey was nodding, tears streaming silently down her face. 'Thank you, Nat,' she said. 'I think Annie would love that.'

We chatted for ten minutes or so before I said goodbye, promising to keep them updated on the adventures of the newly christened Annie's-Whizz.

Obviously, there is nothing that will ease the pain of losing a child. But that short chat and the sight of the pony did seem to have provided a chink of light among the darkness.

That was the power of ponies. Even just seeing them can be

calming and cheering. As I walked Annie's-Whizz down the street, I spotted a trio of eager children with their faces pressed against a window, delighted to see a pony passing by and waving happily. I felt sad for all the people who would be missing their usual dose of horsey happiness – and then suddenly, I had an idea.

The Park Lane community couldn't come to the stables, but what if we could go to them? Could a tiny pony at the window spread the smiles we so desperately needed?

CHAPTER TWENTY-FIVE

Tiny Pony at Your Window

My idea was simple. When we took Mini and Annie's-Whizz for their daily walks, we would take them to the windows of people who were isolating at home. I knew how much our regulars were missing their pony pals, so I hoped this would be a safe way to brighten their day and maintain their connection with the stables.

With my hands full with the kids and home-schooling, and the need to shield because of Woody's Down's syndrome and Dickie's age, I knew I needed help. I'd sadly had to put most of my paid members of staff on furlough, but I'd kept general stablehand Daisy on to help with caring for the ponies. I texted her what I wanted to do – she replied immediately with three thumbs-up emojis and heart eyes.

I started off by posting on social media with a picture of the two ponies – both grey, one little, one even littler – and the caption: 'Fancy a #tinyponyatyourwindow? Park Lane Stables will be providing a National Horse Service to spread smiles during the pandemic.'

I wasn't sure how much uptake it would get, so I contacted some of the families I knew were self-isolating and offered to bring round a pony. Literally no one said no. There was something magical about a pony turning up on your doorstep, and especially at a time when everyone was bored, lonely and scared.

One of Daisy's great skills is that she always takes such pride in the ponies' appearance and when she's finished with them, they look ready for the catwalk. She made sure that Annie's-Whizz looked immaculate on his first day of visiting. Woody, Alice and I waved them off: 'Spread lots of smiles, guys!' I called after them.

One of the first visits was to Dominic, our carriage-driving student. His mum Stacey was beside herself when she saw Daisy and Annie's-Whizz coming.

'The stables is the only place where he really feels welcome and included,' she said tearfully, as her son rocked happily in his wheelchair to show his pleasure at seeing Annie's-Whizz from a distance. 'It's so wonderful that you haven't forgotten about us.'

Daisy did most of the visits, but I pitched in on some at the weekends. Taking the ponies down suburban streets in the middle of the lockdown was a surreal experience. Park Lane was well known in the neighbourhood, where locals were used to the odd sound of horses clopping through the urban landscape, but we tended to stick to certain routes. Now that I was seeking out specific addresses, we were taking the ponies down side streets and cul-de-sacs I'd never visited before. There was barely any traffic on the road too, so the sight of a pony making its way down the street must have been truly bizarre. Sure enough, everywhere we went people stared or waved from windows, amused, surprised and delighted in equal measure.

At first, we were mainly visiting children I knew, taking with us colouring pictures of horses for them to complete and stick in the window alongside the home-made NHS rainbows that had started appearing everywhere.

I remember calling on Lucy, another carriage-driving participant, who was sat waiting by the window with an expression as eager as if she was waiting for Santa Claus himself. Her dad Tony had told me how much she'd been missing the ponies, and it was magical to see them reunited again – even though it was through a pane of glass.

But before long, #tinyponyatyourwindow had taken on a life of its own and it wasn't just people we knew who wanted a visit. I'm not sure if it was social media that alerted people, or simply the sight of us out and about. All I know was that we were suddenly inundated with hundreds of requests from people asking for a tiny pony visit – young and old alike. Even sweeter were the requests from people asking us to visit friends and family that they could not see – whether it was someone celebrating a birthday, elderly people living on their own or simply someone lonely who needed cheering up.

Those surprise visits became my favourites. As you walked down the street, you'd see an array of faces pressed up against windows, wondering where the pony was going. The look when someone realised it was coming to their doorstep was priceless. We made sure safety came first; ringing the door and standing well back when the person answered so that we maintained social distance. Dickie came up with the idea of printing off messages from friends or family, which we'd make into laminated signs to hold up.

One of the most emotional visits was taking Mini to see a lady who was having treatment for breast cancer. Her daughter, who lived in Manchester, was desperately worried about her mum, who was facing such a scary challenge completely on her own. She may have been eighty-one, ill and frail, but the sight of Mini taking a cheeky munch of her rose bush was enough to make the old lady look like a young girl again.

She pressed her hand against the window and watched as we held up the sign her daughter had asked for: 'You're not alone, Mum. We love you and we miss you and are thinking of you always.'

Then her face suddenly disappeared, and I was worried we'd upset her too much. A minute later she was back, holding up a message she had hastily scribbled on lined paper. It was only two words but it meant the world: 'Thank you.'

I didn't want to say no to anybody, so we did as many visits as Mini and Annie's-Whizz could do without being overworked. When they were well enough, Rusty and Red joined our pony support team too. We weren't breaking any rules because the horses had to go out anyway – it was just a lovely way of killing two birds with one stone.

We'd been doing the scheme for a few weeks when the media got wind of it – first the local newspaper, and then the national press. I'd be taking one of the ponies for their daily walk at the same time as fielding calls from journalists. One day I answered the phone en route to surprise a two-year-old girl on her lock-down birthday, Annie's-Whizz decked out with pink balloons, to find I was talking to American reporters from NBC! 'We've gone international,' I told Annie's-Whizz in semi-wonder, when I hung up the phone. He was more interested in trying to grab a mouthful of grass from a nearby lawn.

With so many visits to make, we needed more help – so I put a shout out for volunteers, and was inundated by responses – many from my regular helpers but also from people who were on furlough or living alone and desperate to get out and about.

Annie's parents sent me a lovely email, to say how happy

they were to see Annie's-Whizz spreading so much happiness in her name. It brought them comfort, they said, to know we were constantly telling her story whenever anyone asked about his unusual name. And by cheering people up and trying to be useful, we were embodying Annie's spirit.

I found myself almost as busy as when we were running the riding school: answering emails and social media messages, planning routes, drawing up rotas, talking to the press and all the time trying to keep the stables afloat. However, without money coming in from lessons, we were in serious trouble. The stables relied on participants paying for riding sessions – and on donations, which had also dried up now that times were so tight. We had never built up any reserves – all the income went straight into feeding and looking after the horses and ponies. And just because the lessons had stopped, the costs hadn't. We still needed to buy feed, pay for the vet and farrier – and pay our rent, of course.

I asked the landlord for a rent break, while we were out of operation – he said no. It was our biggest cost, and I didn't know how we were going to cover it. But it was vital we stayed open so our disabled children and adult riders would have somewhere to return once the pandemic was over.

There was a government scheme, sure, but the grant we got didn't come close to what we needed. In fact, a small jewellery shop down the road from the stables, run by a friend, got the exact same grant that we did. But she could close up the shop and sell jewellery online – and she didn't have to feed the jewellery either. We needed more help.

In the end the landlord, perhaps realising he simply wouldn't be able to get the money out of us, agreed to let us use our rent deposit towards some of the rent, but there were still the costs of the horses – which, with zero income, looked frighteningly high. I refused to compromise on their care, so I needed to find the money somewhere.

'You should ask for donations,' said one of the volunteers, sixteen-year-old Bess, when she spotted me poring over the figures on my laptop, perched on the bench outside the stables. 'For the tiny pony at your window service. Why don't you set up a JustGiving?'

It was a genius suggestion. I worked out that every pony cost about £30 per week to keep, so that was the ask – sponsor a pony for a week, or just give whatever you can. Obviously, we weren't going to not turn up to someone who requested a visit just because they couldn't pay, but we found that most people were more than happy to support our work. Thanks to the extra fundraising, we were getting by – just.

Whenever I thought I had problems, though, I had to have a sharp word with myself. Because it was nothing in comparison to the horrors being endured by the brave NHS workers on the front line. Every evening Dickie and I would sombrely watch the Prime Minister's press conference, followed by the six o'clock news. Every day the same harrowing tales of death and desperation. Burnt-out staff struggling to cope with the sheer volume of patients, loved ones forced to say goodbye from grainy iPad screens, key workers killed by the virus in the line of duty. It put everything into perspective. These people were putting their lives on the line to keep us safe, and we were so lucky to have the NHS to keep us going through this crisis.

After one particularly gruelling report about NHS workers forced to use bin bags as gowns because of a chronic shortage of PPE, I had an idea. I enlisted one of the volunteers to help, and with a set of clippers and some animal-friendly hair dye, we turned Annie's-Whizz into a bona fide NHS pony. On one side of his body, we shaved the letters 'NHS'. On the other, the shape of a rainbow – in honour of the drawings so many children had stuck in their windows. I'd heard workers say that it lifted their spirits to know the whole community was behind them. I hoped Annie's-Whizz's new look would do the same.

I thought he looked great – but I couldn't have predicted the reaction he'd get. Daisy reported that after his makeover, when she was walking him to his window appointments, he might as well have been a Hollywood A-lister. People were coming to their doorsteps to applaud him. We'd had an amazing response before, but the new look seemed to take things to another level.

That Thursday evening I took Annie's-Whizz into the street during the 8 p.m. Clap for Carers, and I could have sworn people banged their pans harder and whooped and hollered with more energy. It was like my little pony had become a standard bearer for the NHS, a vehicle for all the hope and faith we put in those brave people.

As I put Annie's-Whizz to bed that night, I made an extra fuss of him. He was a funny little thing – so friendly, the kind of pony who didn't just tolerate people stroking and patting him but actively sought it out. Never boisterous or pushy with the people he met, he seemed to always be able to judge what level of comfort someone had and adjust his behaviour accordingly. And he had a kind of natural cheerfulness, starting every day with his ears pricked forwards and his eyes bright, as if to say: 'What are we doing today then?'

'You're my hero, you know?' I told him, as I gave him one final stroke once he was snugly in his stable. 'Annie would be very proud of you.'

I didn't know then that I was about to get a phone call that would put all of Annie's-Whizz's best qualities to the test.

CHAPTER TWENTY-SIX

The Sweetest Goodbye

It was early when the phone rang – before 8 a.m. Not early enough to wake me, however; by then I'd already been up for hours trying to keep Woody entertained, had fed the ponies and turned out Mini and Annie's-Whizz into the communal gardens of the flats opposite. It was something we'd taken to doing during lockdown – the residents loved having the ponies there, as did passers-by on their daily walks. One man who lived in the flats told me that his toddler's first word was Mini, as they always went to say hello to her when she was in the garden. It also meant the ponies could get a bit of grass – just enough that wouldn't trigger Annie's-Whizz's laminitis.

There was a hairy moment one day when a policeman knocked on the door, asking if the ponies in the garden were mine. I'd had to admit that yes they were, assuming that we were about to be told that we couldn't let ponies graze on council land. But the policeman had just grinned and pressed a tenner into my hand, 'for all the amazing work you're doing.'

That morning I'd planned to let Mini and Annie's-Whizz

have a day off from visits, with Rusty and Red going out instead. Woody was having another bad day, and I was trying to calm him down and get him to eat his breakfast, while Alice sang at the top of her lungs. This was the chaos that was interrupted by the phone.

'Hello, Natalie O'Rourke speaking ... sorry, I can't quite hear you ... DICKIE! CAN YOU COME AND TAKE OVER PLEASE! ... sorry about that. Hello, is that better, can you hear me now?'

The voice at the other end of the line was much calmer than mine. 'Sorry to interrupt you so early when you've got such a lot on,' said the woman. 'My name is Catherine Harris, I'm a palliative care nurse at Great Ormond Street Hospital.'

'Oh, hi,' I said, my mind racing as to why this lady would be calling me. 'No problem at all ... you know how it is in the mornings!'

'Yes, I do,' said Catherine. 'I hope you don't mind me ringing you. A friend of mine's daughter rides at your stables, and she was telling me the lovely thing you're doing with taking the ponies to people in need. And, well, I was hoping you'd be able to help us too.'

'Yes, of course,' I said quickly. Needless to say, many of the kids I worked with had been or become patients of Great Ormond Street, one of the world's leading children's hospitals, and I was well acquainted with the amazing work they did. I couldn't imagine what they needed from me, but if I could help, I would.

'We have a very sick little girl here at the moment,' Catherine went on. 'Her name is Priya, and before she got ill she adored horses. We wondered if you might bring one of the ponies to see her. I think it could be a huge comfort.'

I was taken back immediately to that phone call from David,

180

saying that Annie was in the hospital and me suggesting I come with something from the stable. I felt the same sense of helplessness and confusion. My mind raced. If I was taking a pony to an ill child in hospital, it would have to be Annie's-Whizz, as he was the smallest and cuddliest. But when I'd put him in the garden that morning he'd taken the opportunity to immediately roll in a big patch of mud, so he was a filthy mess right now.

'Sure, I can definitely do that,' I told Catherine. 'The only thing is we haven't washed the pony. He's probably too smelly and dirty right now ... but I can wash him this morning, then be with you this afternoon? Or tomorrow if that's better?'

Catherine paused. 'I really think ... don't worry about washing him,' she said carefully. 'If you can, it would be great if you could come right now.'

The meaning of her words sank in, heavy like lead. If she wanted me to come right now, that meant poor Priya didn't have long left.

'I'll be there as soon as I can,' I said.

Daisy helped me catch Annie's-Whizz and quickly brush off the worst of the mud, then load him into the horse box. 'You'll come with me, right?' I asked her, but she was already climbing into the passenger seat. I was relieved – I wasn't sure I could face this on my own.

We set off towards central London. I hadn't been out in the van for ages – so I hadn't quite realised how bizarrely quiet the roads would be. I was used to queues and busy traffic through Teddington but it was like a ghost town, just the odd cyclist out for a ride in the March sunshine.

When we got into London, it was even weirder. The satnav directed us past Hyde Park, down The Mall and through Trafalgar Square. Everywhere was utterly deserted. It was completely surreal – this part of the city would usually be teeming with tourists, jammed with cars and buses and noisy with honking horns and loud chatter. Instead it felt like we were in a zombie film, as we sailed down silent streets and spotted not a single living soul.

Finally, we arrived at Great Ormond Street, and swung the horse box into the car park where Catherine had said she'd meet me.

'I'm outside,' I texted her, as Daisy hurriedly unloaded Annie's-Whizz and we both masked up.

'We're bringing her out now,' came the reply.

I smoothed down Annie's-Whizz's mane, and patted his neck gently. He snuggled into my side in typically affectionate fashion. 'You're about to meet someone very special, okay?' I told him. 'But I know you'll make her feel better.'

About fifteen minutes later the double glass doors nearest the car park swung open, and a strange, silent procession appeared. There were four nurses in blue scrubs, barely distinguishable from each other as they had so much PPE on – face masks, visors, hair nets, aprons and gloves. I knew that it was totally necessary to protect themselves and their vulnerable patients from the killer virus, but it jolted my stomach as I thought how frightening it must be for a child to be treated by people whose faces you could not see.

The nurses were guiding a trolley which was loaded with so many blankets, at first I couldn't see Priya. As they got closer, however, I could see her. She had a small, very pale face, and long, wavy dark hair. Her eyes were closed, but every so often would blink open. She had tubes going into her nostrils, more tubes attached to her arm – another nurse following behind pushed drips and an oxygen tank.

Behind her came two more masked figures, arm in arm, who I assumed must be her mum and dad. They had the slumped shoulders of frightened parents who had spent too long in a hospital, sick with worry. I could understand a little of what they must have been feeling. Dickie and I had spent such a lot of time in hospital with Woody over the years, and I knew how small your world became during that time, how suffocating that awful hospital smell, how your fear infected the very air that you breathed. It must have been extra hard during the pandemic, with the added threat of Covid and the strict rules on visiting.

One of the nurses broke away from the group and came towards me.

'Hi, I'm Catherine,' she said, her voice muffled by the mask and visor but her brown eyes kind. 'Thank you so much for coming. We'll set Priya up over there, then do you want to bring the pony over? She's going in and out of consciousness, but hopefully she'll be able to sense his presence.'

I nodded, the question I wanted to ask hovering on my tongue. As if sensing what I was going to say, Catherine added: 'It's a brain tumour. She's not got very long left, I'm afraid.'

The other nurses had been fiddling around with Priya's tubes and blankets, but now one of them gave Catherine and me the thumbs up.

'Let's go,' I murmured to Daisy, and together we approached with Annie's-Whizz. As we got closer to the trolley, I could see what a pretty face Priya had, with long dark lashes and high cheekbones. She was probably about ten – the same age Annie had been.

Annie's-Whizz was still chewing a mouthful of hay. For someone who loves horses, that repetitive, mulchy sound is actually very comforting, and I really hoped that it was for Priya too. She wasn't communicating, but her eyes were open. I could sense she was taking it all in.

Priya's parents introduced themselves – Amit and Nisha. 'She will love this, I think,' said Nisha, her mask wet with tears. 'She is – was – totally obsessed with riding.'

Amit was silent, as if the pain was too great to allow him to talk. I wanted to say something that might comfort them.

'The smell will take her back to all those happy times of being with horses and riding,' I said. 'It's totally transportive. And the sound too. She won't be here in the hospital bed any more, she'll be there in her memory having the time of her life.'

I could always count on Annie's-Whizz to know what to do. He shuffled closer to the bed and put his head right on it, next to Priya. I realised with horror that he'd also dropped a load of hay on there.

'Oh, I'm so sorry he's making such a mess,' I whispered to the nearest nurse, but she just shook her head.

'It really doesn't matter,' she said. 'Let's just let Priya enjoy the moment.'

The little girl's eyes were wide open now, and she was looking right at Annie's-Whizz, who simply blinked gently, as if to tell her everything was okay. With Catherine's encouragement, Amit and Nisha took Priya's hands, and put them on the pony's neck. I held his rope and stayed quiet, not wanting to break the spell. I knew that if I was dying, there would be nothing that could be a greater comfort to me than the presence of a horse.

We were with Priya for about half an hour before the nurses decided it was probably time to take her back inside. It was an enormous privilege to be there – due to the tragic circumstances of the pandemic most of Priya's close family and friends would not get the chance to visit her in her final days, as only her parents were allowed. So to be there, and to be able to offer a tiny amount of solace, was a gift. I told her parents as much as we bid them farewell.

Daisy and I stood with Annie's-Whizz and waved as the family and the nurses retreated back towards the glass doors, willing Amit and Nisha the strength to deal with what came next. There can surely be no greater pain than watching your beloved child die, and it broke my heart that they had to endure it. I thought of Annie's parents, and the grief that still engulfed them – and probably always will.

Suddenly I thought of something. When Annie was in hospital, I'd planned to take her a lock of Eliot's hair. It had been too late for her – but it wasn't too late for Priya. I fumbled in my pocket for my keys, which had a little mini penknife as the key ring, and cut off a lock of pony hair.

'Catherine, wait!' I called. She spun round, then hurried back towards me.

'Is everything okay?'

'Yes, take this,' I said, pressing the fistful of hair into her gloved hand. 'Priya will be able to feel it and smell it, and she'll think of Annie's-Whizz – and all the other ponies she's loved.'

Catherine held the horse hair like it was a precious diamond, then gave me a final nod and hurried back towards Priya and her team.

I watched them go, thinking of Annie, my arm draped around the pony that bore her name. For those of us that love them, horses are there for us in our very best times and our very darkest, with the same gentle love and magic touch. I hoped that in her mind, Priya was riding free, wind in her hair and a silken pony's mane clutched in her hand.

CHAPTER TWENTY-SEVEN

Wellbeing and Wellies

Catherine phoned me two days later, to say that sadly Priya had died. Her parents had wanted her to give their thanks to Daisy, me and Annie's-Whizz, who they said was the most amazing comfort for them all.

I felt Priya's death deeply, perhaps because it reminded me so much of Annie. But what could we do but carry on? I felt that in every child who smiled, or older person whose day we brightened, my pavement ponies were making the world a little bit better. If that wasn't honouring the memory of those two lovely girls, then I don't know what was.

It was a strange time – but I tried to hold on to the positives. The fact you could hear birdsong. The unseasonable spring sunshine that gladdened the heart. The amazing feat of a ninety-nine-year-old war veteran, walking laps of his garden and raising £32 million for the NHS.

We queued for supermarkets and took wide berths around strangers in the street and stayed inside our houses, waiting for some word from the government of when the restrictions might ease.

When lockdown was first announced, I'd naively thought it would be over in a matter of weeks. But by early May, when the only freedoms we'd been granted were the chance to sunbathe in the park and exercise outside more than once a day, it was clear we were in it for the long haul. I knew it was the right thing to protect the vulnerable, but my heart ached for my regular disabled riders, who were not receiving their much-needed equine therapy. The longer lockdown went on, the worse the effect would be on their mental and physical health.

I wondered what the horses made of it all. Their routine had completely changed, and although they seemed quite content munching lots of grass, on their unexpected holiday, they were all people-ponies, who loved the attention of humans. I visited the horses up at Oxshott every day, often with Dickie and the kids too, and they were always delighted to see us. But I knew they'd be missing the riders as much as the riders would be missing them.

With lessons still cancelled for the foreseeable, we found novel ways of fundraising – selling painted horseshoes and beautiful illustrations of Annie's-Whizz done by our wonderful volunteer Joy, and hosting a socially distanced street gig with a local musician playing from the stable balcony. Our efforts and the generosity of the local community – plus a few well-timed grants from the RDA, the National Lottery and Sport England – proved just enough to scrape by.

Meanwhile, I tried to keep up communication with the children who were shielding, FaceTiming with the ponies and emailing them horse-related activities they could do at home. For those that were able to go out, we started doing pony story time at the police station at the end of Park Lane. There was a patch of grass there and I'd sometimes walk a pony down with Woody and Alice, then let the pony graze while I sat on the wall and read them a book in the sunshine.

Once other families saw what we were doing, they'd stop and listen – socially distanced, of course. I think the children liked to watch the pony while they listened to the story, and would sit quietly, transfixed. I started taking horse-related books – like Clare Balding's *The Racehorse who Wouldn't Gallop*, or my old favourite, *Black Beauty* – and turning up at more regular times. Seeing if the pony and the lady with the book were at the police station became part of a lot of local people's lockdown routines.

The weeks and months ran into each other, but as summer arrived, so did the news that we'd been waiting so long for. At the beginning of June, the government announced that outdoor sport could resume – and that meant riding.

'I just can't wait to have everyone back!!!!' Verity texted me, obviously glued to the government press conference like I was.

'Me too!' I typed back. 'Although I doubt it will be as straight-forward as it sounds . . .'

I was right about that. The press conference wasn't even over before the phone started ringing and pinging with emails. Everyone was desperate to get back in the saddle – but we couldn't just throw our doors open and go back to how things were before.

Over the coming days, I had what felt like endless Zoom meetings with the team, our trustees and our governing bodies: RDA UK, the Pony Club and Sport England. The focus was on opening gradually and safely, and that meant making careful plans. But I did understand the impatience of our riders and participants, who were still getting in touch in their droves to try and book a session.

After lots of discussion, we had our guidelines and we knew

the plan – which would sadly mean normality was still a long way off. To ensure the safety of all our riders, staff, volunteers and horses, we could only accept competent riders who had their own hat and could mount and dismount unaided. Because of social distancing rules, we wouldn't be able to get close enough to help anyone, which sadly ruled out most of our RDA participants and a lot of our novice Pony Clubbers. We also had to restrict our activities to Teddington and Bushy Park, because the arena at Hampton was in a shared yard. Carriage driving, with its close contact between coach and driver, was very much off the agenda for the foreseeable future.

'It's not ideal, but it's something,' David said to me, as we rode together one balmy evening – him on piebald Dougie, and me on my beloved old faithful, Prodney. Riding your own horse had technically been allowed in the lockdown, but I'd been reluctant, because I couldn't bear the thought of having an accident and then adding pressure to the already stretched NHS. But now that restrictions were relaxing, I felt comfortable getting back in the saddle. Prodney had turned forty at the end of May but he was as sprightly as a colt after his very extended holiday.

'I know,' I sighed. 'Don't get me wrong, I'm so looking forward to taking out rides again. It's just that some of the people who need us most are still shut out, aren't they?'

'Knowing you, you'll come up with a workaround,' smiled David, raising an eyebrow.

As we started to slowly welcome back riders over the coming weeks, it was wonderful to have Park Lane ringing with happy voices once more. The horses were delighted to be working too. Cheeky Jack, who loved to undo the zips on people's jackets, and greedy Marcus, who was always snuffling around for a biscuit, were in their element. My favourite thing in the world is to watch relationships blossom between ponies and humans, and it was wonderful to see them again at last.

But, as David had predicted, I wasn't content to leave people out and I was determined to find solutions. I started to come up with ideas for unmounted sessions, so that the RDA participants and anyone else who wasn't able to ride independently would still be able to benefit from being around the ponies.

Marnie volunteered to help me run our very first stable management session, which would involve bathing a couple of the ponies and filling up the haynets, while also getting lots of horsey cuddles. Philippa and her friend Chris, another RDA participant, agreed to be our guinea pigs, and enjoyed it so much we decided to start offering regular sessions. It was a great way to enjoy the company of horses and fellow humans after so many months of isolation, as well as keeping fit and learning more about pony care.

For the Pony Club members, we put on sessions which would help them get badges that didn't involve riding – like Plaiting or Feeding. The ponies loved getting lots of attention and cuddles from their young friends – and I loved to see the kids back in their favourite place once more.

I was also extremely aware of how lockdown had impacted people's mental health, and wanted to offer the ponies as a much-needed balm. We set up Wellies and Wellbeing sessions, which were basically the chance to enjoy some horsey comfort, and Pony Walking, which did what it said on the tin – participants got to lead, walk, stroke and bond with a pony in the beautiful surroundings of Bushy Park. It was wonderful to see how the ponies instantly lifted the spirits of people who had been ground down by the relentless awfulness of the last few months.

'You really do think of a solution for everything, don't you?'

said Jenny Bear. She'd called by to see me and we were sitting on the bench outside the stable yard in the August sunshine, Woody cuddled up on her lap. Inside the stables we could hear the happy giggles of a small group of RDA participants who were being led through a stable management session by Amelia and Marnie, and we were watching the departing backs of David and a couple of riders heading up to Bushy Park. Behind us was the 'Wishing Tree', a paper design I'd stuck to the outside wall of the stables, for the children to hang with cards stating their goals or a message for the ponies. I'd put it up because it felt more important than ever to hang on to our dreams for a better future.

'It feels like we're over the worst of it, you know,' I said. 'I mean, I don't want to jinx it – but things do seem to be getting back to normal. Slowly, but we're getting there.'

Part Four

Part Four

CHAPTER TWENTY-EIGHT

Chance in a Million

As life often goes, things weren't quite so simple – but I'm glad I'd been so positive in that moment. Innocently basking in the joy of sitting with my old friend and my little boy, with the sound of the ponies and the children's voices ringing down the street, probably gave me a lot more strength than if I'd figured out what was going to come that autumn. Another lockdown. The rumours had been swirling for a week, but it was only when I watched Boris Johnson deliver the chilling news – appropriately on Halloween – that I actually believed it. The country was to stay at home for another four weeks, with everything but essential shops closed down, meaning that once again Park Lane would have to shut its stable doors.

I sat on the sofa, my head in my hands, as Boris droned on about spiralling cases and the increased pressure on the NHS. Woody came and put his arms around me, sensing something was wrong. 'It's okay, baby,' I reassured him, but knew it was anything but. Like many of our RDA participants, Woody was in for yet another disorientating change of routine and difficult period of isolation.

'Looks like we got in there just in time,' said Dickie, squeezing my knee and trying to lighten the mood. We'd finally got married three weeks earlier, at an intimate ceremony at York House in Twickenham, driven there and back in a horse and carriage driven by my friend Rihanna. It had been an incredibly happy occasion, with Woody and Alice gleefully coating us in confetti, but now I felt guilty that we'd shut the stables for a weekend right before we were going to have to close for a month.

'What are we going to do, Dickie?' I asked him, my mouth dry. 'How are we going to afford to keep afloat?'

It was a far more serious situation than it had been when we found ourselves locked down in the spring. Back then the sun was shining and the weather was warm and dry, meaning most of the horses could exercise and graze freely outside. But now winter was here, meaning the horses could not spend all the coming weeks in the field. The grass had stopped growing too, which meant we would need to supplement the horses' diet with feed. With no income this would be very hard, but I would not compromise on their care.

Although we'd been able to operate for some time in the summer, we had by no means been running at full capacity. Any money we'd made in that time had already been swallowed up. Once again, I'd have to turn to the community for help.

'I'll put out another JustGiving appeal, although god knows everyone must be sick of hearing from me by now,' I said, reaching for my laptop. 'And I'll write to the landlord and see if he'll give us a rent break. I know he said no last time, but you never know.'

I fired off an email to the landlord, explaining our mounting overheads and begging him to give us a month's break on the rent, in the hope that we'd be back in operation by December.

Then I started ringing round the people I knew who would take this news the hardest to see how they were holding up – those living alone, those who were still shielding, and the parents of the most severely disabled children.

One small mercy about this lockdown was that you were allowed to meet one person from outside your household for exercise. My mind was already whirring with ideas of how we could use this to support those in need. Perhaps a buddy programme, where you could go for a walk with one of our staff or volunteers – and maybe a pony too?

Meanwhile, the horses were all due a worming treatment, which at more than £20 a horse, across twenty-three horses, quickly got expensive. Then there was the farrier, who came to replace Marcus's shoes – that was £80 for a new set. For each new expense I put out an appeal on social media, and was consistently blown away by the generosity of our supporters. So many people cared about Park Lane and its survival – and it felt good to know we weren't on our own.

In the hope that the lockdown really would only last a month, my team and I were still exercising the horses every day so they would be fit and ready to resume lessons as soon as we were able. Every day I met one of our usual riders going for their daily walk, me on horseback, while they walked beside. It was safe, socially distanced, and most importantly, a chance for people who were desperately missing equine company to bond with the horse.

I had a wonderful ride out one Thursday afternoon with Philippa walking beside me. We were talking and laughing as if everything was normal, and enjoying the twinkling dusk in Bushy Park. Lovely Dougie had walked at Philippa's exact pace without any prompting from me, and I went back to the cottage with my heart full and feeling warm despite the cold.

I let myself into the cottage, the usual noise of two children who had spent too long indoors greeting me immediately. Alice and Woody were wrestling each other on the sofa, while a noisy cartoon blared on the television. Dickie was standing at the stove, stirring what looked like a vegetable curry, but his face was grave.

'Check your emails, Nat,' he said, instead of hello. 'There's something you need to see.'

I realised I'd been having such a lovely time with Philippa that I hadn't been obsessively refreshing my inbox.

'Oh god, is it the landlord? No rent break then?' I said, fumbling in my pocket for my phone.

'Worse than that,' said Dickie, raising his eyebrows.

I opened the message, and started scanning quickly through it. Surprise, surprise, no, he didn't think it was appropriate to offer us a rent break and full payment would still be due at the end of the month, lockdown or not. But he wanted to let us know something else too . . .

'Oh god,' I said, my hand flying to my mouth.

'He rang the landline while you were out,' said Dickie, coming over to read over my shoulder. 'So I know the general gist . . . '

'He's selling the stables,' I said, hardly believing the words that were coming out of my own mouth. 'He wants us out.'

In a year of the most terrible news, where we'd already thought we'd hit rock bottom, here was an even more devastating blow. Ever since I'd taken over the lease for the riding school all those years ago, I'd always assumed we'd be able to stay at Park Lane indefinitely. I didn't believe we could do what we did anywhere else. We were perfectly located for public transport, meaning that anyone could reach us from all over London, and close to a wide open space, which meant that even city ponies could run free. It was the place where I'd fallen in love, made friends for life and raised my children. And we were so deeply embedded in our community – the support and well wishes we'd received over the past year had been proof of that. The people of Teddington felt a part of the stables, just as we felt a part of Teddington. What would become of us if we weren't here?

'This can't be happening,' I said, reaching unsteadily for the counter-top. 'Look, it says he's putting it on the market at the end of the month but wanted to let us know as a courtesy . . .'

I dropped the phone to the counter and stepped away, trying to outpace the tsunami of worries that was assaulting me. Our RDA riders who had endured the toughest year of their lives, mainly in isolation, who had been counting down the days until they would ride again – now perhaps they never would. My wonderful team, who thrived working at Park Lane, but might struggle to find a job anywhere else. The Pony Club children who adored the ponies with their whole hearts and would spend entire school holidays grooming and mucking out. My gorgeous herd of loyal, kind, sweet-natured ponies, who had devoted themselves to the happiness of others, who I might now need to rehome.

I felt really sick. I tried to focus on the silly show Alice and Woody were watching on the telly across the room, but my eyes were swimming. This was the only home my children had ever known. In the grand scheme of things, it was the least of our worries, but I supposed we'd have to say goodbye to the cottage too.

'Nat, wait,' said Dickie. He'd picked up my phone and was still reading the landlord's email. 'He's saying that he wants to offer you the first chance to buy the stables, before he puts it on the open market.'

My head jerked round. Of course! Buying the stables was the obvious solution. And it could actually work out in our favour, in the long run. All the money we spent monthly on the lease, we could instead funnel into new equipment and funding more RDA lessons. The stables were modest in size and hardly state-of-the-art, so perhaps with a mortgage, they might just be affordable.

'How much?' I asked tentatively – I really had no idea how much the stables would be worth.

Dickie was silent, scrolling further down the email.

Then he looked up, and his grimace said it all.

'A million,' he said softly.

One million pounds. I ran stables so skint that when we needed to repair the roof we had to ask for donations. Where on earth were we going to find that kind of money? And what would happen to us if we didn't?

CHAPTER TWENTY-NINE

The Madness of Crowdfunding

My first thought – perhaps naively – was that I'd simply get a mortgage and buy the stables myself. I went straight to the bank the next day, trying to act like a sassy businesswoman who knew her way around the facts and figures. Borrowing a million pounds in the middle of a pandemic when you've never had a mortgage before – surely the bank would want to help me out on that one?

To be fair to the bank, they didn't laugh in my face. Asher, the advisor I was assigned, patiently talked me through all the forms I'd have to fill in and the proof of assets I'd need to provide and the business contingency plans they'd want to see. I spent the rest of the November lockdown struggling through the paperwork, with multiple visits to the bank. Each one seemed to bring a new hoop to jump through.

'They want to know what you're going to do if there's another lockdown next year,' said Asher from behind his face mask, as we went back over my plan for about the third time in his small office at the bank. 'How will you make the repayments if your income stops again?'

'I honestly don't know,' I said, exasperated. 'I'll fundraise again, I guess. People wouldn't let us default, I'm sure of it.'

Asher shook his head sadly. I knew somehow it wasn't going to be good enough.

As I suspected, a few days later, at the beginning of December, I got a formal letter from the bank, rejecting my application for the mortgage. I sat at the kitchen table and stared at it for a while, then screwed it up and chucked it in the bin on my way round to the stables.

Lockdown had lifted on the 2nd, meaning we were able to resume some of our activities – following strict social distancing guidance, of course. It meant that the yard was once again host to children ducking in and out of stables and volunteers chatting happily. Christmas was always a big deal at Park Lane, and even the strict government rules couldn't stop the festive atmosphere. The Pony Clubbers who were mucking out Trigger while he waited patiently on the street were singing 'Last Christmas' to each other, and Daisy was on a stepladder, putting up the Christmas lights.

I hadn't told anyone yet that the stables were at risk. It had been such a terrible year for everyone; I couldn't bear to burden them with this awful news just before Christmas. And I'd been desperately hoping that my mortgage plan would work out. What a wonderful way to finish off the year that would have been – telling everyone that Park Lane was our forever home.

I sat down on the bench outside the stables, underneath the blackboard where one of the kids had scrawled 'Have A Holly Jolly Christmas!' Trigger, a handsome 24-year-old grey gelding who I'd had for years, was tied up to the post next to the bench.

As I sat down he immediately shuffled close to me and put his head on my shoulder. He was such an affectionate horse, who genuinely seemed to think he was a human. I'd lost count of the times he'd tried to follow me into the cottage – I think he thought it was more suited to his status than the stable! He always wanted to be close to you, which made him one of our very best horses for cuddles and sharing secrets.

'What a mess we're in, Trig,' I said, rubbing his nose. I felt totally exhausted by the emotional turmoil of the last month, and I just didn't know what to do next. I couldn't stop the tears from starting to roll down my face.

It was at this low moment that Lucy's dad Tony came round the corner. Lucy hadn't been able to have carriage-driving lessons since last March, but he had been dropping her off for as many activities at the stables as we could offer – whether it was stable management or creative writing or pony crafts. With a disabled child at home, he had enough to deal with on his own – but he was also always keen to lend a hand if he thought we needed it. I tried to compose myself as he approached.

'Hiya, Nat, I just came by to pick up a couple of Christmas packs!' he said cheerfully. The Christmas packs were our latest fundraising wheeze – a packet of pony cards, a home-made tree decoration and a lucky horseshoe for £20, with all proceeds going towards the upkeep of the horses.

'Right, sure,' I said, getting shakily to my feet. 'Let me just run up and get them for you ... '

'Oh Natalie, what on earth is wrong?' said Tony, catching sight of my face. 'Come back here, sit down – talk to me.'

He practically dragged me back to the bench, and I put up little protest.

'It's the stables,' I confided, rubbing my eyes. 'The landlord wants to sell. We can buy it – but only if we can find a million pounds. And god knows how I'm going to do that. I just feel like – like I'm going to let everyone down.'

'Oh Nat,' said Tony gently. 'You've never let anyone down in your life. How long have you known about this?'

'About a month,' I said. 'But I haven't told anyone. I don't want to frighten the kids – not after the year they've all had.'

Tony tutted softly. 'You can't protect anyone if you're shouldering this burden alone,' he said. 'And it hardly helps them to keep them in the dark, does it?'

'You're right,' I said, sitting up and drying my eyes. 'I need to pull myself together. I was just hoping there would be an easy answer, but I don't think there is.'

'Nothing worth having in life is easy,' said Tony, with a rueful smile.

After my conversation with Tony, it suddenly became easier to tell other people. I started with my team, who took the news with impressive stoicism – especially considering their jobs were on the line. Then we started gradually and gently filtering the news to parents and volunteers, with a promise that we were doing everything we could to secure the stables' future.

The landlord's patience seemed to be running out, and I was getting regular messages hassling me about what I'd decided to do. I told him I'd get the money – although I didn't yet know how.

While I was frantically researching the possibility of a grant that might save us, and looking into other ways of borrowing money, it was becoming increasingly clear to me what I'd have to do. I needed to fundraise the money myself. Just like I'd raised a few thousand here and there to keep the stables afloat during the lockdown – except this time, it was a million pounds. No big deal ... right?

'JustGiving won't do the trick – I think we need something bigger,' I said to Nicola. We'd been going through the Park Lane accounts to see if there was any money to spare that we could put towards the million fund – there wasn't – and discussing how on earth we were going to move forwards. 'What about Crowdfunder?'

I frowned – I'd never heard of it.

'I was doing a bit of research last night,' Nicola went on. 'It's a platform where you can ask your community to fund a specific project. And the best bit is it has an "all-or-nothing" option. So if you don't hit the target, everyone who donated gets their money back automatically. Which will save us a hell of a lot of admin.' She paused, seeing my stricken face. 'Not that I don't think we'll get there!' she said hurriedly. 'But just in case.'

I knew what she was saying made perfect sense. Crowdfunder sounded ideal – and she was right to be cautious about whether we'd hit the target or not.

'All or nothing,' I mused, half to myself. 'How very appropriate.'

I knew that fundraising that amount of money would be incredibly difficult. How many people did I know – a few thousand? And if they all gave us a tenner, then that wouldn't even get us to 10 per cent of the target. I'd have to find a way to reach beyond the usual suspects and find new people to support us. This was going to be the biggest and perhaps most stupid thing I'd ever attempted. But what did I have to lose?

London went into Tier 3 restrictions in mid-December, meaning once again we had to limit our activities and deal with a whole new raft of rules and regulations. I had to put my Crowdfunder research on hold for a bit while we tackled the latest challenges thrown our way. But I was desperate to get started on the fundraising sooner rather than later.

Later that week, Nicola joined me to help turn out the ponies. I ran through my thoughts with her as we put rugs on Jack, Marcus and Boyd before we turned them out.

'The landlord won't wait for ever,' I said. 'Every day that goes past, I feel like the stables are slipping away.'

'But you need to get the timing right, don't you, if you can only run a Crowdfunder for eight weeks,' said Nicola. 'You don't want to lose a big chunk of that to Christmas.'

'That's a good point,' I said. Then I laughed, 'Oh Marcus, stop it! I swear he can smell a biscuit that I had in my pocket days ago.' Skewbald Marcus really was the greediest pony I'd ever known; he had a huge heart, but an even bigger appetite. As I pushed his nose out of my pocket, an idea hit me.

'Hey, Nicola, would this be too mad?' I said. 'What if we kicked it off on New Year's Eve? No one can go out this year so everyone will be stuck inside. Maybe they'll think, well, I'm not having a big night, I can donate the money I would have spent to the stables?'

Nicola laughed. 'Either that or they'll be so drunk they'll think it's a good idea anyway!'

I grinned. 'It's a plan then.'

It was only a few days after that conversation that we discovered that it wasn't just New Year, but Christmas that was cancelled too. The government had promised to relax restrictions for the festive period, meaning families would be able to mix together indoors. I'd been desperately looking forward to spending Christmas with Dad, who I had barely seen in the course of this very strange year, and I knew he was dying to see his grandchildren too. But people in the new Tier 4 area, which covered London and much of the south-east, were now ordered to stay at home and see no one outside their household.

I'm sure there were many millions of others who felt exactly like me, watching the news delivered in yet another doom-laden press conference by Boris Johnson. Dejected, exhausted, anxious, frustrated, absolutely gutted. There was really only one thing to do. I switched off the news, poured a big glass of wine, whacked on the Christmas tunes at top volume and danced my heart out around the living room with Alice and Woody.

It was the strangest Christmas I could ever remember – including the one immediately after my house burned down and I had just got divorced. My Christmases were always loud, chaotic and full of people. We had an open door policy, welcoming anyone who couldn't get home or had trouble with their families or just wanted to come, and often invited homeless people too. But in 2020, it was just the four of us. With Woody involved, it was never going to be quiet, and although it was lovely to spend time just as us, it still seemed rather low key. I couldn't help thinking mournfully, as I watched my family tuck into their turkey, paper hats perched wonkily on heads, that this was not how I had imagined our last ever Christmas at Park Lane.

I'd had to accept, one way or another, that we'd have to say goodbye to the cottage. Even if we pulled off the impossible and raised a million, I couldn't use some of that money to buy a home for my own family. Instead, I planned to convert the cottage into an assisted living space where we could offer disabled people from all over the country the chance to come to London for a holiday, spend time with the horses, go riding and see the sights of the capital. My dream was that people from far and wide would be able to experience some of the happiness I'd found here.

But right now, that was all it was: a dream. I felt sick when I thought of the task ahead of me. There's nothing I hate more than failure. I always compare it to marathons, of which I've run many – there's no way I'd ever give up, unless my legs literally collapsed beneath me. I'd rather push through the pain than admit defeat. This fundraising challenge was going to be like running ten marathons back to back. But if we had to go, we'd go fighting.

CHAPTER THIRTY

Starter for Ten

'Do it, Mummy, do it, do it, do it!' Alice and Woody sang, bouncing around, hyper from a week spent mainly inside the cottage. Nicola and I had spent the morning putting the finishing touches to my Crowdfunder page, with its heartfelt plea to 'Save Our Stables'. I'd told the kids that I was just waiting for the right moment to send it live to the world and they'd seized on it as a great game.

I glanced at the clock: 2 p.m., New Year's Eve, with only hours left on the strangest, saddest and most difficult year of most people's lives. Hell, why not, I thought, and hit Enter.

'It's live!' I announced.

'It's live, it's live, it's live,' Alice chanted, grabbing Woody's hands and swinging him round the room as he screamed hysterically.

I stared at the bar at the top of the page which would tot up our total. '£0 raised – 0% of target reached – £1 million to go', it read. It was time to get to work.

The rest of New Year's Eve passed in a blur. Instead of enjoying my usual reunion with Pasty, Sam and Barney – impossible with the pubs shut – I spent hours glued to my laptop, posting the Crowdfunder link first to all the Park Lane social media channels, then to my own. But I wasn't going to stop there, and I started writing personal messages to every single person I had ever met, begging them to either donate, or share our story, or even better, both.

I was right about everyone being bored at home – I could tell by the speed with which they read and responded to my messages. And almost within minutes, the donations started to roll in.

I got a thrill with each new tenner that dropped into the account – and every new donation just spurred me on. There was one from my first boss, the orthodontist, and here was a generous contribution from my old Birmingham mates Jenny and Doug. Lexi, who I'd taught as a girl and was now a riding instructor herself, donated immediately and started sharing the page far and wide. Even when it was time to go next door to see to the horses I took my phone with me, tap-tap-tapping away with one hand and filling up buckets of feed with the other.

The kids went to bed, Jools Holland came on the telly, and I barely noticed, such was my absorption in the task at hand. I was determined to saturate every single Facebook follower, every single stables' newsletter subscriber, with our plight. If you'd crossed my path once in the last thirty years, and you could afford it, then I was determined to have your fiver.

And it was working. The total was creeping up, not just through the hundreds, but through the thousands too. It seemed that the sheer absurdity of my scheme was enough to get it noticed.

'It's a big target but I know you can do it!' a typical message ran. 'If you're mad enough to try, I'm mad enough to support you!'

I scrolled through my Facebook feed, which was now back-to-back with my amazing friends and the loyal stables network sharing our Crowdfunder. I thought of all their acquaintances and contacts who would see it too, and imagined our story spreading out across the internet like a spider's web. I'd got to more than £8,000 in just a few hours – surely this 'impossible task' wasn't so impossible?

'Earth to Nat!' It was Dickie, giving me a gentle shove with his elbow. 'It's about to turn midnight!'

I reluctantly put my laptop aside and squinted at the TV, where the countdown to the new year was beginning. I was sure that no one was sorry to say goodbye to the hardships, loneliness and fear of 2020. I certainly wasn't.

Dickie and I kissed on the stroke of midnight then joined in the singalong to 'Auld Lang Syne'. I knew I should be scared about what this new year could bring when so much was at stake, but that night, all I could feel was bubbling hope. I told myself I had to hold on to the feeling. New Year's Eve fell on a Friday that year, so there was still a whole weekend before the world returned to whatever counted as 'normal' these days.

As London was in Tier 4, we'd had to shut Park Lane's doors once more. It felt like we were in lockdown already, but it was becoming increasingly clear that the Prime Minister was going to announce another national lockdown any day now. The progress of the Crowdfunder, however, cheered me. I drew strength from every new donation or kind message. By the end of 2 January we were on £10,000. By Monday morning, 4 January, we were on £30,000. I could hardly believe how fast it had snowballed, and although I couldn't do the maths as to whether if it continued at that rate we'd hit the target, it was all moving in the right direction. However, walking Rusty through

Bushy Park that lunchtime, I got a phone call that threatened to burst my bubble.

The young man on the line introduced himself as Dale and said he had been assigned to be our Crowdfunder coach. I was pleased; I knew Crowdfunder provided one-to-one support if you were aiming to raise a large amount, but I hadn't expected them to call so quickly.

'Oh hi, Dale, lovely to speak to you!' I said cheerily, imagining he was probably calling to congratulate me on hitting 3 per cent of my target in a matter of days.

'Lovely to speak to you too, Natalie,' said Dale. 'Just one question for you: are you serious?'

I found myself coming to a stop, stumped as to what to say to that.

'Er ... I think so.'

'So you really think you can raise a million in eight weeks,' said Dale. 'Because I don't mind telling you that no one in the office has ever heard something as ambitious as this.'

'I don't just think we can do it, we *have* to do it,' I said, annoyed. 'There are children who come to us, who don't feel accepted anywhere else, and for a few hours a week they get to be just like any other kids. There are people who work for me, bursting with talent, who have been cruelly deprived of opportunities despite everything they can do. There's a whole herd of beautiful, kind, gentle horses, who stand to lose their home. And there's an entire community around the stables, who desperately need it to survive, or their physical and mental wellbeing is going to collapse. So yes, I might be a bit mad, but I simply cannot fail. I will do this, just you wait.'

I felt out of breath when I finished, and couldn't believe such an impassioned speech had just come out of my mouth. I'd meant every single word and more.

'Fair play!' said Dale, and I could tell he was smiling. 'Hey, sorry about that. I had to check how serious you are, but you seem pretty bloody serious.'

'I really am!' I replied.

'Well, I can tell you now, it's not going to be easy,' Dale went on. 'If you hit the million, it will be the second biggest Crowdfunder that's ever been completed.'

'What was the biggest?'

'That was one that raised more than £2.3 million to buy PPE for NHS staff at the beginning of the pandemic,' said Dale. 'It had a lot of support and media attention.'

I gulped. The NHS – an organisation that has a bit more reach than a small stables in Teddington.

'But listen, I like you, and I'm going to help you,' said Dale. 'I can't make any promises, but we will give this our best shot. I can tell you really believe in this project, and that passion is the most important ingredient.'

'Okay, tell me what I need to do,' I said, perching on a bench and fumbling in the pocket of my parka for a scrap of paper.

'We strongly encourage you to set rewards,' said Dale. 'It's what makes crowdfunding different from other kinds of fundraising. Basically, you give someone something in return. I don't know . . . say if someone pledged £1,000, you could promise them a private riding lesson when the pandemic is over. Something like that. They won't necessarily match the value of the donation, but it will be an encouragement to give.'

I liked the idea immediately. There were people who would support us regardless, but most of them had already pledged. This could be a way to entice others.

'Got it, thank you, Dale!' I said. 'I'll go home and do that now.'

'Good luck,' he said. 'I'll check in with you soon.'

Back at home, I opened the laptop and stared at my Crowdfunder page, trying to decide what the reward should be. I looked around the kitchen and my eyes landed on a picture of Prodney stuck to the fridge, which always cheered me up. It gave me an idea.

Half an hour later, I was feeling pretty proud of myself, when the phone rang again. It was Dale.

'Pony positivity cards?' he said, incredulously. 'For a *fiver*?'

'Yes, that's right,' I said cheerfully. The idea was that if you pledged £5, I'd send you a picture of a horse with a personalised inspirational message on the back.

'Nat, I don't think you're getting this,' said Dale, exasperated. 'If you set the reward limit at £5, you're going to end up giving a reward to everyone. You need to put rewards for the higher amounts.'

'With respect, Dale, I do disagree,' I said. 'Anyone can afford a fiver, can't they? It's like a glass of wine or something. I don't want to make it so only rich people can donate, I want to reach as many people as possible.'

Dale sighed. 'You do realise you'll be writing thousands of those things, don't you?'

'I'm not afraid of a bit of hard work, Dale,' I told him breezily.

'Okay, keep the cards,' he said. 'But you need rewards for higher amounts too.'

'Oh, we've got them!' I said. 'Scroll down – if you donate £10 you get a pony hug.'

'Okay, Nat, I'll leave it with you,' said Dale. I could tell he wasn't impressed. 'Think about it, okay?'

Dale turned out to be right about the cards. By the next day, I already owed them to 350 people, and I stayed up until 2 a.m. all that week carefully crafting the positive messages.

I put a shout-out on Facebook to the Park Lane supporters, asking if anyone had anything they could offer as a reward. Local artist Joy, one of our most dedicated volunteers, replied immediately offering to paint watercolours for people who pledged. I rang her excitedly, and we discussed what would be an appropriate price for a watercolour. Her paintings were beautiful and unique; much better than a pony postcard.

Dale was on the phone a few days later. 'The watercolour reward is a lovely idea,' he said. 'Just one problem – do you know how many your friend is going to have to paint now?'

'Um, no,' I said, feeling like a naughty child.

'She's on a hundred already,' said Dale. 'And the reward has only been live for two days.'

'Ah.'

'Two hundred pounds was far too low for that, Nat!' said Dale. 'Joy's going to be painting watercolours until next Christmas!!'

'I really need to think of some big ones, don't I?' I said, finally seeing his logic.

'It is what I've been trying to tell you for a fortnight,' said Dale.

That evening, I added some bigger rewards to the Crowdfunder – for £5,000 you could have a plaque on a stable door, and for £10,000 you could name a pony. I took down the watercolour promise, but couldn't bring myself to remove the pony positivity cards. Yes, they were a pain, but I knew that while we might need some big donors, we'd never hit the million without plenty of fivers too.

Lockdown was in full swing by now, meaning all our lessons had stopped. The horses still needed exercising and grooming and feeding and taking to and from the field, but when I wasn't doing that, I was glued to the Crowdfunder. Friday nights became the crescendo for the week – we'd started on a Friday, so each week it felt important to do an extra push and see what milestone we could hit. On 15 January, two weeks after the Crowdfunder went live, we were hovering just below £100,000. I spent the evening sat on my bed on the phone to our now old friend Peter Laney of H&L Motors, trying to convince him to be the one to push us to 10 per cent of our target. My dignity was well out of the window at this point, and I was literally begging. But Peter is one of the most generous people I know, and he pledged a whopping £5,000. Watching his donation drop in and the bar inch to 10 per cent, I couldn't help but jump up and down with glee, clapping my hands in delight.

Woody and Alice came rushing into my bedroom to see what all the fuss was about.

'High fives, guys!!' I said, holding out my palms to them. 'We hit ten per cent on Save Our Stables!'

'Your mummy is an absolute powerhouse,' said Dickie, appearing at the bedroom door, two freshly poured glasses of prosecco in his hands. We clinked glasses then danced around with the kids, everyone high on the thrill of hitting the first rung of the ladder.

A whole £100,000 in just a fortnight was an incredible achievement, and testament to the generosity of Park Lane's brilliant supporters. Each pound felt like a little drop of love – an unspoken message that said: 'We want you to survive.'

But it was still just the beginning. I'd let us get carried away with excitement and enjoy this moment tonight, but the cold reality would still be there in the morning.

Yes, 10 per cent was a big first step – but it left 90 per cent to raise. We still had a whole £900,000 to go.

CHAPTER THIRTY-ONE

Anisha's Boot Camp

'PLEASE READ – YOUR CROWDFUNDER IS CRAP'.

The email, with its undeniably arresting subject line, sat like an accusation in my inbox. I didn't know whether to laugh or cry.

It was a week on from our 10 per cent milestone, and fundraising had massively slowed down. The initial flurry had not translated into long-term progress. I supposed I must have reached everyone within my immediate network, and they had either already given or decided not to. I was starting to feel dispirited – had we really hit a wall so quickly?

And now, here it was in black and white – someone else out there agreed with all the most negative things I said to myself in my own head. I didn't recognise the sender of the email, but I clicked it open regardless.

Dear Natalie

Forgive me for being so direct and I hope I've got your attention, because you need to see this. My name is Anisha, and I am a marketing consultant. I live in South

West London and have for a long time admired the work you do at Park Lane. Like many others in the area, I fully support your bid to save the stables.

However, I feel compelled to tell you that you will never hit your ambitious £1 million target without some fundamental changes to your strategy. At the moment, you have some major errors with how you are running your Crowdfunder.

This is where I believe I can help. My job is helping brands manage their image and maximise their reach, and I have previously advised on successful Crowdfunder campaigns. I'd love to provide you with some pointers – free of charge of course. Drop me a line if you're interested – I really think you need this advice.

Best wishes

Anisha.

Well, she was certainly direct. I knew plenty of people would be offended by Anisha's blunt approach, but I didn't have time to be prissy about it. I desperately needed help. If this woman was offering it, then I couldn't let a lack of social niceties get in the way.

'Hi, Anisha. Thanks for your email. Please tell me what I need to do,' I wrote, signing off with my phone number and a plea for her to call as soon as she could.

Anisha rang me back that same afternoon. On the phone her tone was the same as her email; no-nonsense, to the point, unconcerned about causing offence. I guessed she was probably in her twenties, but she had confidence beyond her years and I could tell she knew what she was talking about.

'So the Crowdfunder page is basically a mess,' she told me.

'The words are far too waffly – anyone who clicks on it who doesn't already know what you do is barely going to get past the second paragraph. That needs fixing.'

'Okay, rewrite words,' I said, jotting it down, feeling fire rising in my belly. Before Anisha emailed me I'd been floundering and panicking, but suddenly I felt sharp and focused again, happy to put myself in her capable hands.

'You've got an amazing story to tell, Natalie, but you're just totally failing to tell it,' she went on. 'Where's your video? You've got to have a video.'

'Oh, I don't think I can do that,' I said, recoiling. 'I'd have no idea where to start – I've never made a video before.'

'Natalie, that is no excuse!' said Anisha sternly. 'Aren't you literally surrounded by teenagers at the stables? They'll be able to make something social media friendly with their eyes closed. Rope them in.'

'Okay, yes,' I said, scribbling it down, and resisting the urge to call her 'ma'am' – she was like an army general.

'And while we are on social media, yours is an absolute mess,' she said. 'But it's got potential. Do you even know what a blue tick means on Twitter?'

I hardly went on Twitter – although I did try and share the odd update from the stables and pictures of the ponies. 'Erm – is it something to do with the NHS?'

Anisha gave a short bark of laughter. 'No, it is not something to do with the NHS, Natalie,' she said. 'A blue tick means they're verified – it means they're someone important. Someone like a celebrity or a high-profile journalist or whatever. Twitter has gone to the trouble of checking their account is authentic, because it's got a public interest.'

'Oh, right,' I said, not quite sure how this affected me.

'Well, do you know how many people with blue ticks follow you?' said Anisha. 'There's loads of them!'

'Is there?' I said, calling up Twitter on my laptop. I didn't even know how to see who followed me, but Anisha talked me through it.

'It's mad that you're not following those people back,' said Anisha. 'I want you to spend some time following back everyone that follows you. Then once you follow each other, you'll be able to send them a DM – that's a direct message, like you'd do on Facebook. It's a whole new avenue for reaching people who might support you. And if someone with a blue tick gets involved, they'll have loads of followers that they can spread the word to. You've got to get out there, Natalie – it's no good just waiting for something to happen.'

I could tell Anisha wasn't going to be an easy taskmaster, but I'd never been happier to let someone boss me around. Everything she was saying to me felt like a shot of empowerment. She wasn't going to do it for me, but she was going to show me the way to succeed. It was exactly what I needed.

'I'm going to do all of this, Anisha, thank you,' I said, feeling the most enthusiastic and inspired that I had for days. 'Whatever you think will work – I'm going to do.'

'This is just the beginning,' said Anisha briskly. 'But let's get these basic problems sorted out first, then we'll go from there.'

I did exactly what she told me to do. I rewrote the words for the Crowdfunder page and sent them to her to approve – my draft came back with her notes all over it – 'NO! THIS DOES NOT WORK!', 'LAME!', 'UPSELL, UPSELL, UPSELL!' – so I drafted and drafted again until she was happy.

I messaged some of the most tech-savvy Pony Clubbers about the video, immediately sparking a group squabble over who would do it – until they eventually agreed to work on it together. Within a few days, they had sent me what they came up with. I had tears in my eyes as I watched the amazing montage they had put together, the pictures of riders and horses in happier times, little clips of kids larking around or picking up rosettes. The voiceover – which they'd shared out between them – described Park Lane as a 'bubble of happiness'. I couldn't have put it better myself.

Then there was Twitter. I became addicted to it – spending my evenings clicking 'follow' on each individual follower, and messaging them with our plea. I didn't realise I had so many, and it was slow work.

Money had started to trickle in again, but despite everything I was doing, we were nowhere near the pace that we'd been fundraising in the first fortnight. Thanks to Anisha, the Crowdfunder page was a thousand times better, but we still had to get it to the right people. It felt like every donation was hard won – having to convince every new person I messaged that it was a cause worth supporting, then waiting in limbo to see if my pitch had worked. For every donation, there were many more 'no's, people messaging me to say leave them alone, or simply radio silence. I felt like I was pushing an enormous rock up a hill – a rock that kept rolling back towards me and threatening to crush me.

But the slower things went, the more determined I was to work even harder. I started rationing my sleep – I figured I only needed five hours minimum so I would stay up hunched over the laptop, scrolling through Twitter, until I could no longer keep my eyes open. Then I'd set my alarm for long before dawn, to give myself a couple of hours before we had to see to the horses; drafting more requests, following more people, desperately refreshing my DMs to see if anyone had replied to my increasingly deranged messages.

'You need to stop, Nat,' said Dickie gently one night, coming to find me in the living room. He was in his dressing gown, and had been in bed for hours. I squinted at the clock in the corner of the laptop. It was ten past three.

'Right, yeah, sorry. I lost track of time,' I said, closing the laptop lid and yawning. 'I just thought I'd try one more push . . . '

'I don't mean stop for tonight, I mean stop,' said Dickie, taking my hand in his. 'It's making you ill. You can't go on like this.'

'I can't stop!' I said, trying to keep my voice low so as not to wake the kids. 'We've only made £10,000 this week. It's well off the target. The Crowdfunder closes on 25 February. That's only thirty-two days from now – I can't afford to waste them!'

Dickie was looking at me steadily, and I could see there was sadness in his eyes. 'If you're only making £10,000 a week – do you really still think you can get there?' he said. 'Look, you had to try. It's amazing how much you've raised. Maybe you can donate that to the RDA – but the stables, I just don't know if they're going to be saved.'

'You don't understand, Dickie,' I said, tears pricking my eyes. 'We *can* still do it. Anisha says there's still things we can try . . . it's just a matter of connecting with the right people . . . all we need is one lucky break . . . ' I petered out, sheer exhaustion sapping my will to argue.

'Let's go to bed, shall we,' said Dickie, putting his arm around me. I let him guide me to the bedroom, where I collapsed on the bed and was asleep within minutes, still fully clothed.

When I woke the next morning, Dickie wasn't there. I fumbled for my phone to see the time – 9.30 a.m.! It was the longest I'd slept in for, well, decades. I'd somehow managed to sleep through the hullabaloo of Alice and Woody getting up, and missed my usual early start for the horses. Dickie had stuck a

Post-it note to the mirror saying he'd taken the kids with him and they were seeing to the ponies. I smiled; I could always rely on Dickie's selfless and enduring care.

Wrapping my dressing gown round me, I shuffled into the kitchen and put the kettle on, replaying the conversation I'd had with Dickie last night. I couldn't bear the idea of failure. But I couldn't exhaust myself so much I wasn't there for my family and the horses either. Maybe I should scale back what I was doing just a bit – I'd done what I could, and now it was up to fate to decide.

It was a novelty to have the house to myself, and I stretched out on the sofa with my mug of coffee. My laptop was still on the coffee table from the night before. I eyed it warily, telling myself if I was going to detox, I should start now. But once I'd drained my coffee, I couldn't resist any longer. I flipped it open and fired up Twitter. There, in the top corner, was a red circle – I'd got a DM.

There was something about it sitting there, so soon after I'd decided to scale back, that told me it was important. With shaking hands, I clicked it open.

It was from a guy called Nick Luck, one of the accounts I must have followed yesterday in my late-night rampage. Beside his profile was a magical blue tick.

'Hi Natalie, thanks for following back,' Nick's message read. 'I've been waiting a long time for you to get in touch. I really want to help you.'

Nick Luck. Surely with a name like that, he had to be the lucky break I'd been waiting for?

CHAPTER THIRTY-TWO

A Bit of Luck

'Okay, just be yourself, Natalie – and let's save these stables,' said Nick, through my headphones.

I was poised in the stables, gripping an iPad in my hands, Mini, Prodney and Eddy lined up behind me. It was a freezing cold day but it wasn't the weather making me shiver, more the nerves. Nick was giving me an amazing platform to reach a whole new audience who might be able to support Park Lane. I had to make the most of it.

Nick Luck had turned out to be one of the country's leading racing broadcasters. Having presented racing on Channel 4 for years, he was now the face of Racing TV and the BBC's equestrian commentator. He also happened to live just half a mile from Park Lane.

Once we'd got chatting on Twitter, Nick had explained he'd seen our plight and had followed me in an effort to get in touch. He must have thought I was playing hard to get or something – when the truth was I was just bad at social media!

If ever there was proof needed that Anisha's Twitter plan had been worth it, this was it. No sooner had we started talking than Nick had insisted I appear on his flagship racing show, *Luck on Sunday*. That's why I was here in the gloom of the stable block, surrounded by the horses rhythmically chewing their hay. I was glad it was just me, the ponies and my iPad – it was easier to think of it as just any old Zoom call, rather than one that would be watched by thousands of strangers.

Nick was in his studio, and the plan was he'd introduce the story then come to me live to ask me questions about what we did and why it was such an important cause. He was incredibly enthusiastic about the work we did, and I could tell he was desperate to get his viewers just as fired up too.

'So you deliver three thousand sessions every year for Riding for the Disabled, and as well as that you're providing opportunities to less privileged, inner-city kids,' he said to me on the phone, when we were setting up the interview. 'That's a seriously big deal, you know. We've got to do everything we can because that work is too important to stop.'

I smiled to myself; I loved how he said 'we'. From the moment we'd started swapping messages on Twitter, I could tell Nick was going to be an amazing ally. He was a journalist, but he wasn't just interested in Park Lane as a story that he'd cover and then move on. He seriously believed in the need to save the stables, and he was going to do everything in his power to mobilise support around us.

Anisha had been thrilled when I rang her to tell her about how I'd connected with Nick, and he wanted to put me on the TV.

'This is what it's all about, Natalie!' she said excitedly. 'Your profile is about to go through the roof. Think of all the people who are about to hear about Park Lane for the first time!'

She was right, of course – but it was up to me to persuade them to donate to us. I hoped our shared love of horses would help me connect to Nick's viewers, but he'd also advised me to emphasise our connection to the racing industry.

In fact, we were an important route into that privileged world for kids from less traditional backgrounds. Every summer I ran a twelve-week programme for children aged eleven to sixteen who would be referred to me from all over London. These were kids from tower blocks and council estates, who wouldn't usually get the opportunity to ride but had potential – and over twelve weeks I'd train them to be fit and balanced enough to compete in their first pony race. The idea was to leave them wanting more, inspired to want to get into the racing industry. And it worked – several young people who had completed the course ended up getting jobs at racing stables. I saw it as an important first rung on the ladder, as well as a much-needed tool to help diversify racing.

' . . . Park Lane Stables are at threat of closure, they are run by Natalie O'Rourke who is on the line now.'

I adjusted my sparkly pink RDA baseball cap and smiled into the camera. It was time, as Anisha would say, to 'land the message'.

The interview lasted about five minutes, before Nick wrapped it up with a friendly goodbye. I thanked him and ended the Zoom call. I felt like it had gone really well – Nick had asked all the right questions, giving me the opportunity to talk about our outreach work as well as explaining the importance of riding to our disabled participants, many of whom only left the house once a week to come to the stables.

But I'd found the whole experience quite draining – all that adrenalin, the need to say exactly what you wanted to say as succinctly and as powerfully as possible. I yanked out my headphones and put the iPad to one side, sinking to the floor with my back resting against Prodney's stable door. I breathed in that comforting horsey smell and looked around at the three wise old ponies who'd been such excellent support during my first ever TV appearance. Prodney rested his nose on the top of my head, and I shut my eyes, just for a minute, and allowed myself to hope that it would be enough to raise another few thousand pounds.

My moment of reflection was interrupted by my mobile ringing. It was Anisha.

'Natalie, have you seen the Crowdfunder?' she was practically shouting. 'It's absolutely kicking off, oh my goodness, you need to see this.'

Anisha was speaking at a hundred miles per hour, and I could hardly work out if she was excited or angry.

'Wait, what are you saying? What's going on?'

'The racing people, Natalie! They are donating – and they're donating big!'

I had hoped that my appearance on Nick's show would get a bit of attention and prompt a few donations to start trickling in. But instead, it had sparked a flood. I opened the Crowdfunder on my phone and watched in wonder as the total ticked up from £100,000 to £105,000 to £110,000, right before my eyes.

'This is mad,' I breathed.

And the donations from the racing world didn't stop there. Over the next few days, our total continued to spiral. Then ITV asked me to go on their weekend racing show, which turbocharged it all over again. I was getting loads of new tweets and emails from jockeys, trainers, owners and fans, touching messages of support, urging us to keep going. It seemed that suddenly anyone who liked horse racing knew about our little stables – and wanted to help.

'We can't stop here, Natalie,' was Anisha's stern assessment, when we spoke on the phone a few days later. 'Racing is working, but we will have saturated the UK market soon. It's time to go international.'

As far as I was concerned, Anisha was a genius, so when she would email me and say something like 'tomorrow we are doing Australia' I didn't argue. She worked out all the different time zones, and identified key racing people in various countries around the world. Then we'd spend a day tweeting those people at a time they were likely to see the message, in the hope that they'd share our story. To my surprise, it seemed to work – and suddenly we were getting donations from across the globe.

'I guess people can see that the racing bigwigs in Britain follow me, so I look legitimate,' I said to Anisha.

'Or they can see it's just a bloody good cause!' she replied.

As well as Australia, we targeted New Zealand, South Africa, Dubai, Ireland and Canada. A Canadian racing journalist even put us on the radio – it was totally surreal to be speaking live to people thousands of miles away from our unassuming stables. Teddington was well and truly on the map.

'You're doing an amazing job, Natalie!' the presenter told me at the end of the interview, with that gorgeous Canadian twang. 'We'll be rooting for you!'

The donations kept going up and up and up, but with the time differences, I was back to spending all night at my computer, taking ten-minute naps when I could during the day. Canada helped us inch over the £200,000 line, but I barely allowed myself time for celebration, with Anisha moving us straight on to the strategy for Hong Kong.

'I just need to get to quarter of a million,' I said to Dickie, who hadn't said anything but did sleepily raise his eyebrows when I switched on the laptop in bed at 4 a.m. 'Then I'll slow down. Promise.'

Nick Luck checked in almost every day, full of encouragement and offering advice for the best people to contact in various countries. Then one day, he sent me a rather different email.

'Hi Natalie, if okay with you I'm going to give your number to a friend of mine. His name is Jonny – let's keep it at that – and he's a racehorse owner. Might give you a donation but he has some questions. Said best if you talk to him.'

All very mysterious – but I fired back an email saying yes, of course, please do give the guy my number. Nick didn't offer any more information about his friend – except that he was a 'tough customer'. I got the impression that this Jonny might be able to give a pretty sizeable donation, but it was by no means a done deal.

I didn't have to wait long for Jonny to get in touch. He rang me one Sunday morning when I was up at the fields in Surrey, switching over the horses from the stables. Hearing a gruff voice introduce himself as Jonny took me by surprise, and I found myself inexplicably nervous, far more so than I had been going on Nick's TV show or Canadian radio.

'I've got some questions, Natalie,' he said. 'And let me tell you now – my bullshit radar is impeccable.'

'You won't get any bullshit from me,' I said, trying to shelter from the wind so he could hear me properly.

What followed next can only be described as like an episode of *Dragons' Den*. Jonny grilled me on every aspect of the charity – how our management structure worked, what our outreach was like, how I planned RDA sessions, what goals I set, our accounts last year, our projected earnings next year, what plans I had for the stables if I bought them.

I tried to answer everything as best as I could, my brain feeling increasingly scrambled. 'But you know, what the accounts can't show is how much joy the horses spread, or how much confidence each child gets here, or the friendships that are forged,' I said, when I felt he must surely have got to the end of his list of questions. 'It's so much more than a stables. It's a community, a place of empowerment, a safe space for humans and horses alike.'

There was silence at the other end of the line. I instantly regretted what I'd said – had I spoken out of turn? I didn't want him to think I was annoyed about answering his questions.

'I'm going to give you a donation, Natalie,' he said, eventually.

I tried to stay calm. 'Thank you very much,' I said, hoping it might be a big one – was £10,000 too much to hope for?

'I'm going to give you £50,000.'

I felt like screaming and jumping for joy. £50,000! It was our biggest single donation by a country mile – and would smash us through the quarter of a million milestone.

Trying to stay professional, I kept my voice even: 'That is incredibly generous of you, and on behalf of the entire Park Lane community I want to say the most sincere thank you,' I said. 'You have no idea what a difference this could make.'

'I do, actually, have some idea,' said Jonny. 'My mum is blind. And if there's one thing that's taught me, it's that the world needs places like Park Lane, who want to make the world as big and as exciting for disabled people as it is for the rest of us.'

I could feel myself welling up, and any pretence at professionalism evaporated. 'Thank you, thank you, thank you,' was all I could manage, as the tears started to fall.

'I'm sorry to put you through all that, but I had to be sure,' said Jonny. 'I'd give you the whole million if I could!'

Once he'd hung up the phone, I allowed myself a little scream, much to the bemusement of the horses.

I texted Dickie: 'JUST HIT £250K!!!!!!!! :) :) :)'

He fired back: 'Guessing you're not really going to slow down, are you?'

Of course I wasn't.

CHAPTER THIRTY-THREE

The Race is On

By the beginning of February, fundraising had started to reach a new fever pitch.

Yes, big gifts like Jonny's were important – but just as vital were the countless donations under £20 that were continuing to pour in.

Kids pledging their pocket money, older people sending cheques by post because they couldn't figure out the Crowdfunder – it all mattered. And thank goodness for Royal Mail who still managed to find us even when envelopes were addressed to 'The Horses, London'.

As well as donations, we were inundated with thoughtful cards and wonderful letters of support. I got my RDA volunteers busy writing by hand to every person who had left their return address – there was no way we weren't going to say thank you. H&L Motors, who had so generously bought our carriage a few years ago, were kind enough to frank them all.

I could feel the momentum growing, like a tidal wave – our story seemed to have captured imaginations. Although we still had so far to go, people seemed to believe now that we really could do it.

The Park Lane community took matters into their own hands. Lots of our amazing participants and volunteers decided to make videos that we could share on social media. One of my favourites was a short thirty-second clip made by Dominic's sister Keira, with beautiful footage of Dominic in the carriage enjoying 'his most favourite thing in the world'. Although it was short, I thought her video was so powerful – ending with the message that if the stables were not saved, for Dom it would be 'like lockdown every day'.

Meanwhile, the young Pony Club members were busy organising themselves – even though they couldn't meet in person. They came up with the idea of putting SOS: SAVE OUR STABLES plus the Crowdfunder address in the windows of their houses. They also made a brilliant TikTok video showing how you could repurpose the rainbows from the first lockdown to help support Park Lane.

Walking the streets of Teddington, with every other house proudly displaying our Crowdfunder address in the window, was almost overwhelming. Other kids had designed posters for lamp posts and bus stops, and made leaflets that our volunteers arranged shifts to distribute. It felt like the whole community was rallying around us. The local running club organised a sponsored run, the cheesemongers started selling a special cheese with all profits going to Park Lane, various local artists got in touch offering to sell special pony-themed prints. Someone offered to run an online quiz, another person came up with a raffle, a print shop made some Save Our Stables T-shirts. The burden was being well and truly shared, and it was amazing to see people power in action.

A steady stream of locals came to visit the cuddle ponies every day like a pilgrimage, cheering when they saw the latest Crowdfunder total which I kept updated on the blackboard outside the stables. People would always ask me: 'What can I do to help?' I told them to tell everyone they knew and write to anyone they could think of who might support us.

Lots of the letters went unanswered of course – but there was tremendous excitement when one of the kids got a reply from Princess Anne's office. Her secretary said in his kind letter that it was not possible for her to visit at present because of the coronavirus, but that she would love to come and see us afterwards if the fundraising was still ongoing.

Another of my volunteers, Bess, still only sixteen, told me she'd written to the Queen.

'Well, I think that's a great idea, but what did you ask her for?' I said, when she told me. The Queen was even less likely than Princess Anne to visit us in the middle of a pandemic, and you can't exactly ask her for money.

'I asked her for ideas,' said Bess simply. I thought that was absolutely genius. If you want help, why not go to the very top?

We already had some incredible celebrity backing – Clare Balding and the screenwriter Jed Mercurio had tweeted their support. The impressionist Rory Bremner threw himself fully behind our campaign, and even made a brilliant YouTube video asking for money in the voices of Boris Johnson, David Attenborough and Donald Trump. The actor John Altman – best known for playing Nasty Nick on *EastEnders*, but lovely in real life – came by and was kind enough to let us film him making a plea for support, despite the horizontal snow that day!

Every time someone high profile shared the Crowdfunder, or any time we got in the news, there was a surge in donations. But while we had been getting good coverage in the horsey press – publications like *Horse and Hound* – and in the local papers, we weren't yet national news.

Anisha had been incredulous when I told her that I no longer had the contact details for all the journalists who had contacted me when we were doing #tinyponyatyourwindow.

'What do you mean, you lost them?' she said, aghast. We were having another strategising Zoom meeting and she had suggested calling all those journalists to see if they would cover our current plight.

'Well, I didn't think I'd need them,' I said awkwardly.

'Bloody hell, Natalie,' said Anisha. 'Better get back to tweeting then, hadn't we?'

Little did we know it, but another guardian angel was waiting to step in and help us. The very next day, I received an email from a woman who introduced herself as Rachel, another Teddington resident. She ran marketing campaigns for a living, mainly around books, but she reckoned she could help us. I rang her straight back.

'We need to get you on national television,' Rachel said, laying out her plan. 'I'm going to write you a press release, and then we are going to target the news desks of the biggest morning shows. Once the TV gets involved, the rest of the press will follow, it's how it always works.'

'Love it, Rachel,' I said. 'It's ambitious – it's just what we need. Can we do it tomorrow?'

'Leave it with me,' she said. I could tell already that Rachel was quite a different personality to me. I'm frantic and want to do everything fast. She was considered and meticulous. But it was clear she knew what she was talking about.

It was nearly three days before Rachel came back to me to say she was about to send out the press release. I'd left her loads of messages – now I had the idea of national television in my head, I was obsessed with it. Once we'd gone on Racing TV we had made over £100,000 – so if we could get on the national news it would surely prompt an even bigger response.

Rachel told me I had to be patient. 'We've got to phrase it exactly right so it catches the eye of the journalists who get hundreds of releases like this every day,' she said. 'And it has to land at the right time – or it will just get lost.'

I had to take her word for it, even though it felt very unnatural for me to take anything slow. The clock was ticking louder and louder every day. I don't know why I'd done it to myself, but I'd worked out exactly how many hours were left before the Crowdfunder deadline. I had the running total constantly ticking by in my head, which made me feel like any minute I wasn't raising money or getting the word out felt wasted. It's why I struggled to sleep – the ultimate wasted hours – and why I refreshed the Crowdfunder obsessively, like a woman possessed.

At 9 a.m. on 9 February – 471 hours to go – the press release finally went out. I kept checking my phone nervously all morning, waiting for Rachel to call. As each hour went past – 469 to go, 467 – I got more and more panicked. What if no one noticed the release or cared about our story?

Then finally, at about 3 p.m. – 465 hours to go – Rachel called me back.

'*Good Morning Britain* called,' she said, her voice buzzing with excitement. 'They want to put you on the telly, this week.'

'Ohmygod!' I practically screamed with delight.

'Just one thing,' said Rachel. 'They say they want a celebrity to go on with you. So we've got to find one – right now.'

CHAPTER THIRTY-FOUR

SOS to the World

Whenever I was asked about our million-pound target, and what would happen if we didn't hit it – whether it was by a journalist or a supporter – I always said that I didn't waste energy on negative thoughts, so it wasn't something I'd even contemplate.

That was true, up to a point – during the hours of frenzied fundraising, I told myself I needed to stay positive, and I constantly reminded myself that with so many people around me all gunning for the same goal there was no reason we couldn't do it.

But I'd be lying if I said that when I was on my own, in the quiet minutes I spent with a horse in a stable, or watching Woody sleep peacefully in his bed, that the doubts didn't creep in.

There was still so far to go. And I could feel the weight of all the people who relied on Park Lane weighing on my shoulders.

One of my favourite films is *Bridget Jones's Diary*, and there's this bit in it where the character, played by Renee Zellweger, is giving herself a talking to. 'Come the f— on, Bridget!' she says. I would say that to myself too, whenever I had those moments of doubt. 'Come the f— on, Natalie!' Failure was not an option.

So when Rachel told me we needed to find a celebrity willing to plead our cause on national television within a couple of hours, I smiled and told her as calmly as I could: 'Not a problem.'

She asked me for a list of people who had supported us so far. There was Clare, Rory, Jed, Nick – and then a brainwave.

'What about Rob Brydon?' I said.

'He's one of your supporters?' she asked.

'Well, sort of,' I said. The *Gavin and Stacey* star had liked one of the many tweets we had bombarded him with. 'But he lives locally, and he'd be funny and perfect for GMB, don't you think?'

'I'll call his agent right now,' said Rachel.

To our delight, Rob said yes. Two days later, there he was, dialling in from his living room, to tell presenters Kate Garraway and Ben Shephard – and about a million GMB viewers – how 'charming' he found Park Lane.

The GMB film crew had been with us the previous day, interviewing me as well as Dominic's mum Stacey, and filming the ponies and the volunteers working in the stables. Watching with my family at home, it was surreal to see our home and the people we knew there on the screen as Rob spoke. Woody and Alice cheered when I appeared – I had to hide behind a cushion because I found it so awkward!

Rob did an amazing job of summing up just why it was so important to save the stables. 'It's such a force for good in the area,' he said. 'If it were to go, so many people would miss out.'

My phone was off the charts – loads of text messages pinging from friends back in Birmingham, people I used to work with and more, saying they'd spotted me on the television. Everyone assumed that Rob Brydon must be a friend, when in reality I'd never met him! But I couldn't be more grateful for the kindness he showed us when we needed it most.

The thing about celebrities is that they have a superpower. Their profile gives them the ability to reach and influence people in a way that ordinary folk like you and me could never achieve. Some celebrities use their superpower to make themselves richer and more famous; some don't bother to use it at all. Then there are those like Rob who use their power for good. Who see what needs fixing or helping or saving, and they use their superpower to do it.

Within minutes of coming off air, Rob's heartfelt plea had started to work a miracle. I sat at my laptop open-mouthed as donations started to roll in, even faster than they had after my appearance on Racing TV.

After weeks of relentlessly tweeting strangers, now strangers were tweeting me. My phone lit up with notifications, positive messages of support and people sharing the Crowdfunder link. Rachel kept texting me each time a new journalist contacted her – Vanessa Feltz wanted us on Radio 2! The *Sun* wanted an interview! The *Evening Standard* were coming down, the *Sunday Telegraph* were sending a photographer. It was exhilarating and overwhelming all at the same time.

Within two days of Rob's *Good Morning Britain* appearance, we had raised an extra £90,000. I didn't know how to thank him enough for bringing us within touching distance of half a million. Cards and letters were now arriving by the sackful, and the stables seemed to be constantly buzzing with reporters and photographers who'd picked up on our story. The mood among the Park Lane team was ecstatic – the outpouring of support spurred everyone on to work harder than ever on the fundraising campaign.

But as wonderful as it had been to see the total lurch up following the *Good Morning Britain* spot, the fact remained that we still had less than half the money we needed. After the initial flurry, things had slowed down again. And time was running out. There was just a fortnight left to hit the million; it had taken us six weeks to come this far.

Dale was ringing me every day, full of excited praise about what we had achieved. But he'd finish each phone call by asking: 'So what's next, Natalie?'

In the first few weeks, I'd been bursting with ideas. But now I was running out. I had no doubt that if we had all the time in the world, we'd eventually be able to hit the target through sheer willpower alone. Sadly, that wasn't an option – the 'all or nothing' nature of the Crowdfunder meant that come 25 February, if we hadn't hit a million, it was all over.

I'd half thought if we raised a significant portion of the money and got enough attention, a big philanthropist might notice us and make up the difference. But that hadn't happened and I couldn't assume that it would. I knew what I needed to do – but it scared me. So I did whatever I did when I felt frightened: I rang Dad.

'Hi, sweetheart!' he said, picking up on the second ring. 'How lovely to hear from you. I've been so proud watching you on the TV and reading all about Park Lane in the papers.'

I felt bad; I'd been so wrapped up in the fundraising that I'd neglected our phone calls over the last few weeks. Now Dickie was at home with the kids and I was stomping through Bushy Park with the dog, wrapped up warm against the freezing February weather, I finally had time to ask his advice.

'It's really been amazing how much support we've had,' I agreed. 'But I'm worried, Dad. There's only two weeks to go. And still a mountain to climb.'

'If anyone can do it, it's you,' said Dad, his voice full of certainty and pride.

'I don't know, Dad,' I said. 'This might be one challenge too far. But – I think I know a way.'

I took a deep breath and told him what I'd been thinking over the last few days. I could go back to the bank and ask them to lend me the remainder of the money, which I could then put into the Crowdfunder myself. It was a big risk to personally take on that much debt – but I couldn't think of another solution.

'I'm just worried about Alice and Woody,' I told him. 'That much debt is going to saddle us for the rest of our lives. And things are so uncertain – I mean, I don't even know when we can start riding lessons again at this point! Is it too much to burden my family with? But then – what happens if I don't do this? Everything is lost, everything we've worked so hard for.'

Dad was silent at the end of the phone as I poured out my heart, taking it all in. When I had finished, he said: 'The thing is, Natalie, can you put a price on these stables?'

'No, they are priceless,' I said immediately, knowing that was the truth. 'There is nothing that could replace them – either for me, or for everyone that relies on them.'

'There's your answer then,' said Dad. 'It's a lot of debt, and that's scary. But it's just money. And you've never needed much of that to be happy.'

My dad always knew exactly the right thing to say. 'Thanks, Dad,' I said. 'You're a wise old owl really, aren't you?'

'I try my best,' he laughed. 'But listen. I will always be there for you, for Dickie and the kids. Whatever happens, you'll never be on your own.'

As I walked back to the cottage in the gathering dusk, I felt like a weight had been lifted. There was no guarantee that the bank would grant me the loan, but at least I had a plan now. Succeed or fail, I'd know I'd given it everything.

I opened the door to the cottage, and was immediately greeted by a frantically waving Dickie, who was cradling the landline phone under his chin.

' . . . Ah yes, she's just walked through the door now,' he told the person on the other end of the line. 'I'll pass you over.'

'It's *BBC Breakfast!*' he mouthed at me, in an exaggerated stage whisper. Confused, I took the phone; why were they calling me and not Rachel?

'Hello?'

'Hi, Natalie, great to talk to you!' The man at the end of the phone had one of those lovely voices, full of warmth and friendliness. 'My name's Josh, and I'm a producer at *BBC Breakfast*. You probably don't remember, but we were in touch back in March last year when you were doing the ponies at the window.'

Ah, so that made sense. I may have deleted all the journalists' numbers, but they hadn't got rid of mine.

'You've heard about what's happening now, then?' I smiled.

'Yes, it's absolutely devastating to think that Park Lane could be lost, but we've been blown away by what you've been doing to save it,' he said eagerly. 'We'd love to put you on the show, if you'd be up for it.'

Up for it? Of course I was! We'd been over the moon to get on one prime-time news show, and here I was being offered the chance to go on a second. If we could raise another £90,000, like we had thanks to *GMB*, it would massively reduce the burden of debt I'd have to take on.

Josh made arrangements for a film crew to come to the stables in a week's time, and asked me to arrange for some of the children and staff with additional needs to take part in the broadcast.

I punched the air when I came off the phone. 'We're going to get one last push!' I told Dickie. It wasn't ideal that it would be a whole week before we were on air, but it was an opportunity worth waiting for.

I rang Rachel to tell her the good news. She wasn't as excited as I expected her to be.

'Do they know you've been on *Good Morning Britain*?' she said.

'Er, I don't know, does it matter?' I said. Josh hadn't mentioned GMB, so perhaps he hadn't seen it.

'*BBC Breakfast* doesn't usually like to follow *Good Morning Britain*,' Rachel explained. 'And vice versa. They're rivals so they want to be the first to do stories.'

'Ah, right,' I said, suddenly feeling worried. 'Do you think we should tell them?'

Rachel paused. 'Well ... we don't *know* that they don't know,' she said. 'So it's not exactly like it's our responsibility to enlighten them – maybe they're fine with it! Probably best to keep quiet, isn't it?'

I wholeheartedly agreed. There was no way I wanted to do anything that would put the coveted spot on *BBC Breakfast* at risk.

All the same, it made the week before the film crew was set to come a very nervous one. I was half expecting a phone call every day from Josh, apologising profusely but explaining that they couldn't possibly come now they'd spotted a *Good Morning Britain* clip on YouTube. I later found out that they did know about GMB and they didn't mind, but at the time, it was another thing for me to worry about!

With the chance that everything with *BBC Breakfast* could fall through, and with no guarantee that it would get us the money even if it did happen, I spent a large portion of the week filling the necessary forms for my loan application. Once I'd sent them off, I was contacted by the bank to arrange an appointment to talk it through with an advisor. Typically, the only available slot was on the same day as the *BBC Breakfast* pre-record. Whatever happened, that was going to be a make or break day.

CHAPTER THIRTY-FIVE

Last Chance Saloon

17 February 2021. Eight days – 192 hours – to go. We'd somehow made it through a week without a more important news story bumping us from the schedule. The BBC *Breakfast* team of two – presenter Fi Lamdin and cameraman Richard Perry – were at the stables pre-recording the report that they'd play to introduce our live interview the next morning.

My heart swelled with pride as I watched some of our young riders explain on camera what Park Lane meant to them. There was Louis, fourteen years old, who had come to us aged eight when his behaviour was out of control and his parents were at a loss as to how to deal with his Asperger syndrome. With the help of the horses, he'd grown into an articulate, friendly and responsible young man, who was never afraid to get his hands dirty helping around the stables.

'Before I came here, I used to get really stressed and have panic attacks,' he told Fi, who had bobbed blond hair and wore a pleasingly practical red cagoule. 'But it's really helped just being around the animals and being able to have a pony hug.'

Then there was Hannah, with her visual impairment, who spoke movingly about how her job with us had changed her life. 'It's improved my mental health dramatically,' she said. 'It's allowed me to find out what I am good at.'

And there was Philippa, explaining how ten years of riding with us had made her forget about the challenges that her learning difficulties presented. Tom, who works so hard for us at the stables, told them of the satisfaction he gets knowing he is making a difference. Finally Dominic's mum Stacey, who welled up when she spoke of the 'sheer joy' her son got from carriage driving.

I was delighted that BBC Breakfast had chosen to focus so much on our participants, who were the real reason our campaign was so important. And I was blown away by how powerfully they spoke about the stables. Fi's enthusiasm for our cause was wonderful too, and she promised us she'd get an incredible film together. 'We had a guy on the show last week who was raising money for a military charity, and after his appearance he raised an extra £100,000!' she told me excitedly.

I smiled and told her we'd love to be able to do the same. It was my best hope – but would still leave us around £400,000 short.

Fi's attention to detail meant she wanted to know the names and histories of all the horses, see the old black-and-white pictures we had of the stables from over a hundred years ago, and film me and some of the others doing all sorts of random tasks, from pushing a wheelbarrow to forking up hay. I was delighted by how much effort they were putting into getting it right, but I couldn't help but keep glancing at my watch. My meeting with the bank was at 4 p.m., and filming had taken so long we were getting dangerously close to that time.

'Everything all right?' Fi asked me, noticing me take yet

another furtive look at my watch when she asked if we could just refilm some of our earlier interview.

'Sorry, Fi, I didn't mean to be rude,' I said, mortified she thought I was trying to hurry them. 'It's just – I've got a meeting with the bank shortly, about a loan. Just in case we don't hit our target.'

Fi's face softened in sympathy. 'It's a wrap then,' she said. 'I'm just being a perfectionist – we've got some amazing footage in the bag. You get to your meeting. But don't give up hope of hitting the target – the *BBC Breakfast* viewers might just surprise you.'

I thanked her and waved her off, having agreed that she'd be back at 6 a.m. the next morning. The plan was that we'd feature live on the show twice – first at 6.30, then two hours later at 8.30. They'd show the film they shot today explaining the plight of the stables, then Fi would interview me live on air.

I had too much on my mind to get nervous at that point – first, I had to get through the phone call to the bank. The lady I spoke to, Kate, was lovely and patient with me, but she explained that I hadn't provided enough information for her to be able to approve a loan at this point.

'We need a full five-year projection of the business plan, with contingencies for Covid as well,' she said. 'Is that something you'll be able to provide?'

'I can certainly try,' I sighed, my head feeling scrambled already. 'When do you need it by?'

'Well, if you want to know if you have approval ahead of 25 February, we really need them by … yesterday,' Kate said, not unkindly. 'So could you do it by first thing tomorrow morning?'

'Absolutely,' I said, feeling nauseous. It was going to be a long night.

I think I fell asleep around 2 a.m. in the end, unable to keep my eyes open any longer. I wasn't totally happy with the plans I'd written, but as Dickie said, it would have to do.

'They'll either give you the money, or they won't,' he said firmly, prising the laptop out of my hands. 'You've done what you could in the timeframe.'

'I just wish I'd applied for this sooner,' I said, rubbing my temples. 'God, I hope this whole thing doesn't come tumbling down because I was slow off the mark.'

I slept fitfully, in that half-awake state you're in when you know you have to get up early and you can't afford to sleep through your alarm. I'd set it for 5 a.m., to give me enough time to get the ponies looking their very best for their TV close-up. Park Lane had always prided itself on how well our horses were turned out – I wasn't going to let the sheer exhaustion of the last two months change that.

Fi and Richard arrived just as I was giving Prodney's tail a final comb.

'Doesn't he look handsome!' Fi declared, and I had to allow myself a brief moment of pride, because he really did – especially considering he was forty years old and had no teeth. 'I'd like to start the broadcast next to Prodney if that's okay with you,' Fi went on. 'He's going to capture everyone's hearts, I just know it.'

There was something about that decision that gave me a good feeling. Apart from me, Prodney was the only one who had been at Park Lane since the start. So it made sense that he was here to make sure this wasn't the end.

Richard helped me clip on a microphone and asked me to say what I'd had for breakfast, to check the levels. 'Er, does a black coffee count?'

It was time to try and put aside the swirling worries from my mind. The bank, the loan, Covid, the landlord, the deadline that hurtled ever closer – it was pointless stressing about all those now. I just needed to focus on three things. The horses, the children and the community. Their story was the only story that mattered. Everything else could wait – we were going live.

'No pressure,' said Fi – but it's hard not to feel nervous when your future and that of hundreds of people you care about rides on what you say next! I looked down the barrel of the camera and tried not to focus on the slow trickle of cold sweat making its way down my back. If we didn't succeed, then hundreds of local children and adults with disabilities and mental health challenges who relied on us for comfort and happiness would suffer an unimaginable loss. No pressure, indeed.

'I feel like I've got sick in my mouth, Fi,' I told her as we waited for Richard's signal that we were going live.

Fi's megawatt smile never faltered. 'Don't say that on air, Nat,' she said. 'The viewers don't want to hear that. So like we discussed, the studio presenters will have a quick chat with me and then I'll come to you, okay?' I nodded, glad we'd done a run-through earlier. Richard held up his hand for the countdown.

5 … 4 …

My stomach churned, and I felt so grateful for the presence of the ponies behind me, Eddy and Marcus. I reached out a hand to Eddy's sturdy shoulder to steady myself – having a pony by my side always made me feel like I could do anything.

3 … 2 …

I thought of all I'd been through to get to this point; the heartbreak and hard work of my early years in London, worth enduring because by building the stables I'd made my dreams come true. Finding friendship, finding love – finding joy in the faces of extraordinary individuals discovering the power of connecting with a horse. Park Lane was my whole world.

... and ACTION!

Fi was chatting to presenters Naga Munchetty and Jon Kay in the *BBC Breakfast* studio. I knew that all across London the Park Lane family would be tuned in and holding their breath, hoping against hope that this last roll of the dice would work.

'... and now we can talk to Natalie O'Rourke, the manager of Park Lane Stables. Natalie, half a million is such a huge amount. Do you really think you can get there?'

I had to believe we could do it. I took a deep breath.

'Absolutely, and we have to do it for the people that need us,' I said. 'We will get to that target and then Park Lane will be our forever home, and the people who need us won't need to worry any more.'

I hoped I sounded more confident than I felt. Would the British public find it in their hearts to provide a happy ending to this incredible story twelve years in the making? It was time to find out.

CHAPTER THIRTY-SIX

The People's Stables

'And ... cut!' said Richard. All the phones had started ringing, even before we'd finished the 8.30 a.m. slot, and I hoped they hadn't been audible on TV. As soon as the camera snapped off, Bess, Daisy and Hannah all rushed to answer them – my mobile, the landline for the stables, the cottage handset which we'd brought with us.

'A donation!' Daisy mouthed at me, taking down some details on a notepad. She hung up the phone, then stared at it in astonishment as it immediately started ringing again.

Fi and Richard had started to pack up their equipment, but I could see Fi watching with interest as the girls and I juggled the phones that just would not stop ringing.

'Are people calling to donate?' Fi asked, as I briefly hung up my mobile.

'Yes, I can't believe—' I began, then my phone started ringing again and I had to answer it before I could finish my sentence. I had no idea how people had got my number but I didn't care. Every single call was from someone wanting to give us money.

Then the cars started arriving. I'd never seen so many on our quiet street – Park Lane was starting to look like the M25 at rush hour. People were leaning out of their windows, brandishing £10 or £20 notes.

'We saw you on the TV!' one old lady called from the passenger seat of a Ford Fiesta, her husband beside her at the wheel. 'We drove all the way from Guildford to tell you to keep up the good work!'

'I think you're going to do it, you know,' said Fi, climbing into the BBC van which she and Richard were driving back to Bristol. 'Call me – as soon as you have news.'

'We will. Thank you so much, Fi, you did this!' I said, gesturing to the increasingly chaotic scene behind me, as the volunteers tried to wrangle phones, cars, people and cash. The BBC van was just pulling away when I spotted Anisha hurrying down the street towards me, an open laptop in her hands.

'Nat, it's going absolutely mad,' she said breathlessly. We perched together on the bench outside the stables and I looked at the Crowdfunder page for the first time since we'd been on *BBC Breakfast*.

'Bloody hell!' I gasped. We were on £723,000 – and the number was ticking up all the time.

By 10 a.m., Fi was back on the phone. 'What's going on, Nat?' she said. 'I can see the total on the Crowdfunder – it's nearly there!'

'Fi, it's absolutely bonkers,' I told her, trying to make myself heard over the volunteers, who were all still taking donations over the phone, and the tooting car horns outside. 'We've got more than what you can see because people are giving over the phone or in person. A guy just arrived who got the train all the way from Leatherhead to give us a tenner – said he didn't have a car or a computer but still wanted to donate!'

'Right, I'm turning the van around,' said Fi. 'You're going to do this – I can feel it.'

'Oh don't be silly, Fi!' I said. 'Just come back next week, like you planned.'

'No, I'm coming back, Nat,' she said. 'We need to get this moment on film.'

What moment? I thought, as she hung up. The money was flooding in but I still could hardly believe that we would hit the target today. Maybe this week, if we were lucky, but—

The phone rang again. It was Dale.

'Natalie, what on earth is going on?' He was so excited that he was almost shouting. 'I've never seen anything like it – your Crowdfunder is going *wild*!'

'I know, I know,' I said. 'And we've got some other money we need to add in, can you talk me through how I do that?'

'Never mind that, Natalie, you need to add a stretch,' said Dale. 'It means you'll be able to keep fundraising even after you hit the million. Otherwise, it's just a hard stop.'

'You really think we're going to get there?' I said, flabbergasted.

'Natalie, you're already on £920,000!' he boomed. 'Anyway, haven't *you* been telling *me* all this time that you would?'

'Yes, but—'

'No buts. You've got ten minutes to decide what your new target is and what you'd spend the extra money on, then we'll add it to the page.' And with that, Dale hung up.

I'd been dreaming of hitting the target for so long that now we were on the precipice of doing just that, I could hardly dare to accept it. I sank down on to the bench, Prodney still calmly chewing mushed-up carrots beside me. I allowed my mind to go to all the things I'd wanted for Park Lane all these years but assumed we'd never be able to afford. We could buy the fields where we kept the horses instead of renting them. I could get a proper arena where I could hold lessons. A new lorry for moving the horses around.

I quickly dialled Dale's number and told him the plan.

'Put the target at £1.5 million, please,' I said, my voice shaking.

'You've got it,' Dale said. 'And Anisha has emailed me the details of the other donations you've got so far, just putting that in now. Which takes you to . . . wow.'

'Takes us to what?' I said breathlessly.

'£989,324,' said Dale. 'Stay on the line, Nat! I think you're going to get there, like, right now!'

Anisha had realised just how close we were too and rushed over with the laptop, Hannah, Daisy, Stacey and Dominic, Louis and his dad, Dickie and the kids following behind her. We sat like that, a small crowd around the laptop, me with the phone to my ear still talking to Dale.

'It's going up, it's going up!' he was yelling. We stared at the numbers on the screen, watched them shuffling and changing until—

'ONE MILLION!!!!!!!'

Everyone started jumping around and screaming and the people in their cars on the street started beeping their horns. Alice threw her arms round Woody, Dickie pulled me in for a kiss. Dale was still going absolutely mad on the end of the phone.

'YOU SMASHED IT, NAT! YOU DID IT! YOU'VE HIT, LIKE, ALL MY TARGETS FOR THE YEAR IN A DAY!'

I couldn't even find the words to reply. I handed the phone to Anisha, who started talking to Dale about practicalities. I rose slowly to my feet and walked back inside the stables, feeling like I was in a dream.

I looked around the familiar space, small and comforting, full of memories. I patted each pony in turn, all of them oblivious to the life-changing chaos going on outside.

After twelve years here, I'd never wanted to say goodbye to Park Lane. It was my home; an unassuming stable block that I'd filled with the kindest, gentlest ponies and, with the help of my incredible community, transformed into a lifeline for people in need.

Horses were my world – their love and dependability had saved me during the darkest times of my own life. And I'd made it my mission to spread that special pony magic as far and wide as possible.

I'd watched time and again how friendships blossomed, confidence grew and people who the world had written off discovered the power of what they *can* do – all thanks to that horsey superpower.

But it could all have so easily been taken away. My mind was jumbled with snapshot memories of the last two months – the relentless slog of barely sleeping, staying up all night racking my brains for new ways to fundraise and begging money from friends and strangers alike. But the incredible generosity of our community, here in Teddington and further afield, had saved us.

We really had done it. Dale said that thirty-two thousand people had donated to our cause – a fact that was simply mind-blowing. All those people had heard our story and dug deep because they wanted us to survive.

Against all odds, we had the money to buy our forever home. It was the people's stables.

CHAPTER THIRTY-SEVEN

A Royal Knockout

The joy that we felt at Park Lane that day was monumental. So many people had worked so hard on the campaign, and so much had been at stake. To achieve our goal, and then watch in wonder as the money still kept coming, was the most incredible feeling. The only thing I could think to compare it to is the scenes after the Second World War ended. After toiling for so long, with a looming threat over our heads, our happiness was uncontained.

Fi was as good as her word and came straight back, and the report she filmed featured on BBC *Breakfast* the next morning.

As the week wore on, the phone didn't stop ringing – but now it was journalists calling, wanting to cover the story. The BBC's coverage ensured we were still making headlines days later, and we were getting requests from TV, radio, newspapers and even international media.

But for me, after the elation came exhaustion. I had barely slept for two months, and I hadn't realised the toll the stress had taken on me. I felt like an athlete that had just run the race of their life. Every part of my body ached, my mind couldn't focus on anything, and all I wanted to do was sleep.

I found the whirlwind of attention completely overwhelming. It wasn't just the media requests and the constant phone calls and emails, but people were even knocking on my cottage door. It was lovely, because they were stopping by to congratulate us, but I felt like there was nowhere I could rest. And I'd gone from being a woman who ran a riding school to someone who had to manage press requests, run social media, deal with the financial and legal implications of our next steps and also look after my own kids and the horses too. It was all getting too much.

As I lay in my bed early one evening, with the duvet pulled up over my head, I scrolled through the contacts book of my phone and knew who I needed to call. Ali. My old friend, who had ridden at Park Lane more than a decade ago, had gone on to have a glittering career in the showbiz world as an agent to top celebrities. If anyone knew how to deal with media attention, it was her. But would she pick up after more than ten years? I dialled her number hoping she would.

Ali picked up on the second ring. 'Nat? Oh my god! I'm so happy you've called! I've been watching you on the news and – oh heavens, what's wrong?'

The sound of her familiar, kind voice had caused me to burst into tears. Through gulping sobs, I tried to explain to her what had happened – how I didn't want to complain about it, because it was wonderful and all from a place of kindness, but how I was struggling to cope with all the attention. Ali listened carefully, adding soothing words when I took a breath.

'You can't do this on your own any more, can you?' Ali said, when I'd finished. 'I'm going to find you someone who can help.'

'Thank you, Ali, but it's okay, I just wanted some advice really,'

I began. But then I thought – can I really cope on my own? I felt completely broken by the last few months, and if I kept this up I wasn't going to be any good to anyone.

'Actually, forget that,' I said. 'Any help you can get me – I would really appreciate it.'

It's not easy to admit you're struggling, especially when you're someone like me – a tough, stoic woman used to relying on herself and herself alone. But I was so glad I did, because a few days later Ali put me in touch with two guys who would prove to be absolute lifesavers.

The first was Paul, who had previously been a high-powered PR executive for Sony Music. These days he ran his own communications business, but was based near Teddington and loved what Park Lane was doing. Ali told me he'd offered to help us out for free, for as long as we needed it.

I couldn't believe someone with that much experience could be so generous, but I rang Paul straight away. He put me instantly at ease with his friendly manner.

'You've done the most incredible thing, Natalie,' he said. 'But I'm sensing it's what happens next that scares you. Well, you shouldn't have to worry about that – you need to focus on what you do best, which is running the stables.'

It was exactly what I wanted to hear. Paul asked a lot of questions, and got me to give him the contact details of various people. 'And now just leave this to me,' he said. 'You get some rest.'

I could hardly put into words my gratitude. Paul was a ball of energy, who immediately appointed himself point of contact for the media. He filtered requests and only arranged interviews which he thought would be helpful, making sure none of the media stuff impinged on the time I needed to spend with the horses.

The second of Ali's contacts was Neil. When I googled him, my eyes nearly popped out of my head. He had previously been the managing director of Fulham Football Club – did he really want to take on my little stables?

The answer was, yes he did. And we really needed him. Our team of trustees were brilliant, but they were kind-hearted volunteers who were used to managing small budgets and the everyday running of the charity. We needed someone who could deal with the legal and financial implications of our million-pound windfall, and oversee the purchase of Park Lane. With Richard having recently resigned as a trustee because of ill health, Neil stepped in to be chair.

The Crowdfunder had actually finished on an astonishing £1.35 million, and with Neil on board, the trustees met every week to discuss the sale and how to ensure that the extra money would secure a sustainable future for Park Lane.

But I hadn't heard anything from the landlords, which was a little bit strange. They had supposedly been desperate to sell, and they couldn't have missed the fact that we'd raised the amount they'd asked for. I thought perhaps they would have congratulated me and we could get the ball rolling. But no – just silence.

The trustees would be the ones to handle the sale, and with charity guidelines and legal framework to abide by, it wouldn't be a quick process. 'It's really important we do things by the book,' Neil explained to me on the phone. 'But don't worry – we're working on it.'

It was frustrating not to be able to do the deal and call Park Lane ours immediately, but I understood that these things have to be done properly. Meanwhile, there was plenty to keep me busy – even though we still couldn't start lessons because of the ongoing lockdown.

We did, however, have a date for reopening – 29 March, all being well. Sadly, we still wouldn't be able to welcome everyone back but we could offer lessons to confident, independent riders and to some RDA participants, as long as they had a fully trained parent or carer to help them with mounting and dismounting. I had to work through all the new Covid guidelines and make sure everything was in place for a safe reopening. I couldn't wait to see our participants again.

Hundreds of letters of support and congratulations cards continued to arrive for several weeks after we hit our target. I was still determined that we would reply to them all, although luckily, I wasn't doing that on my own. Many Pony Club members and RDA participants had volunteered to help. But it was still a logistical challenge arranging who was doing what, dropping off the cards, picking up the replies then taking them to H&L to post them out.

All of the messages we received were heart-warming and wonderful in their own way. But Bess dropped by one evening when I was putting Dougie into his stable with a particularly exciting envelope clutched in her hand.

'Natalie, I've got something to show you,' she said, her eyes shining.

'What is it, love?' I said, bolting the door and giving Dougie a quick pat.

'Here,' she said, and held out the letter. I took it and immediately gasped when I saw the words 'BUCKINGHAM PALACE' beneath the royal seal at the top of the letter.

'The Queen wrote back!' Bess said, still grinning. 'Well, not exactly the Queen ... this guy called the Crown Equerry ...'

I was speed reading the letter, barely able to take it in. I started to read it aloud:

'The Queen has asked me to reply and was delighted to hear that your amazing campaign has raised the money necessary.

'As part of our recognition of the hard work of all of the team at the stables I would like to extend an invitation to visit us at the Royal Mews at Buckingham Palace when circumstances allow. It would be a pleasure to show you how we look after and manage the horses who play such an important part in our work.'

I looked up at Bess, my mouth hanging open. Then back at the letter, which said that they could entertain up to twelve volunteers for the visit. It was signed by someone called Colonel Toby Browne, of the Royal Mews.

'Can you believe it?' said Bess, her face a picture of delight.

'It's like some kind of fairy tale,' I said incredulously. I was so proud of Bess, and so happy that the volunteers were getting this recognition. They kept us going, mucking out in every weather, cheerfully pitching in when they were needed, and never complaining about the hard work. Going to visit the horses at Buckingham Palace would be a reward they richly deserved.

'Well, you've got a tough decision now, Bess!' I told her. 'It's your invitation, so you've got to pick the eleven people who get to go with you.'

We sat on the bench and reread the letter together again, Bess chattering excitedly about what she thought it might be like at the palace. 'It will definitely be posher than Park Lane, won't it?' she said.

'Just a bit!' I laughed.

She'd just left when I spotted Paul's car coming down the road, and I waved excitedly at him.

'We've had some amazing news!' I called over, as he got out of the car. 'The kids have been invited to Buckingham Palace!'

But Paul didn't grin like I expected him to – in fact, his face looked grim.

'That's great, Nat,' he said. 'But I'm afraid I've got some rather worrying news for you.'

'Oh god, what is it?'

'It's the landlord – he's raised the price.'

I couldn't understand what I was hearing. After all our hard work to get to a million, how could they move the goalposts like this? According to Paul, the landlord was saying he had another buyer, who was offering more than our £1 million. In fact, this buyer was supposedly offering £1.35 million – coincidentally, the exact amount we had in the Crowdfunder, publicly available on the internet for all the world to see.

'It's a serious problem, Nat,' Paul was saying. 'Even though we've got the money, it might not be in Park Lane's interest to try and match that offer. It's higher than the independent valuations the trustees have had done.'

I felt like I had been winded.

'So what does this mean?' I asked.

'Obviously, we're still trying to negotiate,' said Paul. 'But they're playing hardball on this. I don't think they'll budge. And if they won't, well ...'

He trailed off. He didn't need to finish the sentence, I knew what it meant. After everything we'd been through, were we really about to become homeless after all?

CHAPTER THIRTY-EIGHT

Shifting the Goalposts

I could have screamed with frustration. We'd worked so hard to get to £1 million, moved heaven and earth, and yet here we were, still facing eviction.

Paul tried to calm me down. 'We've got to leave it to the solicitors now,' he said. 'There might be a way we can resolve this.'

It didn't matter what he said – I just felt, in the pit of my stomach, that there wasn't going to be a happy outcome. The landlord knew how much I loved the stables, and how I would have done literally anything to hold on to them. I'd proved that in the last few months. But the £1.35 million in the Crowdfunder wasn't mine. It belonged to the charity and needed to be treated very carefully.

'You've got to stay calm, Nat,' Paul was saying, as I paced up and down the street in front of the stable block. 'The lease doesn't expire until the end of May, so there is time for things to change. It's not over yet.'

I nodded, knowing I had many more months of stress ahead of me. People were already asking daily when the sale would be complete. Naively, in the immediate aftermath of hitting our fundraising target, I'd promised we'd have a big street party to celebrate and say thank you, as soon as Covid restrictions allowed. There were questions about that too. How would I explain that we might not be able to buy Park Lane after all?

'What happens to the money, in the Crowdfunder, if we can't buy Park Lane?' I asked, panicked, feeling the entire future of our charity slipping away. 'It's all or nothing, right? So would we have to give it back?'

'The trustees are looking into it,' said Paul. 'But we think it's possible it will still fulfil the terms of the agreement as long as you spend it on buying a permanent home in the borough, even if it's not Park Lane.'

'Where on earth will we find that?' I said. 'Stables in London aren't exactly ten-a-penny. Oh god, what are we going to do? It has to be Park Lane, it just has to be.'

We had two and a half months before our lease expired. Over the following weeks, I tried to hold on to the hope that everything would be resolved, but it was so hard. I was back to hardly sleeping, and the knowledge of what was going on behind the scenes felt like a poisonous secret. We had decided not to tell anyone so as not to jeopardise the ongoing negotiations with the landlord. One of the few people I confided in was Nina, and we went on ever longer runs together, discussing the predicament over and over again as I tried not to let it overwhelm me.

Meanwhile, the lockdown restrictions gradually lifted, and life at Park Lane almost felt 'normal' again. At first, we were only allowed to have groups of six or less, meaning that we couldn't cater to as many riders as usual, but by mid-May we were allowed to hold larger classes once more.

Even better, we were able to resume carriage driving. It was such a joy to welcome back some of our carriage drivers, who hadn't been able to do the activity they loved for more than a year. Watching Dominic, who'd been such a huge part of our fundraising appeal, light up as he rode in the carriage was the perfect reminder of what we were fighting for.

However, time was running out on the lease, and the landlord had made it clear that if we couldn't offer £1.35 million, there wasn't room for further negotiation. Paul was busy getting ready for a coordinated media announcement of our awful news. I felt constantly sick about what on earth we were going to do, and how we would explain the mess we were in to everyone who had so generously supported us.

Yet May brought a drop of good news amid the ongoing worry – fans were allowed back into football stadiums! Which meant Woody would be able to go back to Brentford.

If one thing had stayed the same throughout all the lockdowns, it was that Woody had started each day hopefully signing 'Brentford?' Every day, I'd had to sadly shake my head no. I'd tried to find other ways to make him happy, like taking him out on a pony. The truth was, Woody wasn't at all bothered about horses – but he did discover he had a bit of a taste for it once I bought him a riding hat in the Brentford FC colours!

So when the club rang me the day before their first match with a limited crowd to offer us a pair of tickets, I couldn't contain myself. 'Tomorrow, Woody, we are going to Brentford!' I told him. He looked confused, like he didn't trust himself to get excited.

But something must have sunk in, because he was awake at 4.30 a.m. the next day, tugging on my pyjama sleeve and signing 'Brentford? Brentford? Brentford?' I told him to go back to bed, but it was no use – his emotions were running too high. We ended up setting off to the match ridiculously early, and Woody was tense and moody on the way. I think he was half expecting it to be a cruel joke.

Then, as we got off the train at the station nearest the stadium, I saw him start to relax. He spotted other people in red-and-white shirts, and spied the Giant Bee which told us we were in the right place. His little face turned to me, a smile of wonder spreading across it.

The next ninety minutes were nothing short of magic. It was like a sensory explosion for Woody. In the stands he got to be his true self, make noise, join in and feel whole again. It was as if the last fourteen months of hurt were dropping from his shoulders, and the energy in the stadium was healing him from inside out.

On the train home, Woody fell asleep on my lap, exhausted by the overwhelming emotions of the day. Looking down at his face, the picture of contentment, I felt for a moment like nothing bad could happen in the world.

My phone rang. I fished it out of my pocket, managing not to disturb Woody, and answered it in a low voice. It was Paul.

'I hope you're ringing me with good news,' I said. 'Because I've had the most perfect day.'

'I'm afraid not,' said Paul, ruefully. 'I've spoken with the trustees, and they agree that the time is right to go public with the news that our negotiations have stalled. We'll do it on Monday, which is a week before the lease is up. We'll say we intend to leave on 31 May if a deal hasn't been done – and that might be enough to bring the landlord to the table.'

'Okay,' I said slowly. 'And what if it doesn't?'

'Well, then there really is only one option,' said Paul. 'We'd have to move.'

I had known it would come to this – it had been the nuclear option we'd discussed in endless trustee meetings. But there was one big flaw in that plan which we still hadn't resolved, despite endless discussion.

'But where will we go?' I said.

Paul took a deep breath. 'Well, we've got a week to figure that out.'

CHAPTER THIRTY-NINE

Miracle Stable

Ever since I'd received that very first email from the landlord back in December, saying he wanted to sell, my greatest fear had been that Park Lane would have to cease operations. And now, just as the easing of lockdown was allowing us to resume our activities, that was becoming a very real possibility.

There was nowhere obvious we could move to where we could continue operating as a riding school and RDA centre. My best hope was to find temporary places for my ponies while we searched for an alternative home. I had no idea if we'd ever find one. It needed to be easily accessible by public transport, somewhere we could stay for ever, and in the borough of Richmond upon Thames, if it was to fulfil our obligations to our donors and fit the needs of our participants. Did such a place even exist?

I started ringing round all my friends in the horse world, explaining our predicament and asking if they could take a couple of ponies for a short while. Almost everyone was happy to help, but I felt devastated by the idea of breaking up my little herd. The twenty-three Park Lane ponies were a family, and it was so sad to think that soon they'd be scattered across the country, even though I knew they'd be well taken care of.

Worse than that was the prospect of having to stop our much-needed services. I desperately hoped we could find a way to keep operating even if we didn't have a proper base, because there were so many people who relied on us to get through the week.

Dickie, Woody, Alice and I were also about to become homeless, but Julie the physio owned a house in Hampton which she offered us to rent, on mates' rates. There was so much else to stress about that I tried not to think too hard about how difficult it was going to be to uproot my entire family from the only home we'd ever shared. But as always, I was ridiculously grateful for the generosity of my friends, and accepted the offer of the house immediately.

Paul and Rachel had put together a killer press release, and arranged interviews with the BBC, *Evening Standard*, *Teddington Nub*, *Richmond and Twickenham Times* and more. If we had to go, we weren't going to go quietly. It was our duty to our supporters to fight for the stables. Ahead of the announcement, I began the arduous process of individually contacting our participants or their parents, to warn them of the news that was about to go public. Shock and dismay started to echo through our community. No one could get their head round what I was telling them. Everyone believed that the fundraising had been the hard part – but here I was telling them we were back to square one. It was emotionally draining trying to reassure others everything was going to be all right when I didn't know if that was true, and trying to field questions that I had no answers to.

The day of the announcement passed in a blur – Paul by my side, handing me the phone at various points to speak to different media outlets. Even the journalists seemed to be wrong-footed – we were meant to be the stables with the happy ending, and this was a twist that no one wanted.

'I can't believe this is actually happening,' I said to Paul at the end of the day, as we shared a well-earned drink at The Anglers pub (the Queen Dowager had shut its doors many years earlier). 'There's always another mountain to climb, isn't there?'

My phone started ringing; an unknown number. I groaned.

'Paul, I thought you said we were done for the day,' I said. 'Is this another journalist?'

Paul frowned, and consulted his notebook. 'Shouldn't be,' he said. 'Let me answer it.'

'Natalie O'Rourke's phone?' His face changed as he listened to the person at the other end of the line, but I couldn't read his expression.

'Okay, yes, she's here with me now, let me pass you over,' he said. I shook my head frantically. Paul put his hand over the microphone.

'Believe me, you want to take this call,' he said.

Reluctantly, I took the phone. 'Natalie speaking.'

'Hello, Natalie,' said the voice at the end of the line. 'My name is Peter. I just wanted to let you know that I have a yard with thirty-five stables available, just across the river from where you are now. And, well, you can have them, if you need them.'

I felt a wave of shock, almost immediately followed by fury.

'Is this some kind of sick joke?' I thundered. 'There aren't any stables like that round here, don't you think I've been looking and looking!'

'Natalie, no, it's really not a joke,' said the man, and the panic in his voice made me pause. 'I really do have a stable yard, but not many people know it's there because it's tucked on the edge of Ham Polo. Please, allow me to explain.'

It turned out that Peter worked for King Power Polo, which had been owned by the Leicester City owner, Vichai Srivaddhanaprabha, before he was tragically killed in a helicopter crash in 2018. Before that, Peter had worked at Ham Polo Club, and had some stables right next door which were now standing empty. Ham Polo was in Petersham, just across the river from Teddington. He'd seen our predicament on the news, and said he knew he had to help.

'The thing is, Natalie,' he told me a little shyly, 'I have a sister who has a learning disability. I was trying to imagine what this would be like for her, if she was one of your riders. I know what she'd need most is continuity, and I'm sure it's the same for people you help.'

I was astounded. This guy just totally got it. And here he was, offering us a lifeline I never thought was possible.

'It's an incredible offer,' I said. 'How much would you be looking for in rent?'

'Why don't you come and see the place tomorrow?' said Peter. 'And then you can tell me what you think you can afford.'

We made the arrangement to meet the next day, then I hung up the phone, in a total daze. 'I think – a miracle just happened?' I said to Paul.

'Cheers to that!' he said, and we chinked glasses.

The next day, Amelia and I set off together for our recce of Peter's stables. I drove us up through Teddington, across the river and down the elegant streets of Petersham.

'It's really not that far, is it?' I said to Amelia, who nodded, both of us trying hard not to get carried away.

'I make it about twenty minutes,' she said, as we approached the address Peter had provided.

'Gosh, this looks posh,' I said, as we drove past an elegant gatehouse and down a long, tree-lined gravel driveway. At the end of the drive, there was a sign pointing one way to Ham Polo club, and another to Manor Farm. As advised by Peter, that was the way we went, and soon found ourselves at a set of white double gates.

Amelia hopped out to open the gate, then turned back to me, wide-eyed.

'This is absolutely nothing like Park Lane!' she said.

It really wasn't. I steered the truck through the gates and parked up. The stable yard was enormous. There was space for about fifteen cars to park among some beautiful oak trees, then a sweep of perfectly maintained tarmac yard leading to the stable blocks – modern, spacious and painted a spotless powder blue.

'This isn't real,' I said to Amelia. It was the kind of yard I'd dreamed about when I was a little kid – the sort you thought couldn't exist in reality.

'Natalie, hi!' A man in his late forties, wearing a loose polo shirt and shades, was bounding towards us. 'I'm Peter, so happy you've come.'

'Thanks for having us,' I said, a little awkwardly. 'This is my colleague Amelia.'

Peter shook both our hands vigorously, and repeated again how happy he was to have us.

'So as you can see, plenty of space,' he said. Amelia and I exchanged glances; now that we were closer, we couldn't believe how big the stables were. The ponies would love it here.

'So there's these stables out here, and as you can see on this side of the yard there's lots of space to tie up the horses while you wash or groom them,' he waved at a hitching rail opposite.

'And then there's the barn here.' We stepped inside – it was wonderfully cool, spotlessly clean and about three times the size of the Park Lane block. 'So room for even more horses!'

Amelia and I were completely speechless at this point. I couldn't believe that this facility, which we couldn't have imagined in our wildest dreams, was sitting here empty – just twenty minutes from our front door.

'Peter, I don't know what to say,' I said, turning to face him. 'This place is just incredible.'

'All I want you to say is yes, we'll move in,' said Peter, smiling. 'So what do you think?'

I turned to Amelia, who was nodding furiously. I laughed. 'All right then . . . yes, we'll move in!'

We stayed to talk to Peter about the practicalities, and he said he'd get a contract drawn up that our trustees and solicitor could take a look at. I was already thinking what a mammoth task it would be to move the ponies, all the equipment, our supplies, and everything that made Park Lane the magical place it is before the end of May. And then there was the small matter of how our members with additional needs would adjust. Many of them relied on routine, and coming to a whole new place would be a big upheaval.

As if reading my mind, Peter said: 'I want you to do whatever you need to do to make it feel like home. Bring your Park Lane signs, decorate the stable doors, put up anything you need to make it feel familiar to your riders. It's yours to do what you like with.'

Amelia and I couldn't stop talking on the drive back to Park Lane. There were plans to be made and tasks to assign – it would be all hands on deck to move us across the river to Petersham. I knew our army of volunteers and supporters would step up once again, but it was going to be hard work.

'Can you even believe that place is real?' I said eventually, as Park Lane drew into view.

Amelia smiled. 'Yes, for the tenth time, it's real,' she said. 'And it's proof everything happens for a reason, you know.'

She was right. If we hadn't tried to raise £1 million to buy Park Lane, then Peter would never have known we existed. And if he didn't know about us, we certainly would never have found out about him – or his secret stables which were perfectly suited to our needs.

I parked the Nissan in the usual spot, outside the cottage door. I killed the engine and took a moment to survey the squat whitewashed building, adjoined to the scruffy little stable block next door. God, I was going to miss this place. I'd come here with nothing, and I'd found everything.

Peter's place really was incredible, but no matter how luxurious the facilities, could anywhere ever match Park Lane? This tiny stables was stuffed to the rafters with memories, good and bad, and humming with the spirit of all the people and ponies who had made it such a special place. It was the result of a dream my mum had given me as a little girl, and I'd held on to tightly ever since. It was time to say goodbye – but, I desperately hoped, only for now. We'd be back one day – wouldn't we?

CHAPTER FORTY

Prize Ponies

The stables at Petersham really were a miraculous gift – sent to us at just the time we needed them.

I was worried about how some of our members with additional needs might react to the upheaval of moving there, but not a single person made a fuss. Whether it was Daniel mastering a new bus route to the stables on his own, or Hannah finding her way round unfamiliar surroundings despite her visual impairment, they all just got on with it. Ever since we first started fundraising back in January, everyone connected to Park Lane seemed to have found an extra reserve of can-do attitude. If this time of upheaval had taught us anything, it's that you never give up.

We brought with us the black Park Lane Stables sign which had been outside the stables ever since I started the riding school, and attached it to the white gates of Manor Farm. The significance of that familiar sign couldn't be overstated. I watched as participants tentatively made their way up the sweeping drive, looking anxious at the new and strange surroundings. Then they caught sight of that sign, and beyond it, the familiar faces of volunteers they knew and ponies they loved. That little reminder of our former home seemed to help their anxiety drop away.

The horses settled in brilliantly too, loving life in their new, luxurious surroundings. I was so relieved I had been able to keep their horsey family together.

The move itself was, predictably, a mammoth task. First I had to do a mountain of paperwork, new risk assessments, re-registering the charity's address and changing all the rotas based on how easily people could reach us in our new location.

Then came the day itself. My team, aided by our incredible volunteers, worked from half past six in the morning until seven at night, moving our entire operation across the river. It wasn't easy, but the spirit of togetherness that came out that day was something to behold.

But even though I loved the new stables, with generous Peter dropping off ice creams and pizzas as treats for the kids, a bit of my heart still yearned for snug, unassuming Park Lane. There was some undefinable magic about that place that was impossible to replicate anywhere else – that's why I'd fought so hard to raise the money to buy it. And Manor Farm was lovely, but it wasn't for sale, so it could never be a forever home.

What's more, I'd asked the British public for £1 million to buy Park Lane Stables – nowhere else. I couldn't give up on fulfilling that mission until we'd tried absolutely everything to get what we'd promised.

The alternative buyer that the landlord claimed he'd had mysteriously dropped out not long after we moved. The good news was that meant negotiations between the trustees and the landlord's solicitor could start again. The bad news was the landlords said they had another offer, from yet another buyer – and that meant there was still lots of haggling to be done over the price. There was only so much we could offer while sticking by the Charity Commission guidelines. Neil and Paul kept me abreast of every twist and turn, and it felt like an ever heavier weight that I was carrying on my shoulders. The legal wrangling made me so stressed, and the worst part was trying to explain it to our supporters, some of whom were demanding to know why we hadn't used their money to do what we set out to do.

There was a degree of confidentiality around our negotiations, which meant I wasn't able to give the whole picture. I could feel some people were starting to doubt me, and I hated that I couldn't fully explain what was going on. It was unbearable that loyal supporters and donors might think I was a fraud.

'Sit tight, Natalie,' was what Paul would always say, when I felt like I had reached the end of my tether. 'We're going to get that happy ending – just you wait.'

I tried to do as Paul said and remain positive, but as the weeks turned into months I was losing hope that we'd ever go back to Park Lane – and that was a really painful thing to accept.

I tried to keep myself as busy as ever to take my mind off our uncertain future. Riding lessons in the hot July sun, jogging along the river with Nina, taking Woody to scream himself hoarse watching Brentford – all these things made me feel a little lighter. But at night I'd lie awake, worrying about what we'd do if the Park Lane purchase never happened. Peter was a wonderful host, but we couldn't stay for ever – and where would we go next? And how would we explain the change of plan to all our supporters, donors and participants?

Amid all this turmoil Paul called me one muggy afternoon, and told me the *Sun* newspaper wanted to visit the stables later that week, to do an interview with me and film some of our work. I agreed without asking too many questions – ever since the Crowdfunder there had been a lot of media requests, and everyone was pleasantly interested in what we did. Paul only passed on the interviews he thought would be beneficial to our work or profile, and I trusted his judgement implicitly.

'That's no problem, Paul,' I told him, as he ran me through the timings, my mobile hooked under my chin as I stirred bolognese for the children's supper. 'I'll ask Philippa and Daniel if they'll come too and talk about what the stables mean to them.'

'That's a lovely idea, Natalie,' said Paul. 'But listen, this interview is a bit different because—'

'MUM! Woody's dropped his glasses down the toilet again!' Alice was bellowing from the hallway, and I could tell from Woody's mischievous laughter echoing from the bathroom that she wasn't wrong.

'Oh god, Paul, sorry, I've got to go,' I said, hurrying towards the source of the chaos. 'Two p.m. on Thursday, yeah? I'll be there.'

'Yes, but—' began Paul, but I couldn't hear him over the shrieking children and had to hang up.

I hardly thought about the interview until Thursday arrived, and with it the team from the *Sun* as promised. Amy Jones, the reporter, was bright and bubbly, and put us instantly at ease. She chatted easily to the participants who'd agreed to be in the film while her videographer, Marc, set up his camera.

'Right, we'll just do a few questions with you now, Natalie, for the video, if that's okay?' Amy asked when Marc was ready.

'Of course,' I said, adjusting my RDA cap. I knew the drill by now.

'Okay, brilliant,' she said, manoeuvring me into position. I put on my special telly smile. 'So to start, can you just tell me how you feel about being nominated for this award?'

'I'm sorry, what?' I said, the telly smile falling instantly into a puzzled frown. 'What award?'

Amy's blue eyes widened in surprise. 'You've been nominated for the *Sun*'s Who Cares Wins awards, in the best health charity category,' she explained. My brow furrowed further.

'Who Cares Wins is our annual awards ceremony recognising all sorts of heroes across the health sector,' Amy went on patiently. 'This year it's going to be screened on Channel 4. That's why we're here, because you've been nominated ... and, well, you're a finalist!'

I was flabbergasted. Park Lane Stables – nominated for a prestigious award? I could hardly take it in. Until January this year, it felt like no one outside Teddington had even heard of us. Now Amy was saying we were going to be on national TV!

'Well, that's amazing,' I said, as I pulled myself together. 'We're so incredibly grateful – and it will mean the world to all the volunteers to get this recognition. I'm sorry, I had no idea we were even in the running!'

Amy flipped back through her notebook. 'It was a lady called Nina who nominated you,' she said, checking her notes. 'She said says you're a, er, "force of nature who has built something incredibly special".'

Not for the first time that month, I could feel tears pricking behind my eyes. But this time, they were happy tears – not tears of frustration. Lovely Nina – always there as a shoulder to cry on, who knew how much I'd been through these last few weeks. And now she'd put us forward for an award without me even knowing. Amid all the uncertainty, it was exactly the boost I needed.

Once Amy and her team had got what they needed, word started to get through the Park Lane community about our nomination. I mean, Philippa was there – so it was hardly surprising that the news spread like wildfire. Then when the article about Park Lane appeared on the *Sun*'s website, my phone really started going crazy with messages of support and delight.

It turned out that Who Cares Wins was a pretty big deal. Not only was it going to be broadcast on Channel 4, hosted by Davina McCall, it was also going to be attended by some serious VIPs, including Prince William, Prime Minister Boris Johnson – and even David Beckham! It would be a black-tie occasion with a full red carpet, champagne, canapés, the works.

Obviously, the first thing I did was drive straight round to Nina's to give her a big hug.

'I can't believe you've done this,' I said, laughingly. 'You'll come with me on the night, won't you? Amy said you can.'

'Of course I will!' said Nina. 'Oh Natalie, why wouldn't I nominate you – no one deserves this more than you.'

'Come off it,' I said, giving her a friendly shove. 'There's no way we'll win. But it's so lovely to be nominated all the same.'

'Do you know what you're going to say to David Beckham?' Nina teased, her eyebrow raised.

'Never mind about that!' I said. 'I've got a much bigger problem – what on earth am I going to wear?'

CHAPTER FORTY-ONE

The Winner Takes It All

By the time the week of the Who Cares Wins ceremony finally arrived in mid-September, there still hadn't been a resolution in the ongoing discussions over the sale of Park Lane.

I was totally exhausted by the back-and-forth between the trustees, our solicitors and the landlord. Every time it seemed like we might be making progress, a new legal issue would present itself. It felt like we were so close, and yet so far. Every day I snatched up the phone when Neil rang, hoping he was calling to say a deal had been reached. But instead, every day seemed to bring even more disappointing news.

'We're so close, Natalie,' Neil told me on the phone one Monday evening, sounding as weary as I felt. 'We've agreed a price, and the landlord has agreed to sell. But during their searches our lawyers have found some extra legal issues around the property. We're working on that now – but we can't move forward without a resolution.'

'And do you think there will be a resolution?' I asked tentatively, dreading the answer.

Neil was quiet for a few seconds. 'Honestly, Nat, I don't know,' he said eventually. 'We're doing our best but ... it might be an idea to prepare yourself for a situation where we can't make this happen.'

His words were like a kick in the stomach when you're already on the floor. I knew Neil and all the trustees were moving heaven and earth in an effort to get the sale through. But maybe it was just doomed to fail.

'You've got the awards ceremony tomorrow, haven't you?' Neil went on. 'Listen, the best thing to do is to try and switch off from all this, at least for a day. It's an incredible achievement, and not the sort of thing that happens every day, so you've got to enjoy it.'

He was right, of course. It wasn't every day that I got picked up by chauffeured car and driven to a luxury hotel to get glammed up by a squad of professionals – in fact, that had literally never happened to me in my life before! But that was the plan for the day of the awards, as arranged by Amy from the *Sun*. She'd said I could bring three guests, so I'd chosen Nina, Alice and, because she was such a loyal participant and had helped out so much with the filming, Philippa.

The taxi picked Alice and I up first, then called for Nina before finally stopping at Philippa's house. To say she was excited was an understatement. On the hour-long drive through London to the Marriott Regent's Park, where we would be getting ready, she didn't stop talking about all the celebrities she hoped to see, whether or not the cameras would be on us, how pretty her dress was and the new silver shoes she'd bought. It was impossible not to get swept up in her infectious enthusiasm. Alice was almost as excited, buzzing with a sort of nervous energy, as she gripped my hand in the back of the taxi.

We were greeted at the doors of the hotel by a grinning Amy, who ushered us up into the lift and to a hair and make-up room where the air was thick with hairspray and excited female chatter. And just like that, we were in the Who Cares Wins bubble.

The next few hours passed by in a blur. Nina, Alice, Philippa and I all had our hair crimped and curled, our lips carefully painted, our cheeks dabbed with shimmering powder blush. I barely recognised myself in the mirror brandished by the wonderful make-up artist, Lisa, who had somehow managed to transform an unkempt horse lady into an elegant swan. Then I was hurried down the hallway to a room where a team of stylists had hung up rows of beautiful gowns to choose from. With their help, I picked an elegant, floor-length dress in green silk, paired with slender gold heels. It was a far cry from my usual uniform of skinny jeans and mucky riding boots – but I had to admit, it was rather lovely. Alice gasped in delight when she saw me, and Nina huddled all four of us together for the first of a million selfies.

I'd worried that it might feel like a lot of waiting around at the hotel, but the truth was by the time we were ready it was pretty much time to head to the lobby where a bus would collect us to take us to the Roundhouse, the venue for the ceremony. During our hours getting glammed up, we'd also had the chance to meet the other finalists in the Best Health Charity category. They were Look Good Feel Better, which supported women undergoing cancer treatment by offering therapeutic beauty treatments, and TheRockinR, an incredible charity set up by grieving parents Jonny and Carol to provide gaming carts to kids in hospitals, in memory of their own son Reece. The representatives from both charities couldn't have been more lovely or inspirational – and would be tough competition.

'We've got no chance,' I muttered to Nina, as we carefully clambered the stairs to the bus, tottering slightly in the unfamiliar heels. 'And I'm okay with that. They're all very worthy winners.'

Nina simply smiled serenely. 'I wouldn't write yourself off just yet,' she said.

It was just a short ride to the Roundhouse, and as we disembarked and were shown inside, all thoughts of the competition went right out of my mind. That was because the room we were ushered into was, quite simply, breathtaking.

'Oh my god,' I murmured, reaching for Alice's hand again, as a waiter with a silver tray and spotless uniform offered me a glass of champagne. The vast space sparkled with lights, which swirled up to the vaulted ceiling in a perfect heart shape. Round tables were laid with stiff white tablecloths and glittering glasses, in front of a massive, spotlit stage. Big screens were lit up with moving images showing the nominees and the heart logo of Who Cares Wins.

But as beautiful as the studio was, what really stopped me in my tracks were the exquisitely dressed people moving through it. Look to your left – it's David Beckham! Over there to your right – it's Rod Stewart, chatting to Kate Garraway! I recognised the footballers Tyrone Mings and Troy Deeney, saw the chancellor Rishi Sunak greeting *The Apprentice*'s Karren Brady, while Gary Lineker gave a knowing nod to TV presenter Piers Morgan. It was completely surreal to find ourselves surrounded by so many familiar faces.

'Look, this one's our table,' said Nina, pointing to where our name cards were written in elegant cursive. 'We're sitting next to the cyclist Mark Cavendish!' Philippa and Alice excitedly looked for their own name places, while I gave a rueful look to where the teams from Look Good Feel Better and TheRockinR were being ushered to tables in the front row.

'It must be one of them,' I said to Nina quietly. 'They've put them right by the stage.' I felt kind of relieved. The idea of going up there, under all those lights, was pretty terrifying.

Then all of a sudden we were being urged to sit down, because Prince William and Boris Johnson were about to arrive! All eyes spun to the back of the room, where the Prime Minister and the future King of England were striding in. Philippa could barely contain herself. 'This isn't real!' she squealed. I noticed even the celebrities were craning their necks trying to get a good look at Wills – well, it's not every day you get to rub shoulders with royalty.

With Boris and William finally seated, it was time for the show to begin. It felt like all the chaos of the last few hours fell away as, rapt, we listened to some of the incredible stories of the nominees. There was the doctor who had come to the UK as an Afghan refugee, and now ran a charity connecting British doctors with those in war zones. The paramedics who were stabbed while out on duty, but risked their own lives to save each other. The young man who had bravely dived into the River Thames to save a stranger's life, and lost his own life in the process.

'Oh Nina, I'm a total mess,' I whispered, while the singer James Blunt and the NHS choir set up on the stage for a performance halfway through the show. I hadn't been able to stop crying!

'Don't worry, you still look beautiful,' she replied, giving my arm a squeeze. She was flicking through the programme on the table in front of us. 'Oh my goodness, Best Health Charity is up next!'

My stomach clenched. Winning really wasn't the most important thing, but I could just imagine how much it would mean to everyone at Park Lane if we pulled it off.

The host, Davina McCall, introduced Chris Evans, who would

be presenting the award. He made a short speech about how the winning charity put the 'zing' in 'amazing' and was a lifeline to people in need. So far, so vague. It couldn't be us – could it?

'Let's have a look at the incredible work they do,' said Chris, gesturing at the big screen behind him. It lit up, with a glorious aerial shot of a part of the River Thames I'd recognise anywhere.

'That's Teddington!' squeaked Alice. It was – and I could feel the words stop in my throat. All of a sudden, there were our ponies Marcus, Eliot and Annie's-Whizz, and some of our incredible participants too, filling this strange showbiz room with their calming presence.

The film ended with Philippa telling the cameras that 'I love Park Lane, so much.' Then there it was in gold letters, on the screen. Best Health Charity: Park Lane Stables.

I felt frozen to the spot – an affliction that did not seem to affect Philippa, who was already bounding to the stage. I hurried to my feet and followed her as fast as I could, trying to take small steps so I didn't stack it in my towering shoes. Philippa bounced up the steps and made the whole room roar with laughter as she leapt in the air and gave Chris Evans a flying high five.

She grabbed the mic and started making her own accept-ance speech, while I hung back. Davina had caught my eye, and I knew I'd get the chance to say something. I was already planning in my head how I'd dedicate the award to the whole RDA family, spread across the whole country, all part of the same amazing mission to heal with horses. But for now, it was important for Philippa to speak, because she spoke for all our participants.

I had tears in my eyes as her excited voice rang out across the studio as clear as a bell. 'Park Lane Stables makes me feel on top of the world,' she said. 'I don't know where I'd be without it.'

I couldn't have put it better myself.

When I woke up the next morning, my head still bleary from the late night and the free-flowing champagne, I had to check that it hadn't all been a dream.

But reaching for my phone, and flicking through my camera roll, I saw that yes, I really did get a selfie with Prince William. He'd come over to our table – not the other way round – and I'd just started chatting to him about football. That was something to tell Woody! I kept flicking through – yes, David Beckham really had stopped by and spoken to Philippa by name, telling her how amazing she'd been on stage. And there was a snap of Alice, clutching the glass heart trophy. So we really had won.

I sat up, rubbing my eyes. Dickie had already got up to see to Woody, so I had a rare moment to myself to reflect on the magical events of the night before. I wondered what my mum would make of it all. Her dying wish was that I'd achieve my dream of running a stables. Well, look how many more dreams had come true since then!

I grabbed the notepad I kept next to the bed and started jotting down a list of things to do. I needed to talk to The Anglers pub to see if we could rent the upstairs room on Sunday night, so we could host a viewing party of Who Cares Wins when it screened on Channel 4. Amy had told me I had to keep our victory under wraps until then. I couldn't wait to see the faces of my team-mates and the volunteers when they realised that we'd won the award. It would be bittersweet of course, because although the prize was for Park Lane Stables, I'd also have to tell them that it looked like we probably weren't going to be able to go back to Park Lane. Perhaps, I thought ruefully, this moment of joy might be enough to cushion the blow.

My phone rang shrilly, shaking me from my reverie. It was

Neil, and when I answered, he greeted me with uncharacteristic excitement.

'Natalie, I can't believe it!' he practically shouted.

Gosh, news travels fast, I thought. 'Who told you?' I said, too happy to be cross. 'Our win was meant to be a secret!'

'Win?' said Neil, momentarily confused. 'You won? Last night? Bloody hell! Congratulations!'

'Isn't that what you're ringing about?' I said, puzzled.

'No!' he roared. 'I had no idea, but that's just incredible, the icing on the cake ...'

'What do you mean?' I said, barely daring to hope it was what I thought it was.

'We've got a deal, Nat,' said Neil, and even though I couldn't see him, I could hear in his voice that he was grinning ear to ear. 'There's just some paperwork to sign, but that's it, Park Lane is ours. We're going home.'

I was, for once, truly lost for words. I felt the phone fall from my hands on to the soft bed beside me, poor Neil still calling my name. Dazed, I reached for leggings and trainers, and without even thinking about it I was out of the door and pounding along the street, my feet thudding in time to my racing heart.

I powered down familiar roads where we'd walked Annie's-Whizz at the depths of lockdown, rainbows in the windows and eager faces at the door. I ran through Bushy Park, where the memories of twelve years' worth of riding lessons fluttered through the autumn leaves like the breeze. I took the familiar turn past the Queen Dowager, long since shuttered up, but still humming with the love and friendship I'd found there.

Finally, I turned down Park Lane. The place where my children had grown and played, where my horses had thrived, and where hundreds of people had come searching for companionship, empowerment and a little bit of magic. Against all odds, in the face of fire and financial ruin, amid uncertainty and fear, we'd delivered it – time and time again.

At last, I reached the stables and stopped, doubling over to catch my breath. Tears were streaming down my face, and I didn't even try to stop them. I looked up, trying to take it in, that this funny little building was going to belong to my community for ever.

The blackboard on the outside stable wall hadn't been cleaned before we left, and although it was very faded, you could still see how it had been decorated with coloured chalk drawings of flowers and butterflies by some of the children. In the middle, someone had written our motto: 'It's what you can do that counts.'

I smiled to myself. I couldn't wait to see what we could do next.

BONUS CHAPTER

The Perfect Present

'You know there's only one thing I want for Christmas this year.'

It was mid-December 2021, and Dickie and I were on fairy-light festooned Teddington High Street, wrapped up in our winter coats and diving in and out of the shops, picking up stocking fillers for Alice and Woody.

'I know, Nat,' said Dickie, taking my gloved hand in his. 'But don't be too disappointed if it doesn't happen, ok? You've just got to be patient.'

I knew he was right. But I'd been being patient for almost an entire year, and I was losing the knack. It was three months since that magical day when Neil had rung me to say we'd got a deal with the landlord, and I'd run to Park Lane brimming with hope. We'd exchanged contracts now, but the lawyers were still wrangling over the finer details. There still wasn't a date in the diary for completion, when we could finally pick up the keys and call Park Lane ours for good.

'This whole journey began last Christmas,' I reminded Dickie. 'It was New Year's Eve when I started the Crowdfunder, remember? So wouldn't it be nice to end it this Christmas? I don't want to go into another year not knowing when we are going home.'

We were now in the bookshop, where we both spotted the Brentford FC calendar at the same time and smiled at each other. That would be perfect for Woody.

I was still worrying about the completion date as we made our way home, laden with shopping bags. We'd already decided we wouldn't be having a Christmas party this year because of the growing number of Covid cases – thanks to a new variant called Omicron – and the vulnerability of many of our participants. So it would be amazing if we could instead tell our supporters that the gift they'd be getting this year was the re-opening of Park Lane Stables – after how they'd stuck by us through thick and thin.

'It's not like you'd be moving in straightaway, anyway,' said Dickie, as we jumped onto the bus.

'I know, but it's symbolic!' I insisted. 'And I just want to get going on all the improvements as soon as possible.'

Now that we had the temporary base at Petersham for the foreseeable future, we had the perfect opportunity to carry out works at Park Lane which had been needed for years.

The plan was to strip centuries of paint from the old fabric of the building to reveal any structural work needed. Then we'd get going on refurbishment work, which would make the stables more comfortable for horses and humans alike. And I was most excited about the idea for a 'wall of bricks', each bearing the names of 1,200 supporters who contributed to the appeal, an idea we'd come up with as a way to commemorate the incredible generosity of the people who supported us. I couldn't wait to get started.

But there wasn't too much time to dwell because Christmas is always a very busy time for us. Our tradition is to throw our doors open on Christmas Day, and only a worldwide pandemic had stopped us last year, when the combination of the bleakest Covid lockdown yet and knowing that the landlord wanted to sell had conspired to make it very strange and sad. So this year, I wanted to make it extra special – even though a new Covid variant meant we'd be limited in what we could do.

The next day I was up at the yard at Petersham, stringing tinsel around the stall doors, 'Step Into Christmas' blaring out of the portable radio. The vet was coming at lunchtime to make sure all the horses were happy and healthy ahead of the festive season. Then I was heading over to Jenny Bear's place to finish packing up presents for our visit to Kingston Hospital the next day. Build-A-Bear had generously donated teddies for all the poorly kids on the children's ward, and we'd also been given some pampering bits from a beauty charity so we could make up parcels for the nurses too. The plan was to take two of the ponies, Marcus and Squiffy, to cheer up the sick children along with our special gifts. Amelia and Daisy had even agreed to dress as Santa's elves.

'Are you going to open on Christmas Day, like usual?'

I turned to see Anita, one of our volunteers, a Santa hat perched jauntily on her head.

'Yes, definitely,' I said, reaching for the gold ribbon. 'It was such a shame we had to keep things so low-key last year.'

Anita smiled. 'That's great,' she said. 'I've got a neighbour who I think would really appreciate it.'

Not everyone likes Christmas. If you're lonely or bereaved, it can be a particularly difficult time of year. So where better to spend the day than with our ponies, who have no idea that it's not just another day? Christmas or not, our animals still need feeding, grooming, mucking out and taking for a walk. And we invite anyone who wants to join us to come and help – to get away from whatever pain the day brings them, so they can feel like they are doing something useful instead. Quite often the people who come are faces we've never seen before, and might never see again, who have just heard on the community grapevine that we are looking for help. We never ask what brings people to us on Christmas Day, we just make them welcome.

When we lived in the cottage adjoining Park Lane Stables, Dickie would get the turkey going while I oversaw the chores around the yard. Then, we'd asked over anyone who wanted to join our family for Christmas dinner, and it would inevitably be a day filled with love, laughter and good spirit, no matter who was round the table. Now that Dickie and I were living so far from the temporary stables, that wasn't going to be possible, but we had plans to serve up mugs of tea and bacon butties instead.

'Marcus is ready, I think!' said Anita, standing back from the little skewbald pony. She'd been getting him looking perfect for his trip to Kingston Hospital, his coat brushed until it shone.

'He looks gorgeous,' I smiled. But then, when did Marcus not? He would always have a special place in my heart, because of his infinite kindness. There was something about his gentle nature that just inspired confidence, and he must have taught hundreds, if not thousands, of children to canter.

Now semi-retired, his wonderful character had been put to a new use, and he had become our go-to pony for hospital and care-home visits where his special brand of magic came into its own.

Marcus was actually the star of one of my favourite Christmas memories. It was a few years ago now, when a woman I'd never met before phoned me up, her voice thick with tears. She'd only just found out that her little boy's cancer was terminal, and, understandably, she could barely get through a sentence without breaking down. Eventually I managed to establish why she was calling. Her son, AJ, had always dreamed of riding a horse. It was his Christmas wish that he'd finally get to do it. His mum was determined to move heaven and earth to make that wish come true. Several stables she'd tried had said they weren't open on Christmas Day – so she was calling me as a last resort.

We didn't generally offer riding on Christmas Day either, but you'd have to have a heart of stone to turn her down – and so it was, that on Christmas morning AJ's mum woke him up to tell him there was a pony waiting for him in London. They'd driven nearly two hours to Park Lane, where Marcus and I eagerly anticipated his arrival. AJ's little face shone with pure delight when he saw Marcus, so much so that you barely noticed his skeletal limbs, shaven head and pinched cheekbones. I lifted him into the saddle and we set off towards Bushey Park, AJ chattering all the way about the books he'd read on horses and the various pony facts he'd memorised. My heart overflowed with so many emotions as we walked along the familiar pathways of the park, this poorly little boy joyfully shouting 'merry Christmas!' to everyone we passed, while his mum silently wept beside me. Marcus carefully kept perfect pace with me, carrying AJ like he was the most precious cargo.

I was shaken from my memories by the sound of the phone ringing from the office.

'I'll get it,' said Anita, clocking my hands full with baubles and tape. Ten seconds later she was back, phone in hand, and she was grinning.

'It's your solicitor,' she said.

My eyes widened in shock, and I dropped the decorations I was holding immediately. Taking the phone from her, I tentatively answered.

'Natalie, it's good news,' said the solicitor, getting straight to the point. 'It's all happened quite last minute, but it looks like we're going to be able to complete today.'

'Today?' I squeaked, barely able to believe what I was hearing. 'I'll be able to pick up the keys, today?'

'Well, maybe tomorrow,' he replied. 'I'm not sure we will have them until closing time this evening. But I'll let you know as soon as I do.'

I hung up the phone, and Anita and I just started jumping and dancing around madly, to the bemusement of poor Marcus. It was a Christmas miracle!

The next few hours passed in a blur of phone calls as I rang round the trustees and everyone else who needed to know the good news.

'We've got to let Fi Lamdin know,' said Paul, when I called him. 'She keeps saying she wants to come and film the moment you go back in for the first time as the rightful owner. I'll ring her now.'

I thought there was no way Fi would be able to come down at such short notice, but ten minutes later Paul was back on the phone.

'She's going to be there first thing tomorrow morning,' he said. Goodness, I thought. I better hope I get the keys tonight!

Later that afternoon, Alice and I were at Jenny's, sitting cross-legged on the floor next to her glittering Christmas tree, wrapping the gorgeous toys Build-A-Bear had sent. Jenny had made us steaming mugs of hot chocolate, and she had Christmas carols playing on her old record player. It was the perfect December afternoon, but I couldn't stop staring at my phone, just willing it to ring with the good news that the deal was complete.

'Oh for goodness sake – why don't you just call them!' laughed Jenny, as I looked at my phone for about the 1000th time.

'I can't, he told me he'd ring me!' I wailed. And then, I almost jumped out of my skin as the phone actually started to ring – for real!

'It's done, we've got the keys!' said my solicitor. I could have kissed him. 'Come by tomorrow morning to pick them up.'

'Can't I get them tonight?' I said. Alice and Jenny were crowded round the phone, their faces pressed next to mine, their arms around my waist.

'Um, well, we close at 5.30.'

I looked at my watch. It was 5.11.

'I'll be there!' I said, already heading for the door, as Alice and Jenny cheered.

I drove as fast as the speed limit would allow, praying I'd get a parking space. My prayers were answered, and I rushed into the office as fast as my legs would carry me. The moment the keys were placed in my hand, I felt the most enormous rush of joy come over me. They were finally ours!

I had made it to the office just in time – which was just as well, because Fi and her cameraman were going to be at Park Lane by 6a.m. the next morning. That meant a very early start for Amelia, Daisy and I. Our quickly formulated plan was to head to Petersham to get Marcus and Squiffy in their Christmas regalia. We'd drive them to Park Lane in the van, do the filming with Fi, then head straight to Kingston Hospital as planned. That meant the girls would be on national television in their elf outfits! Luckily, neither took themselves too seriously.

With the busyness of the festive period, I hadn't been past the little stables in weeks, so when I turned up there in the early hours of December 17, I got the shock of my life.

Fi and her cameraman, Richard, were already there when we pulled up in the horsebox to the dark street. I'd barely opened the door of the van when Richard announced sombrely: 'Natalie, we've got a big problem.'

'It's not a problem – I'm sure it's easily dealt with!' trilled Fi, trying to stay positive. But I could see immediately what Richard meant. The stables were completely boarded up.

I'd never seen Park Lane like this. You couldn't even tell it was a stables – it was totally concealed by chipboard. I supposed because it had been empty for so long, the landlord had decided to take extra measures to keep squatters out. But it meant that the keys I'd so eagerly picked up yesterday were basically useless because we couldn't even get to the lock – the door was completely boarded up.

'It's ok, I think we can fix this,' I said, thinking fast. I looked down at the t-shirt I was wearing. It was one of the bright pink ones we'd sold as part of our campaign, but with one crucial difference – instead of Save Our Stables it read Saved Our Stables. There was one thing that had got us that all-important 'D', and it was the same thing that could get us into the stables today. People power.

I told the team what we needed to do. Amelia and Daisy, still dressed in their bright-green and red outfits, started knocking on doors. I rang volunteers who I knew lived nearby. Within minutes, the street started to fill up with bleary-eyed friends and neighbours armed with tools. Half an hour later, Dickie turned up with Woody and Alice, then Daniel, Philippa and Nina. Despite the dark and cold on that frosty December morning, everyone, Fi and Richard included, set to work, hammering and unscrewing and sawing our way into the home we had dreamed of for so long.

I could have cried when we finally tore enough of the boarding away to see the door.

'Ten minutes until we go live!' yelled Fi. The creeping dawn light had revealed a total chaos of sawdust and woodchip and discarded tools, which we all hurried to clear up. Then, before I knew it, Fi was manoeuvring me into position, fixing a mic to my lapel, and shushing everyone around us as the camera started rolling. The keys jangled in my hands like jingle bells.

'Park Lane Stables is just about to reopen, after a real roller-coaster ride!' Fi told the presenters in the studio, Charlie Stayt and Naga Munchetty. 'This morning we've got the screws out, we've got the boarding off and in a minute – Nat has got the key – we are about to go in.'

That was my cue. I felt like I'd left my body and was hovering above it as I stepped forward and slipped the key into that familiar lock. Then just like that, the old black door was open – and we were home.

As Fi played a clip reminding viewers of our bumpy road to get to this point, Amelia and Daisy lead in Marcus and Squiffy. The ponies barely blinked – they just made themselves comfortable in their familiar surroundings as if they'd never been away. Seeing them there, in their stalls, I could hardly believe we'd been away either. After all the hard work, all the heartbreak, all the triumph and disaster, we were back where we belonged.

'How do you feel, Nat?' Fi asked me eagerly.

'I'm almost lost for words,' I said, and meant it. 'We are here forever, and nobody can take that away from us. It means we can make horses accessible for even more people.

'I just want to say to anyone watching: believe in your dreams, because dreams can come true. This was our dream, and we made it happen with the power of the people.'

The little crowd that had assembled on the street cheered, and Fi handed back to the studio. I looked around at the faces of the people I loved, who once again had come to my aid in a time of need. We simply would not be here without them. It was the best Christmas present I'd ever had.

'You can relax now, Nat!' said Fi, once the camera had stopped rolling and Richard was packing up his kit.

'Relax?' I smiled. 'There's no time for that – we're off to Kingston Hospital with the ponies.'

Fi laughed. 'It never stops, does it?'

And she was right. Our work never stops, and nor should it. We had our Christmas miracle – now it was down to us to make some more.

THANK YOU

To everyone who donated to keep Park Lane Stables going . . . you are the true heroes of this story.

So many people have touched my life; I have been very fortunate. A huge thank-you to those that have never faltered in their belief in me.

My Park Lane Stables Trustees past and present: Richard Sharp, Jayne Ellis, Jane Mawer, Kath Dillon, Rachel Maund, Paul Baines, Neil Rodford, Ruth Kelly and JP Prayag.

A very special thank you to my team, our wonderful army of volunteers and all our participants who make the magic happen.

To all the heroes mentioned in the book, and additionally: Ed and everyone at the RDA. Marcus and all at the Pony Club. Everyone at 21&Co. All at the Teddington Society and Stuart and Ellie at the Teddington Nub. Amy and the Who Cares Wins team. Our MP, Munira, and the local councils. Everyone in our Brentford football family. And the Bearcat Running Club!

To Emily Barrett and her team at Little, Brown for believing in this book, and Emily Fairbairn for catching my voice.

To my family. x

Park Lane Stables is very proud to be part of the Riding for the Disabled Association (RDA)

Their horses benefit the lives of over 25,000 disabled children and adults annually. With fun activities like riding and carriage driving, the RDA provides therapy, fitness, skills development and opportunities for achievement – all supported by 18,000 amazing volunteers and qualified coaches at nearly 500 centres all over the UK.

The RDA is an inclusive and diverse organisation. It welcomes clients with physical and learning disabilities and autism, and there are no age restrictions. Through its network of member groups, the RDA is at work in every corner of the UK, in our cities and remote rural areas, bringing the therapy, achievement and fun of horses to as many people as it can.

The RDA is a charity, and it can only carry out its life-changing activities thanks to the generosity of its donors, the dedication of its volunteers and the good nature of its fantastic horses.

At the RDA it's what you can do that counts!

To find out more about the RDA and see where your nearest centre is: www.rda.org.uk

To keep up with Natalie's story: www.parklanestables.co.uk or follow us at:

Instagram: @park_lane_stables
Facebook: ParkLaneStables
Twitter: @ParkLaneStables